Hannah Kent's first novel, the multi-award-winning international bestseller, *Burial Rites*, was translated into over 30 languages and is being adapted for film. Her novels *The Good People* and *Devotion* have been translated into multiple languages, shortlisted for numerous awards and are being adapted for film. Her original feature film, *Run Rabbit Run*, was directed by Daina Reid and starred Sarah Snook. Hannah is also the co-founder of *Kill Your Darlings*, and has written for *The New York Times, The Saturday Paper, The Guardian, The Age, The Sydney Morning Herald, Meanjin, Qantas Magazine* and *LitHub*. She lives and works on Peramangk and Kaurna country.

Fiction by Hannah Kent

Burial Rites
The Good People
Devotion

BURIAL RITES

'A story of swirling sagas, poetry, bitterness, claustrophobia ... Holds an exhilaration that borders on the sublime.' SUNDAY TELEGRAPH

'Kent's debut is assured, moving and incredibly well researched and written. It's the perfect mix of literary and historical fiction, giving an insightful and empathetic look at a woman demonised in her lifetime.' BOOKSELLER, Books of the Year

'So gripping I wanted to rush through the pages, but so beautifully written I wanted to linger over every sentence.' MADELINE MILLER, Winner of the Orange Prize for Fiction

'*Burial Rites* is an accomplished gem, its prose as crisp and sparkling as its northern setting.' GERALDINE BROOKS

THE GOOD PEOPLE

'*The Good People* takes us to a place utterly unexpected and believable, where amidst the earnest mayhem people impose on each other, there is no patronising quaintness, but a compelling sense of the inevitability of solemn horrors.' TOM KENEALLY

'Dark, poetic, and intense, *The Good People* is a fascinating and atmospheric tale of the ancient fairy lore of Ireland and how it shaped the people who believed it. One of my best reads of 2016.' KATE FORSYTH

'The world Kent depicts is richly and convincingly layered with superstition, ritual, and religious belief.' AUSTRALIAN BOOK REVIEW

'Kent's prose is tied to the earth in its evocative description of the villagers' hardscrabble lives but is also otherworldly in its treatment of malicious fairy folk blamed for all manner of misfortunes.' SUNDAY AGE

DEVOTION

'Hannah Kent's latest novel is stunning – full of magic and adventure. I fell in love with language again reading it. So beautiful and so raw. *Devotion* is impossibly good.' EVIE WYLD

'Such a glorious love story. And the poetry of the landscape had, for me, a Whitmanesque sensibility. A mighty impassioned cry to love and the land.' SARAH WINMAN

'*Devotion* is rare and exquisite, both beautiful and muscular in its portrayal of love found and denied. It's a story of love as a radical act, and a celebration of place and persistence. As we've come to expect from Kent, this is masterful storytelling with pull-no-punches stakes. It's taken root in my heart.' KIRAN MILLWOOD HARGRAVE

ALWAYS HOME, ALWAYS HOMESICK

'a tender account of how Iceland captive her and forged her literary career.' JASON STEGER, THE BOOKLIST

'a personal and intimate memoir' ENGLISH TEACHERS ASSOCIATION OF NSW

'she has given back to the culture that nurtured her own gift for storytelling' THE WEEKEND AUSTRALIAN

HANNAH KENT

Always Home, Always Homesick

PICADOR
Pan Macmillan Australia

Pan Macmillan acknowledges the Traditional Custodians of Country throughout Australia and their connections to lands, waters and communities. We pay our respect to Elders past and present and extend that respect to all Aboriginal and Torres Strait Islander peoples today. We honour more than sixty thousand years of storytelling, art and culture.

Some of the people in this book have had their names changed to protect their identities.

First published 2025 in Picador by Pan Macmillan Australia Pty Ltd
This edition published 2026 in Picador by Pan Macmillan Australia Pty Ltd
1 Market Street, Sydney, New South Wales, Australia, 2000

Reprinted 2026

NATIONAL LIBRARY OF AUSTRALIA
A catalogue record for this book is available from the National Library of Australia

Typeset in 11.5/15.5 pt Adobe Garamond Pro by Midland Typesetters, Australia

Printed by IVE
Illustration by iStock.com/Ida Setyorini
Cartographic art by Laurie Whiddon Map Illustrations
Photographs by Hannah Kent

For those who call me daughter

CONTENTS

AUTHOR'S NOTE

To write this book I have relied on my personal diaries, notebooks and correspondence. I have also called upon my own memories, as subjective and fallible as they may be.

I have changed the names of some individuals and places mentioned in this book. Many who retain their true names have given their consent. Aboriginal and Torres Strait Islander people should be aware that this book contains the names of people now deceased.

I would like to acknowledge that this memoir was written on the unceded, sovereign lands of the Peramangk and Kaurna people, and pay my respects to Elders past and present. I am deeply grateful to write stories on such storied Country.

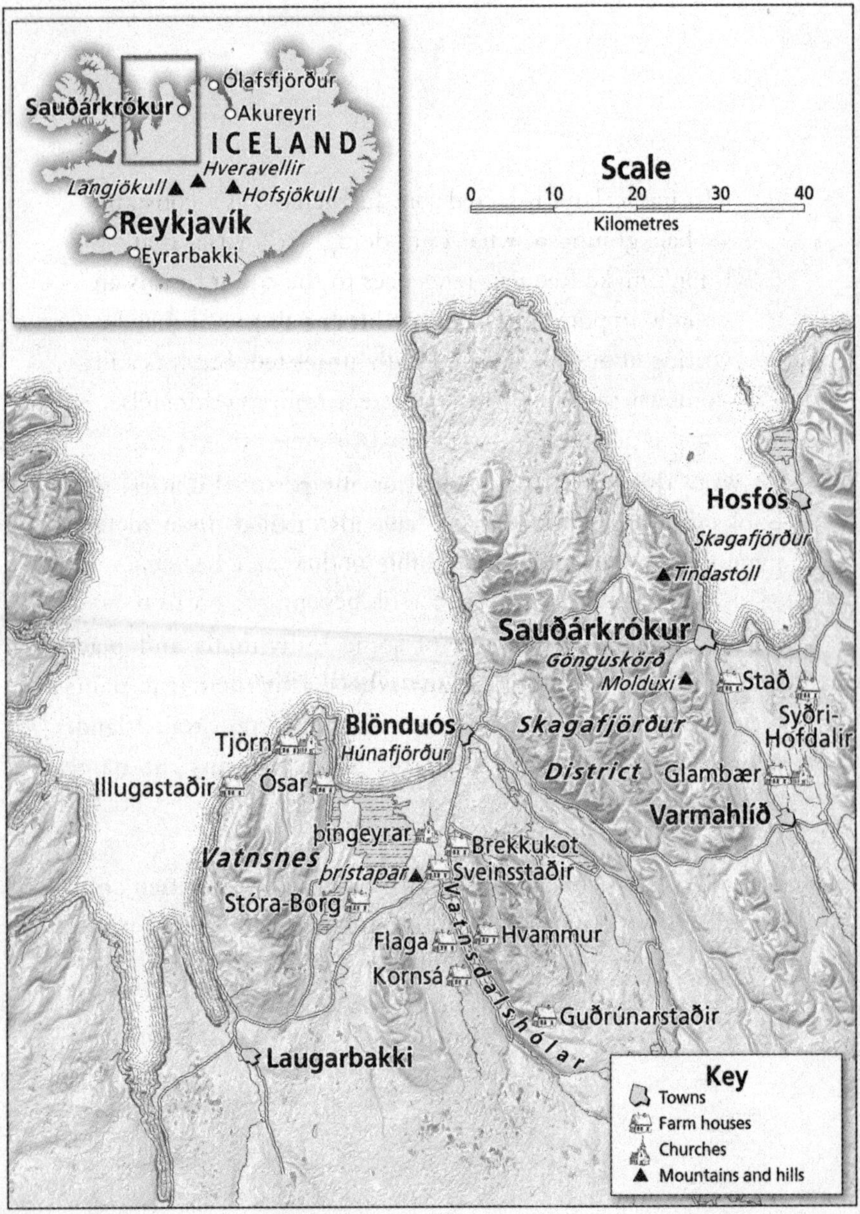

Ólafsfjörður
Sauðárkrókur
Akureyri
ICELAND
Hveravellir
Langjökull
Hofsjökull
Reykjavík
Eyrarbakki
Scale
0
10
20
30
40
Kilometres
Hosfós
Skagafjörður
Tindastóll
Sauðárkrókur
Gönguskörð
Molduxi
Stað
Syðri-Hofdalir
Blönduós
Húnafjörður
Skagafjörður
District
Glambær
Varmahlíð
Tjörn
Illugastaðir
Ósar
Þingeyrar
Brekkukot
Vatnsnes
Þrístapar
Sveinsstaðir
Stóra-Borg
Flaga
Hvammur
Kornsá
Vatnsdalshólar
Guðrúnarstaðir
Laugarbakki
Key
Towns
Farm houses
Churches
Mountains and hills

'To me Iceland is sacred soil. Its memory is a constant background to what I am doing. No matter that I don't make frequent references to the country; it is an equally important part of my life for all that. I may be writing about something totally unrelated, but it is still somewhere close by. It is different from anything else. It is a permanent part of my existence, even though I am not continually harping on about it. I said it was a kind of background, that's right. I could say that Iceland is the sun colouring the mountains without being anywhere in sight, even sunk beyond the horizon.'

~ W.H. Auden, April 1964

A field of lava crowned with moss

Kvöldvaka
Evening Wake

2020

I stand at a place of wild liminality, upon a shore of black sand. There is a raw and seething ocean before me and the sky is a lowered brow. Behind me is a field of lava crowned with moss and, beyond that, a scoured glacier. The wind whips my hair against my neck, my skin is tight with cold, and I am alone and waiting. My waiting is of the enduring, desperate kind; something is going to happen and it shall be momentous. Something is coming and I must meet it.

The sky threatens blizzard – I recognise the heavy, yellowing pall of the clouds – and I turn away from the rage of the sea and walk towards the lava, stopping before a crevasse. Somewhere, deep within the dark rock, I know a river runs.

*

When I wake, it is to the warm glow of a salt lamp and the sound of a newborn inhaling as he prepares to cry. My body, dislocated from my mind, is already pulling itself up against the wooden bedhead and reaching into the bassinet at my side. As the baby latches, my thoughts orientate themselves. There is no ocean here. There is no cragged lava. I touch my cheek, and it is soft and creased and bears no mark of cold or salted air. I am in my bedroom, my sleeping wife radiating warmth at my side, and this tiny creature, hand splayed on my breast, intent and quiet again, is our son.

Again, I think. Again and again, in one form or another, I am returning to Iceland.

At three o'clock in the morning, our house is a womb. The bedroom is suffused with the lamp's pink glow, smelling of sleep and milk. Tender things. I can hear a smattering of rain upon leaf litter as it drips from the trees outside, the hissing of possums in the feijoa.

I am in Australia, I tell myself. I am beneath the canopies of my childhood.

Closing my eyes, I summon back the feeling of my dream. It felt premonitory. I come from a line of women who sometimes do dream things that are other and strange and not quite dreams at all, and there have been times in my life when my sister and my mother and I have known things, avoided things, warned of things dreamed. We don't usually speak of it outside of our tight trinity. It spooks people. But we three know the feeling of these not-dreams and I recognise it in that northern sea, in the boom of its crashing waves and their spray against my face, and the hidden river running to meet it. I lick my lips and anticipate salt. I wait for a greater understanding.

But it is gone.

I open my eyes to switch the baby to my other breast and the fugue that might have offered meaning dissolves in the realities of the t-shirt stretched down my front, the horror-novelty of veins across my chest, the mug lipped with stains on the bedside table. I stare at the unread books stacked precariously beside it and feel dumb with fatigue. I am supposed to be writing my third novel. In a recent mood of forced optimism, I brought in a pile of titles for research I should, by now, have already read. I have not read them. I have not been reading anything. These past two years of unremitting exhaustion have acted like a riptide on my mind. I have been dragged beyond language.

I notice that my son is finished, his mouth finally slack on my nipple, a thread of milk running down his cheek. I place him on my chest and feel his entire weight balanced over my heart. The wound on my abdomen twinges as his eyelashes flutter against my neck. He is more than what I may hold. He is dreaming of his own strange landscapes.

I have been existing in a state of unknowing for some time now.

Outside, things I did not believe would happen have happened. Rory was born fourteen days ago. Australia has been in lockdown for sixteen. I feel alone and lost as all parents of newborns sometimes feel alone and lost, but I also feel utterly unmoored from myself in a way that feels unusual. The claustrophobia and disconnection that can come from being homebound and endlessly occupied with tiny, urgent tasks – feed, soothe, change, clean – has compacted into something harder, something not so easily dissipated, by mandated confinement. My usual worries have seeped wider and deeper to combine with the dread and restlessness rising like a flood line in the world. I am worried all the time for my parents and their vulnerability to this virus. My sister is six months pregnant. Heidi's parents, who live in another state, will not be able to meet our son. I am aware that our problems are not as bad as others' and I am grateful that we are safe. But I prickle with unease. I am unsure if I will recognise the world my children will come to know, and in my many unsleeping hours I reach tentatively into catastrophe so that I will not be caught unawares. I wonder what will fall apart and how, and do not recognise these new routes of thought.

The sleeplessness is not helping. I have not slept for much longer than four hours at a time since Anouk was born, and at two years old she is still a poor sleeper and not easily returned to rest. Rory wakes every few hours for feeding. They take it in turns to fracture the night. Sometimes Heidi and I do not sleep at all. We refer to these nights as 'Night Xs' and joke of being tortured. Sometimes one of us will retreat to the bedroom to cry out our overwhelm into a pillow.

I am so tired that I feel as though I am hallucinating most of the time. The floor tugs to the side. The walls warp and ripple. I walk into furniture constantly. I am covered in bruises, pitted with fatigue and anxiety.

Adding to this dissociation is the unfamiliarity of my body. In acquiescing to the creation of others it has transformed into another self entirely. Beginning with the discovery of my first grey hair the morning after I gave birth to my daughter – a harrowing emergency of a birth that left me with knuckles bloodied from punching the hospital bed – my body has shifted and ebbed and changed so rapidly I simply do not know it as my own. There are mornings when I startle at my reflection in the mirror. I do not recognise my own breasts nor the way they now lie upon my chest. My skin, once smooth, is now puckered with scars and bears the punctuation of gestational diabetes' ritual of needles. I am not so much saddened by this metamorphosis as I am bewildered.

And the changes extend beyond the physical. I hardly know who I am when I am not writing. Not reading. All my life, words are where I've found my handholds. Now I feel as though I am scrabbling for purchase on a sheer wall. Language has left me in devastating, funny ways and it feels like an undoing. Last week, when I broke a bone in my foot, I tried to tell Heidi what had happened but realised I had forgotten the word 'toes'. As Heidi had raised her eyebrows, waiting for me to get to the point, I snapped in pain and frustration, 'Like teeth for your feet!' She laughed at me. I laughed too. It *is* funny, my searching for simple nouns, my reliance on hand gestures and miming to communicate the most basic information. But beneath the laughter, I feel uneasy.

I am supposed to be writing a novel.

I am not writing a novel. I cannot even remember the word for toes.

I do not know how to write as a parent. Everything I have ever written came from practices that can no longer be accommodated. As a child, I wrote alone, mostly outside in nature. Now I am tethered to the house. In my twenties my mind was reliably keen in the morning. I could move into a creative space with ease, shutting myself off from others and the world to give myself over to thought and imagination. Perhaps I always knew this freedom was a privilege, but since my daughter was born I have appreciated it as such on a much deeper level. I can no longer close myself away. I must be helplessly open all the time. My body has sharpened itself into something ever attuned to my children; worn down by demand into nervous response. I am ever coiled.

I tell myself, in the middle of these wakeful nights, that an incomplete novel does not matter; it is certainly wildly insignificant compared to the suffering in the world. But it is hard to contextualise my greater fears about what might happen if I remain distanced from language. It's not that my identity rests on 'being a writer'. I am worried that the bright wick illuminating my way has burned out.

It begins raining again at five o'clock in the morning. Rory is grizzling, spine arching, mouth tremulous, and I pick him up before Anouk wakes at the sound. He settles but it is too late. I hear the thump of her feet hitting the floor as she slides off her bed, her patter down the hall.

The door creaks open and our eldest, bundle of brown curls and quilted pyjamas, pads in on her customary tiptoes. She does not like to let her heels touch the floor.

'Mama.'

Heidi stirs, looks to me bleary-eyed and smiles. Lifts her head to kiss me. 'Happy birthday,' she says. She gets up to change

Anouk's nappy and the morning begins. I hear the cupboard open and shut as clothes are fetched, a mild protest when a head is presumably stuck in a jumper. The hallway light comes on, the coffee machine is whirring. Outside, it is still dark, but the birds are singing. The birds are always singing here. Even in the wet.

As I feed Rory, I reach for my phone and look up death tolls. They are rising. I know my constant monitoring of the pandemic is unwise, but there is a hunger for knowledge that overrides my better sense. If I can control so little, I can at least learn the nature of what is controlling us.

Heidi brings me in a mug. I drop the phone into the blankets and sip the coffee carefully over the tender whorl of Rory's ear.

'How did you sleep?' she asks.

'I dreamed of Iceland again.'

Heidi gives me some painkillers, a glass of water.

'It's strange,' I continue. 'In these dreams I am always on the precipice of something.'

While we can't have a party, Heidi has gone to a lot of trouble to make my birthday feel cheerful and celebratory. By the time Rory and I make it out to the kitchen, she has put up bunting, set the table with candles and flowers and started cooking waffles. Anouk dances around our feet to PJ Harvey's 'Good Fortune', and then the morning passes with breakfast and the opening of presents and video calls from friends and their kids.

Just when I think the celebrations are done, Heidi tells me to go sit down in the lounge room. She then screens a twenty-minute video full of birthday messages secretly collected from friends and relatives. I hold it together until I am surprised by the faces of Pétur and Regína. The realisation that Heidi has gone to the trouble of contacting them, and the sound of their voices wishing me a happy birthday in Icelandic, make me sob.

'Hæ elsku Hannah, innilega til hamingju með daginn.'

'Hannah mín, hey, it's been eighteen years since you came to live with us. It was wonderful. Have a great birthday, hugs from us to you and Heidi and the kids.'

The video goes on and I am completely undone. There is my dear friend Hera and her husband, Donni. My host brothers Gunnar Stefán and Óli Björn, Gunnar holding his newborn daughter, Óli kitted out in protective headwear at work. Pétur and Regína's other four children (Birgitta still in bed, good-naturedly mumbling, 'Til hamingju með afmælið,' with her eyes half-closed), my old boss from Kaffi Krókur, relatives and their children.

'How did you get in touch with them all?' I ask Heidi afterwards. I am exhausted from the unexpected emotion. 'How did you even know who to contact?'

'Well, I messaged Pétur and I asked if he could send a video,' Heidi says. 'I thought you might like that. He sent me one from him and Regína, and then a few seconds later he messaged to say that he was getting on his bike and would be in touch. A few hours later he sent all the others.'

There were videos sent from neighbours' houses, the local cheese factory, construction sites, even the ski field.

'He must have gone around the whole of Sauðárkrókur calling in on people,' I say.

'I think that's exactly what he did.'

*

The video messages from my friends in Iceland, together with my dream, put me in a quiet mood for the rest of the day. I am happy but my heart is aching.

I leave Heidi playing with the children to have a moment alone in the room I have claimed as my study. I shut the door behind me and sink into my chair. My desk is in a state of neglect. The keyboard is uncharged, left on a pile of unread books. Three glasses with various amounts of water in them, all filmed with dust, sit next to opened mail, crochet hooks, notebooks. Several yellow post-its have fallen from my computer screen and are now curled amid the detritus like fallen leaves.

Adding to the general mood of disorganisation and abandonment is a cardboard box that my mum dropped off shortly before Rory was born. She'd gone through her filing cabinets, she told me, and this was my 'stuff'.

'What stuff?' I asked.

'You know, school stuff. Things we kept from your childhood. Certificates.'

'I thought you kept them because you wanted them.'

Mum laughed as though I'd made a good joke. 'Anyway, you might want to show your kids one day,' she said.

Heavily pregnant, I had dragged the box into my study and left it on the floor, wondering when I'd get the chance to go through twenty kilograms of paper considering I struggled to shower myself regularly.

Now I slide off my chair and sit cross-legged by the box. I pull out a page at random. A school report.

Hannah is anxious about doing the right thing, I read, then flip the paper over to see the date: 1990. I was five.

Next is a photo of me at around four years old, scribbling in a notebook while sitting on the toilet with my socked feet dangling. I remember this, remember pretending to write before I had learned how, remember the privacy of the bathroom and my indignation at being interrupted by the click of a camera and my parents' laughter.

I take out a milk carton, folded flat. The expiry date reads 4 January 2004. The carton shows an illustration of one of the Icelandic jólasveinar, or yule lads. The picture is of Kertasníkir, the Candle Beggar, who steals children's candles of tallow to eat. I don't remember bringing this random milk carton home with me, but now I am glad I did.

I realise then, that the ache and dread and dissociation I have been feeling is homesickness.

I am homesick for Iceland.

I am homesick for my body.

I am homesick for writing, and the understanding that writing brings me.

That night I clear my desk and wipe it down. I place my books in neat piles and stick the photo of myself on the toilet onto the wall above my computer. This funny little four-year-old will be my talisman, the photo a reminder that I was writing before I knew what to say and how to say it; that I must have faith in the act of writing itself.

I have decided that, tonight, I will keep a kvöldvaka. An evening wake.

Kvöldvaka is one of my favourite Icelandic words. It does not translate easily. Kvöldvaka describes the time when Icelanders, confined in their turf houses by the winter dark, would gather in the baðstofa, the communal living room where everyone slept, to listen to the recitation of stories or poetry or scripture while knitting or mending in the evening. It is a word born out of a culture that has long used storytelling to alleviate the oppression of the dark.

I am between bodies. I am outside of language, a writer outside of practice. The world beyond our home holds no reassuring stability. Everything is in flux. I am waiting for something to fix in permanency so that I may find my bearings. So, I do as Icelanders used to do when in the confinement of their winters, and I stay awake into the dark evening to forget the gloom outside through storytelling.

This night, I begin my novel.

It makes sense, I think, in this great in-betweenness, that my sleeping self is reaching for Iceland. A stone-cairned country, mindful of journeys. My original land of redirection.

PART I

Heimþrá
A Longing for Home

1989–2003

When I swing, I dream

CHAPTER ONE

Sensitive

1989–1993

My kindergarten is a small place in the Adelaide Hills where the children wear skivvies in primary colours and the radiata pines pierce the sky. I do not have any close friends, but I am not unhappy. I am too young to understand that friends are an expectation, or that solitude is so often conflated with loneliness by those looking on. I am never lonely: I like to give myself over to play without the interference of others. Already, at four, I have discovered the secret of utter absorption. I have learned that if I surrender to my imagination, I am able to leave my own body. I can be anywhere. I can be any age. In solitude, with the wide invitation of my own mind, I disappear out of time. I am elsewhere, unencumbered by an awareness of myself among others.

I very often do not hear my own name being called. In those moments when I am elsewhere, I am not Hannah. I am not anything.

'Hannah. Hannah!'

I must be summoned back with repetition. A voice laced with enough frustration to inspire a flicker of worry in my stomach, which reminds me that I have a body situated in time and place. At four, I do not think that what I do is forbidden, but I am embarrassed to be caught outside of myself. To be so suddenly returned to the kindergarten yard and its masses of damp woodchips knocks the breath out of me. To realise I am being stared at, that I am amusing my teachers or, worse, annoying them, or to suddenly have the dreadful awareness that I have missed some vital instruction, makes me want to cry.

My favourite part of kindergarten is the single swing in the yard, because to go on this swing is to escape into the sky. When I swing, I dream. I don't hear the squeak of the metal chain. I am soaring. I am a bird. I hear feathers holding air and below me is the world. Everything is small, and the smaller it becomes the more I feel joy and love for it all. I lift, and lift, and lift.

But I am not alone in my love of the swing, and when I am in my body I do not feel brave enough to speak out when children who do not notice that it is now my turn clamber on ahead of me. I would never push in front of anyone. How do other children not notice me? Why don't the teachers see? I don't understand why I am overlooked when it comes to turn-taking. Sometimes my throat screams at the unfairness of it, but I know that I am not making a sound.

*

One day, I wait in what seems like an endless line for the swing. Two other children have taken longer than is right, and already a bell has been rung to warn that outside play is ending. There are more children waiting before me and I am very anxious that I will miss out when, in spectacular and startling fashion, the sky turns to water. The other kids shriek and flee for cover, and suddenly the swing is empty. My moment has come. I climb onto the seat and thrust my feet skywards. The rain on my face is like a blessing. The sky is limitless, and I am filled with happiness to be flying, to be feeling so free, to be weightless and alone, my skin tingling with cold and water. I love the cold. I want to be cold forever. I am flying higher and higher, and I am nothing but a spirit above the world. I am so happy.

'*Hannah!*'

I plummet. I am returned. I search for the source of the voice and see my teacher sheltering with the kindy kids, her hands raised in exasperation.

'What are you doing? Come inside, please.'

I put my sneaker down and feel the toe drag in the dirt. I come to a stop. Slipping off the swing, I make my way to the teacher.

'You're soaked,' she says.

I like this teacher. She has kind eyes, but sometimes she laughs at me and not with me. Once I drew a purple tree and she told me that trees were green, which I knew was not always true. Another time she pointed out that my Father Christmas was hovering in the air and not standing on the ground. 'He's jumping for joy,' I replied, but it was a lie, and I felt ashamed of my mistake and betrayed by her implication that art was right or wrong.

As I take my place on the carpet inside with my wet bum and hair tangled down my back, I realise that I should not have wanted to swing in the rain, that it was the wrong thing to do and I should have known that, as I should have known to make my trees green. It doesn't matter that rain feels nice and the plum by our letterbox is a deep and velvet purple in leaf and fruit. All the other children ran. All the other children knew what to do. And suddenly I feel that I do not quite belong like other children belong, and that being weird is not simply something others call me, but something others wish I wasn't. Suddenly, I feel illiterate in a common tongue of childhood.

I have been born into story, as the luckiest of children are.

Mum is a primary school principal. When I was three, I asked her to read me 'Goldilocks and the Three Bears' every single night for a year, and she did so. Perhaps she knew that I was teaching myself how to read through memorisation or recognised that I was learning the shape of crisis and resolution.

Dad is a man of great imagination. At home he allows himself the creativity he is not permitted at his job in the city and he tells me and my little sister Briony stories of his own invention after he tucks us into bed. He calls them dreaming stories. Each night he stops short of their ending and gives us the responsibility of finishing the narrative in our dreams.

Both Mum and Dad see that words are something that make sense to me.

Not everyone does. My reception teacher does not believe that I am able to silent read. She makes me sit on the mat with the rest of the class and chant aloud as she slaps a ruler against words in a 'big book'. The slow wait for the turning page is so excruciating that sometimes I lie down on the carpet and scrunch my eyes shut. I hold out for my family's trips to the library, Dad's stories. I know every book we have by heart. But I yearn for more. I am word hungry.

One day I am sheltering from the rain in the shed of Kay, the woman who takes care of me and my sister after school. Kay is one of the first truly mean people I have ever met, loathsome in her open contempt for children and her refusal to allow us the sanctuary of her warm living room when it is raining.

On this cold afternoon, I find a large cardboard box of books. They are more grown up than the ones I have at home and have few pictures, but I discover I can read them. I sit down on the concrete floor and read, and suddenly I am not stuck in this horrible woman's backyard, I am in an enchanted forest. I am elsewhere. When Kay's voice suddenly announces that my mum is here, I am surprised to find that I am still somehow in her shed. I ask her if I can borrow the book to finish it.

'Take the whole box,' Kay tells me. 'I was going to dump them.'

I come home with thirty hardback books, my glee all the more pronounced for having recognised treasure where the woman who afflicts my afternoons saw only rubbish.

At six, I am officially 'very sensitive'. It is what all the grown-ups in my life say. Sometimes I know that this word means they are curious about me, that they think I am different but in a way that is interesting. An aunt, when I tell her I can see colours around people's heads, or my parents, when I am moved into reveries by music. Often, though, 'sensitive' is offered as a criticism, such as when I fly into rages at my sister's teasing, kicking her in bursts of violence that horrify me and everyone else, or when I run away in frustration when I am unable to do something on a first attempt, or when I cannot stop sobbing after I read a book in which no one comes to a girl's birthday party. It is true that I feel everything, all the time, and it is so much. And when it is too much, I nest in language. I make a home in stories and let them hold me. Words become the bird wing that enfolds me and hides me from the world. I feel safe among them. I forget the plummet that surrounds me.

Around this time, I tell my parents I want to be a writer. It makes sense: if books are magic, then there must be those who wield it. I long to be able to summon such magic. I feel it running in the world like groundwater. I know that there are times and places where it breaches into the open air, where it might converge with my life. This magic is wild and abundant and precious, and I want to learn how to divine it, like my uncle who can make dowsing rods swing. I want to learn how to draw it from the source.

My parents are supportive and unsurprised. I take a book with me everywhere. I beg for five more minutes in the library.

I get the 'Stationery' show bag at the Royal Adelaide Show, one of the few completely bereft of lollies, much to Briony's confusion. I read when we are driving at night, stealing a sentence each time we pass under a streetlight. When I tell my parents I want to be a writer, I have just finished my first short story. A fish discovers his family has been killed by a fish-and-chip shop, so he seeks to destroy the business by placing sea junk on every hook thrown in from the jetty. He succeeds, although his family are gone forever.

If my parents find my story of murder and revenge a little dramatic, they hide it well. 'The first of many,' Dad says, smiling, and I light up inside, as though a match has been struck in the cavity of my chest. I ask for a desk in my room to write at, and Mum says she'll see what she can do. A few days later she brings home a tiny wooden desk procured out of a storage shed from her primary school.

With the desk comes a talk. My parents want to encourage me in my writing and say that if I want to be a writer then I should absolutely do that, but they ask me to keep in mind that writers also do other things. I might like to be a writer 'and something else'.

I nod. It makes sense. Why be one thing when you can be many?

From that point on, whenever someone asks me what I want to do when I grow up, I reply, 'A writer and a teacher,' or, 'A writer and a doctor.' The something else changes. The writer does not.

For my seventh birthday my parents give me a diary with a lock. I recognise the gift as a sacred thing. It is entirely mine.

In my best handwriting I commit myself to the diary's unfilled pages.

I will be writing lots of storys in this book.

It is a bright and secret feeling. If reading is a portal, then, I am discovering, so is writing. A place where I may go for relief from the burden of being. A place where I may become other people.

In 1993 we move to a house on seven acres. We have sheep, chickens and a dam. There is an enormous oak tree and a little forest of steepling pine, and a pond whose banks are pocked with fox holes. I see the foxes sometimes when I wake early, peering out of my bedroom window to see the grass silvered in frost and a lithe rust-red body streaking across it. Sometimes I hear the foxes kill the wood ducks at night, and in the morning I count the remaining ducks as they waddle from the dam to the oak tree. Sometimes families disappear overnight. Sometimes they are only docked a duckling or two.

Mum has told me many stories of the 'dreaming spots' she had growing up in her country town, places where she would go to be alone with her thoughts. Now that I am almost eight, I find my own. There is a stile separating the paddocks and I like to stand at its summit, looking out over the stringybarks sloughing off their skin and the soggy run of water leading in and out of the dam. I also like to scramble up onto the roof of the rainwater tank by the stand of alder trees, where I can lie back against the heat of the concrete to cloud-watch and dream. There is also the dam overflow, the grass streaked with duck poo, the water host to frog call and the shush of reeds. I sit there and watch the rippling of every movement. But my favourite dreaming spot is under the oak tree. The trunk is patched with lichen in summer and moss in the winter. The canopy is so big that the branches touch the ground, and to stand under it is to stand in a room of leaves, the light soft and green. I often wrap my arms around the oak's trunk and press my forehead against the bark. Sometimes I whisper things to it. The tree feels very alive and I feel very alive when I am with it. When Dad loops a swing over one of its lower branches, the oak becomes a refuge where my happiness reaches its zenith. I lean back and feel the generosity of the tree as it holds my weight, feel its bark brush against the tips of my toes as I swing, and am tranced into that divine elsewhere.

It is here, under this oak tree, that I find it easiest to tap into the witcheries of the world.

It is here that I begin to write in earnest.

Words pour from me like water.

What then, would be wondrous to you?

CHAPTER TWO

The Decision

2002

When I am sixteen, one month into my first term of year twelve, my grandfather dies.

I am at home, unwell and snotty, watching *Dancer in the Dark* and crying my eyes out as Björk's character, Selma, stands singing on the gallows before her execution. When the phone rings, I assume it is Mum calling to see how I am feeling and don't bother to disguise my tears.

'Hello?'

'Hannah? It's Christopher.' One of my uncles. Hearing my voice already thick with tears he says, 'Oh. You already know.'

*

So many people come to my papa's funeral that the little country church cannot hold them all. A crowd gathers outside in the red dirt. Someone props open the door.

During the service people speak of my grandfather's many kindnesses. Already there is talk in the community of putting a plaque up in his honour.

They speak too of Papa's great love of life, his capacity for pleasure. He was tall and robust, with a loud, contagious laugh and a childlike delight in toys and novelty, always carrying a bouncing ball in his pocket, always filled with music. His life had not necessarily been an easy one. He had experienced war, had lost a daughter when she was twenty-three. But as one of his beloved grandchildren, I knew Papa only within the prism of his extraordinary positivity.

At the reception following the funeral Dad tells me a story I have not heard before. Once, on a camping trip in the Riverland with his father-in-law, Dad had got up in the middle of the night to have a piss. As he stuck his head out of the tent, he had noticed someone standing on the riverbank. It was Papa.

'He was standing there with his face lifted to the night sky, which was filled with stars. You know what it's like out in that country. The sky was full of them. There was a full moon and a pelican throwing a wake on the river. And Papa was standing there with his arms extended out wide, looking up, smiling. Embracing all that beauty.'

When I return to school, I find it hard to engage with my teachers' definition of success. Every time they emphasise the importance of getting a good Tertiary Admission Rank, something in me revolts. I keep thinking of death and what it means to live and how nothing is certain. I keep thinking of Papa with his arms thrown wide to the night sky.

Many of my peers have selected subjects that will allow them to get into specific degrees at university, but I am studying biology, English, art, drama and history, the five-fingered handprint of an adolescent yearning for culture over career. I have no idea what I want to study at university. I have safe-harboured the desires of my six-year-old self – I hold the yearning to write at the heart of me – but it is the 'something else' I must inevitably do that preoccupies everyone around me. They read careers into my year twelve subjects as if they were tarot cards.

A family friend advises that if I enjoy writing I should be a journalist.

'I don't want to be a journalist,' I tell him. 'I want to make up stories.'

'Some would argue that that is journalism,' he says, chortling.

Relatives (all teachers) recommend teaching. A regular at the cafe where I work part-time tells me I should apply for medicine because I get good grades. My biology teacher hands me a pamphlet about additional science courses I can do to meet university prerequisites.

Everyone is kind. Everyone is encouraging. But the pressure to plan out a career is paralysing. I think of Papa's love of the transcendent, his ecstatic praise of the vast and exquisite beauty of the world, and an appetite for freedom rises in me until I feel

I might levitate in my desire to notice life. I want to be wide awake to the divine mystery of the world in the same way my papa was, to keep my face and heart turned to wonder. This, I think, is success. This is what I want for myself.

One morning in March we are sitting, cramped and cross-legged, on the concrete floor of the main hall for an assembly. There is a routine roll call of announcements, sports results, reminders about the chocolate frog fundraising drive. Then the counsellor, a woman who earned begrudging respect for her stony-faced insistence on 'sexual intercourse' as the only permissible term to be used in health classes, gets up to run through some work experience opportunities. I am zoned out, poking the plastic tip of my shoelace into the holes of my sneaker, when something she says captures my attention.

'The Stirling Rotary Club are currently accepting applications for their overseas student exchange program. Anyone under eighteen who might be interested in living abroad for twelve months, come see me for forms after assembly.'

In that moment I know that this is for me.

I know it.

I know it in my bones, with a surety that runs through my body and makes me sit up as though I have been prodded in the back by life itself. This is what I need to do. This is the thing that will lead me further into life, that will allow me to breathe lung-deep of it. My certitude feels miraculous.

My parents meet my declared intention to live overseas with their characteristic support. If they have any qualms about their sixteen-year-old being suddenly set on a year abroad, they don't show it. There is a moment as they absorb the information, a slight glitch in their responsiveness, but they listen patiently as I describe my yearning for travel, how I want to throw myself into living. Thinking fast, I tell them that the year away will also give me time to think about what I want to study when I get back.

As a family we have hosted several exchange students over the years, although the Thai and Taiwanese students who stayed in our home were part of larger exchange groups, not solo students, and their visits only lasted for a few weeks. The friendships born of these programs, though, alongside my parents' familiarity with Rotary, bodes well for me.

'Papa was a Rotarian,' Mum says. 'He tried to get me to go on exchange when I was your age, but I didn't want to leave the horses.'

'What do you think he would say about my going?' I ask.

'He mentioned it once, actually,' Dad says. 'I don't know how it came up, but I do remember what he said.'

'What was that?'

'"She'd shit it in."'

After submitting an expression of interest, my parents and I are interviewed by the local District Youth Committee. I am terribly nervous, but I have worked casual jobs since I was thirteen and have been interviewed before. After this initial assessment, I am asked to provide considerable information about my personal particulars, an overview of my interests and abilities, my school activities, a report from my principal, doctor and dentist, and an endorsement from my local Rotary Club.

I am also asked to nominate five countries I would like to be considered for.

It is here that I am a little stumped. I know from the exchange program pamphlet that priority for certain countries is given to applicants who have studied those languages at school. France, Germany and most South American nations will be out for me. It is also stressed that there are no guarantees applicants will be sent to any of the countries they nominate.

As I read through the list of places available, I realise that I haven't given any thought to where I would like to go. It was enough to simply have the offer of travel. Now that I must consider actual destinations, I find that I don't have one in mind.

I go down to the oak tree to think it through.

Why are you doing this? The question comes from the tree.

I want wonder, I think.

What then, would be wondrous to you?

The answer comes to me swiftly. Snow.

I am delighted by the simplicity of my desire. If I don't include the few flakes that fell during an English class in year ten (leading to five minutes of whole-class hysteria), I have never seen snow before. Snow feels otherworldly to me. It has only existed within story.

I give the oak tree a pat of thanks and walk back up to the house. I find the forms and tick Sweden, Norway, Finland, Switzerland and Canada, and hope the committee gets the gist.

My final interview is in front of a panel of four rather serious-looking Rotarians. I am dressed in clothes that make me feel like an accountant, sitting on a hard-backed chair, trying to make sure my knees stay pressed together.

This interview, it has been stressed to me, is crucial. It is when applicants must articulate how they will meet the challenges of a year away from home and family in an unfamiliar country. It is an opportunity for us to pre-emptively problem-solve the possibility of excruciating homesickness, language barriers, logistical challenges, and social and cultural integration.

The man on the far right adjusts his glasses. 'Hannah, in your application you speak a lot of your family and their support. How will you cope without them in close proximity?'

I nod. I've rehearsed this answer. 'It's true that I'm close to my family and it's inevitable that I will miss them. I think that I will be homesick for them. However, it is my family's support that has given me the confidence to apply for this kind of experience. I plan to make the most of it and to do everything in my power to engage in the culture, to make friends, to learn the language. I know that this will help the homesickness pass.'

I'm pleased with myself, but the panel gives me nothing.

'How would you cope if you were sent to a place where it is dark a great deal in winter?'

I am not expecting this question. Honestly, I haven't anticipated darkness might be something I'd have to problem-solve. I have always lived in a place of abundant light.

'I'd love to experience that,' I say quickly. 'Coming from Australia, I'd love to experience such difference.'

The Rotarian studies me for a moment then picks up his pen. I am certain he inscribes a mark next to my name.

*

The voice on the phone a few weeks later is formal, male. 'Hannah, I have some good news.'

I press the receiver to my ear, walk into the lounge room as far as the telephone cord will allow me, and make wild movements with my arms to get the attention of my parents and sister. 'It's Rotary,' I mouth.

'You've been selected for our exchange program. Congratulations.'

'Thank you,' I squeak. 'That's wonderful news.'

I make a gleeful face to Mum, Dad and Briony. They return my grin and offer enthusiastic thumbs up.

'I bet you're wondering where you'll be going.'

There's a long silence. I get the impression that the Rotarian is enjoying himself, holding back the news like the host of a television game show. I can hear him smiling.

Finally he says, 'You're going to Iceland, Hannah.'

'Sorry, where?'

'Iceland.'

'Oh, wow,' I say. I look over to my expectant family. 'Iceland!'

I see them all glance at one another, eyebrows raised.

I thank the Rotarian for calling, say my goodbyes and hang up. My family rushes forward. We're all staring at each other, slightly dumbfounded. Then, without quite knowing why, we start to dance around the living room, laughing.

News spreads fast and I become the recipient of odds and ends of information about Iceland which, after a wide sweep of family and friends, I realise no one knows much about. No one has been there. A schoolteacher quotes a *Mighty Ducks* film at me.

An aunt sends me five torn-out sheets about fish from an issue of *Gourmet Traveller*. A drama friend recites every fact he knows about Björk. At lunchtimes I go to the school library and hunt for information online. Resources in English are scant, and what I turn up is either cold statistical fact (population of 250,000, land area of 103,000 square kilometres, primary industry is fishing), or suspect descriptions of a 'strange' population that believes in elves and defends the purity of its language with perplexing bureaucratic ferocity.

Of all that I read, it is the prospect of encountering Icelandic which makes me most nervous. I have been raised in a monolingual, English-speaking home. Neither of my parents speak another language and neither do my grandparents. Another generation back and there are some German-speaking Lutherans on Dad's side, but there has been no cultural or linguistic inheritance other than something my family refers to as our 'Protestant work ethic', which is only ever mentioned to explain our collective inability to relax and do nothing. When pressed I can offer a handful of Bahasa Indonesia, but an apathetic teacher whose pedagogical approach was to give us Indonesian Kopiko lollies and let us play congklak while she napped failed to awaken in me any great love for the study of languages. I have no idea how to go about it.

That the tongue I will have to learn is old and insular, most frequently described as 'difficult' and 'inflected', makes the prospect even more daunting. One friend, who speaks several languages and studies several more, says it's a shame I won't have much use for it. When would Icelandic come in handy, living in Australia?

There is a moment when I mourn the impracticality of learning a localised language, but as the weeks pass, I realise that I like the idea of Icelandic's exclusivity. I want to be someone who speaks an uncommon tongue. Why must everything be utilitarian and outwardly useful? I tell my friend that at least I will be able to swear profusely in public without recrimination. Privately, I wonder what strange roads Icelandic might lead me down. Who knows what gifts it might bring?

In April, the Rotary Exchange Committee hold an information day for all outbound students. Of the twenty-three successful applicants, only five of us will be going alone to our country. I am one of these five. In 2003, Iceland will receive the smallest contingent of exchange students from Australia. It will just be me and a boy from New South Wales.

Mid-morning, we are asked to divide into our destination countries to meet previous exchange students and learn about what to expect from them. The past exchanges seem worldly and wise, and as I wait for my own ex-student to find me, I listen to their exuberant recollections. Many tell the new applicants about opportunities to travel around Europe on special Rotary trips, of the social events for exchange students arranged by district clubs. Over the course of a twelve-month exchange, we will stay with two or three families, and many alumni speak of this as a good thing, an opportunity for different experiences. One boy who travelled to the USA talks of how his first host family took him to the Grand Canyon, the second around the Bahamas on a yacht. The likelihood of my yachting around Iceland seems small, but it's hard not to get excited listening to his adventures.

After ten minutes I am still on my own. An apologetic committee member comes up to me and explains that no one has been to Iceland for quite a few years, so I'm welcome to have a break. I make a cup of coffee and sit apart, swinging my legs, while everyone else interrogates the past students about cultural faux pas to be mindful of, useful phrases to learn. Another committee member pauses by my chair to tell me they're going to try to track down someone who has been to Iceland from Australia before, so that I can get a sense of what to expect.

My apprehension about learning Icelandic mounts as the year passes and I am unable to find any examples of what it sounds like. There are no teach-yourself resources readily available. The only extended title on Iceland I have found is a single Discovery Channel travel guide, last updated in 2000. I pore over it, contemplating its sweeping cultural observations such as: 'Anyone would be a little bit crazy after centuries of long cold winters and a struggle for survival against a hostile environment.' It does include two pages of suggested vocabulary, but the list is restricted to nouns one might use in a restaurant and random geographical terms. The section concludes with the dismissive reassurance that 'most Icelanders, particularly the young, speak English fluently'.

I begin to listen to Björk's albums *Post* and *Homogenic* on repeat, and her voice becomes the soundtrack to my year twelve studies. Amid the rising pressure of exams and academic expectation, I take comfort in the wildness of Björk's music.

Her artistry and originality become a bolster against my own tendencies towards perfectionism. A promise, too, of something greater awaiting me beyond the pedestrian anxieties of Australian Tertiary Admission Ranks.

In October I finally receive a brief email from another Australian who went to Iceland as a Rotary exchange student. She tells me she is now living there.

The people are fantastic and the landscape amazing, she writes. *Things are so different from what we are used to in Australia. But it is all an experience.*

She invites me to respond to her with questions. I am filled with them.

In what way is it so different?

How many families did you stay with?

What are the people like?

Are there any customs I should know about?

Is the food very different?

Can you tell me about the language? What words do I need to know? It would be so helpful as there is very little information I can find.

What are the high schools like?

I also ask her if there is any way I can find out where in the country I am going, as Rotary have not yet provided the name of my host club.

A few weeks later she writes to me again, saying that she'll get in touch with the exchange committee in Iceland and see what they know. She tells me to pack a scarf, gloves, warm hat and some slippers, as shoes are never worn inside.

Clothes are very expensive here, even when on sale. The Australian dollar is about 48 Icelandic krona, and you can get nothing for that, not even candy. Just to give you an idea, something you could buy for $5 in Australia will be $15 here. Rotary will give you a monthly allowance, but in summer school is off for about three months, so you will be helped to find work.

As for my questions, she tells me that a travel guide will answer them.

I write back saying that I have a travel guide, but some more specific information would be appreciated, especially any personal anecdotes. Also, I'm confused about her mentioning employment as it is not allowed by Rotary. Is she still in touch with any of her host families? What about Iceland has led to her living there? It's all I can do to limit my email to an acceptable ten questions.

I don't hear back.

November is a month of exams. My world condenses to study and nerves as, one by one, I cross off each of my subjects. Every time I walk out of the exam room, I calm my pounding heart with thoughts of Iceland.

No matter what happens, I will have travel. I will have adventure.

Then, suddenly, I am done with school. I throw a going-away party and impulsively invite most of my school year, asking them to come as movie characters. Regret sets in soon afterwards. I have not forgotten that awful picture book about the sad birthday girl. What if no one comes? What if no one dresses up?

But people do come, and most of them come in costume. My grandmother wears little wings as Tinkerbell. Several boys from school arrive sans trousers as Tom Cruise in *Risky Business*, one comes covered in glitter as Ewan McGregor in *Velvet Goldmine*. My sister paints herself entirely in green as Kylie Minogue's absinthe fairy from *Moulin Rouge*. It's a good party. I have a wonderful time.

I help Dad pick up empty bottles from the lawn the next morning and then sit with him in the sun. We talk about my impending January departure date, and I tell him I am struggling to fathom the great lengths I am about to travel. In these moments, confronted with the prospect of distance, my own existence feels miraculous. How great is the world, how vast. I look down at my hand, the tiny ridges uniquely mine on the pad of each finger.

'I am just a little speck,' I tell Dad.

He covers my hand with his own. 'Yet here you are.'

One month before I leave, I finally learn the name of the town where I will be living. I receive the news via letter, opened in great trepidation as my family stand around me, television muted, mashed potatoes steaming on plates. The letter states that I will be hosted by Rótarýklúbbur Sauðárkróks, or the Rotary Club of Sauðárkrókur.

'Is that near Reykjavík?' asks Dad.

'I'm not sure.' I attempt to pronounce the name of the town. 'Soda-croakur.'

'Soda cracker?'

'Let's look it up,' Mum suggests.

We go to the bookshelf that holds our encyclopedia, medical textbooks and atlas, and look up the single map devoted to Iceland, Greenland, the Faroe Islands and Northern Scotland. The page is awash in blue, the landmass depicted small. Half of Iceland is ominously coloured white, the coastline corrugated. A small black dot on the south-western shore indicates Reykjavík. There is another, in the north, for Akureyri. No other townships are indicated.

'It's not on the map,' I murmur.

'It must be a small town.'

'Didn't they say most exchange students sent to smaller countries stay around the capital?'

We turn on the computer, disconnect the phone line and wait for the internet connection. I keep staring at the letter, my heart hammering. This feels momentous. It feels adult and exciting, and I have a strong feeling that I am doing something a little bit scary and possibly misguided, but perhaps also truly wonderful.

'Here we go.'

We peer over Mum's shoulder at the computer screen. She's found a basic map of the country. About twenty towns are listed and it takes several seconds before one of us spots Sauðárkrókur. It is nowhere near Reykjavík. It is in the north, tucked against the bottom of what looks like an extended finger of land reaching into the North Sea.

'There it is,' Dad says, nodding. 'You can't get much further north than that, Hannah.' He taps the screen, indicating the line marking the Arctic Circle, which brushes the ocean just north of the town. 'If you travelled any further, you'd start coming home again.'

A town more than a capital

CHAPTER THREE

Þetta reddast / It Will Work Out

2003

I should be tired. My journey has taken three days and I have slept very little, but now that I am here my teeth clench with nerves and anticipation. During a stopover in Amsterdam, I saw a group of Dutch Rotarians welcome two Brazilians on exchange. There had been flags and balloons and a homemade sign. I brace myself for a similar welcome as I exit customs.

The doors open and I step through. I am finally in Iceland.

The arrivals hall of Keflavík Airport, fifty kilometres outside Reykjavík, is cold and brown. I scan the waiting crowd and, though glances are thrown in my direction, I can't see anyone who looks like they are expecting an exchange student. There is no sign. Nothing that indicates welcome. I stand still for a few minutes, gripping the handle of my giant suitcase, watching as my fellow passengers are greeted. I check the time on the arrivals screen. It's midnight. My plane was neither late nor early.

A man comes running in, a little flustered, and I perk up. But his eyes slide over me to the woman waiting nearby. I look on as he takes her luggage. My smile fades.

The possibility that I have not been recognised by my contact does not seem likely. I am wearing a green blazer riddled with pins, ribbons and badges, as though a discount tourist store has vomited a layer of Australiana onto my chest. The jacket is mandatory, I have been told, so that I will be easily identified as a Rotary exchange student. I feel like a Christmas tree. Standing in the emptying hall, I feel a surge of hate at how conspicuous it makes me among the dark-clad locals welcoming friends and family. I don't want to be an outsider here. I want to belong. The blazer is not an auspicious start.

I look through the glass doors of the airport. Beyond the dull shine of cars and a large white bus that pulls up outside, lowering onto its front right wheel to admit a handful of waiting passengers, I can see nothing of the country I am to spend the next twelve months in. I had expected darkness, arriving this late, but the black expanse beyond the airport car park seems overwhelmingly thick, unpunctuated by any lights other than a grim row of streetlamps illuminating a single road, continuing in a straight line until they, too, are pinched out by the night.

The bus leaves. Cars pull out of the lot. They are all soon swallowed by the dark.

It is quiet inside the airport now. I can hear the familiar, ubiquitous sound of late-night vacuuming. I glance up at the arrivals screen and see that only one more flight is expected. I wheel my suitcase to the nearest wall and sit down beside it.

An hour passes. Perhaps the Rotarian is late. My hope lifts as, outside, several pairs of headlights cut through the darkness and pull up in the adjacent car park. My eyes seek out those of every person entering the terminal, watching as they take off gloves and beanies, or unbutton the fronts of their heavy coats, but aside from a few curious looks at my stupid jacket, no one approaches me. When the passengers from the last flight finally pour out from customs, greet those waiting and then disappear once more into the waiting dark, I finally acknowledge to myself that I may have been forgotten.

Squatting down beside my suitcase, I open my backpack and pull out my passport, my Walkman, a collection of mix CDs, some peanuts I saved from my flight from Singapore, the notebook I prepared as a journal for my time away, a dog-eared copy of Michael Cunningham's *The Hours*, until there, at the bottom of my bag, I find the envelope I am looking for. I take out the thick wedge of folded documents and find the details of the man who was supposed to have met me before tomorrow's onward flight to my first host family in Sauðárkrókur.

Jón Ásgeir Jónsson.

Gathering my courage, I approach a man behind a nearby car-hire counter and ask whether he speaks English.

He nods.

'Can I please use your phone?'

He gestures, unsmiling, to a payphone a short walk away. I drag my stuff to the payphone and then, realising I have no coins, return to the car-hire man. Breathlessly, I explain my situation. He gives me an impassive look then hands me a bunch of coins. Every krona features a fish. I haul my bags back to the payphone and dial the number of my contact.

A woman answers.

'Talarðu ensku? I am Hannah, from Australia. I've arrived.'

The woman responds in a pleasant-sounding but entirely undecipherable stream of language. It is so unfamiliar I can't make out where the words begin or end.

'Excuse me,' I say. 'Talarðu ensku?'

I am speaking to the dial tone.

I call the number again, the same woman answers, and this time I realise I am listening to an automated message.

I'm out of money so I return to the car-hire counter, but the man is nowhere to be found. I look around the airport and notice that all shops and booths have closed, and half of the overhead lights have been turned off.

For one horrifying moment I feel my throat tighten with tears.

Unsure of what to do, I sit down next to my suitcase and dig my fingernails into my palm, until I notice a woman with a blonde plait striding towards me with some urgency. I stand to my feet, relief washing through me. Finally, someone has come.

She does not return my smile. Says something I don't understand.

'I'm sorry, do you speak English?'

'The airport is closing,' she says with a thick accent, pointing to the exit. I realise then that she is wearing the uniform of a security guard. 'You have to leave.'

The story tumbles out. I tell her I am an exchange student, that I've been travelling for three days, that I've come all the way from Australia and that someone was supposed to meet me but no one has come, and the phone number I was provided isn't working and I don't have any more coins.

'Can you give it to me?' she asks. 'The number?' She pulls out a mobile phone. 'What's their name?'

'Jón Jónsson.'

'He's Icelandic?'

I nod.

She gives me an appraising look. 'How old are you?'

'I'm seventeen.'

The security guard nods, enters the phone number, listens for a moment, then pulls a face and hangs up. 'This number is not connected. You said his name is Jón Jónsson?'

I nod. 'Jón Ásgeir Jónsson.'

'He lives in Reykjavík?'

'I think so.'

'Okay. I'm going to try to find him, but you can't stay here.'

'Should I wait outside?'

She looks at me as though I am extremely stupid. 'No. Do not wait outside. You need to take that.' She points to a bus idling in the dark.

'But where should I get off?'

'Just take it until the last stop,' she says. 'Okay, you have to go now.'

'I don't have a ticket.'

'Just go, it's leaving. It is the last bus. You must go now!'

The bus door is closing so I make a run for it, hauling my stuff behind me, the sudden cold slamming against my body as I trip through the sliding doors, breaking the handle on my suitcase.

The bus is already pulling away from the kerb, but I manage to smack my palm against its metal side, and it jerks to a stop. The doors hiss open and, pulse racing, I climb up into the dark interior.

'Sorry, I don't have a ticket,' I say to the driver.

He shrugs.

As I push my bags into the rack at the front of the bus, I see the security guard standing in the terminal, phone to her ear, one of my gloves stranded by her feet.

I sit down. Look at my watch. It's nearly two o'clock in the morning. As the bus pulls onto the main road, I press my face to the freezing glass of the window and see that I have arrived in a country of deep night. As we pass under orange street-lights, I see illuminated circles of black asphalt, their border of gravel and, occasionally, flickers of a twisted mass. Lava fields? Beyond that is black. I have no idea whether the land I am travelling through is a vast plain or whether it is populated by animals or people. It feels as though I have been suspended in time, caught up in an eternal witching hour comprising only darkness and rock.

Forty-five minutes later the airport bus enters a sleeping city and its dull halo of light. I can finally see more than an infinity of black. As the bus does a quiet round of incongruous stops, halting at sleepy hotels and random suburban roads to let the other passengers off, I gaze with interest at the city.

Reykjavík seems very small and neat, a town more than a capital, blocks of grim-looking pebble-dash apartments alternating with older, steep-roofed houses clad in corrugated iron.

The street signs are filled with words so long and alien I wonder whether I'll ever be able to pronounce them.

I am the last passenger on board when, at half past two, the bus finally pulls up next to a single-storeyed bus terminal. The driver eases himself from his seat, hoists his belt over his hips and nods at my bags.

'This is BSÍ.'

I have no idea what that means, but I stand up, sling my backpack over my shoulder and drag my suitcase down the stairs by its broken handle. Stepping out into the cold is like walking into a knife; my lungs seize on the air, and I look up to see an older man in glasses grinning at me, his white hair mussed. He is wearing a dressing-gown, his arms thrown open to the night.

'Hannah!'

'Jón?'

He makes his way over to me and gives me a hug. 'Velkomin til Íslands! Welcome to Iceland!'

I smile at him, deeply relieved and suddenly, impossibly weary.

Jón apologises as he leads me over to his car. He was sure I was arriving in a week's time; he had mixed up his days, but þetta reddast, everything works out, he'd been woken up by a phone call. Yes, airport security had found him; Iceland is small, you see, it is not so hard to find someone, even with such a common name as his. 'John Johnson!' He laughs, popping the boot and setting my bag inside before stopping and tilting his head to the sky. I glance upwards.

'Hannah,' he says. 'Look.'

It has begun to snow. And something in me, a breath I have held for the past three days, is released. And when I breathe in again, it is of a cold and pure air that strikes me to my bones.

Jón pulls into what looks like a large, gated housing complex, and leads me up to a small apartment where his wife, Jónína, is waiting, also in a dressing-gown. She offers a firm handshake and lets me use their phone to call home. No one answers, but I leave a message to say that I have arrived safely. Then I climb into the makeshift bed Jónína has made up for me in their study. It is nearly three o'clock in the morning, but my body tingles with jet lag and the adrenaline of arriving and sleep does not come. I get up and look out of the window. Reykjavík is silent and still. The only movement comes from the falling snow.

I watch it for a long time before returning to bed and picking up *The Hours*. The last pages feel like prophecy.

> There's just this for consolation: an hour here or there when our lives seem, against all odds and expectations, to burst open and give us everything we've ever imagined, though everyone but children (and perhaps even they) knows these hours will inevitably be followed by others, far darker and more difficult. Still, we cherish the city, the morning; we hope, more than anything, for more.

I wake up at ten o'clock, just as Jón is leaving the apartment. He tells me to make myself at home and that he'll be back at lunchtime. I let myself into the bathroom and, turning on the taps, am astonished by the sulphuric stink of the hot water. As the steam rises and I wash the days of travel from my body, the stench of rotten eggs is so repelling as to be almost exciting.

I dress, make my way into the kitchen and – unwilling to intrude on these strangers' pantry – take a slice of bread from the plastic bag on the counter. The apartment is high enough to afford a clear view of the surrounding streets. It is not pitch-dark outside, but it is not light either. Everything is steeped in blue, and as I chew my dry bread and watch the occasional passage of cars and pedestrians below, I am aware of its slow lessening until, at eleven o'clock, there is enough light to quantify something akin to day.

I flip through a copy of a newspaper – *Morgunblaðið* – left folded on the table, until Jón returns with a teenage boy and a bag of takeaway in tow. The boy, tanned and friendly, introduces himself as Roman, and I realise that he is the other Australian exchange student sent to Iceland this year. We sit at the table and eat chicken and hot chips, and Roman tells me about the six other Rotary exchange students currently in Iceland. Most of them have already been here for six months. Roman says he has been billeted nearby in an outer suburb of Reykjavík and gets along well with his first host family. He expects to stay with them for six months before moving to another home for the remainder of the year. At Jón's suggestion, we walk into downtown Reykjavík after lunch. I am astonished when, rounding a corner of a building, I see a glassy bay of water and, beyond it, a large, snow-covered mountain.

'Mount Esja,' Roman tells me.

'Are there more of these?' I ask him.

'What?'

'Mountains.'

Roman laughs. 'Yeah. But I haven't been up north yet, so I don't know what your area looks like.' He hesitates. 'Strange that they've sent you all the way up there.'

By the time we return to the apartment the light is fading, and I need to leave almost immediately to catch my plane to Sauðárkrókur, a forty-five-minute flight north. Jón Ásgeir bends down to kiss me on the cheek in farewell. His mouth smells like an open grave. Jónína explains that her husband has been out eating rotten shark.

'Rotten shark?' I repeat.

Jón claps me on the back. 'In Australia the sharks eat the people, but in Iceland the people eat the sharks!'

I want to point out that my horror has less to do with the animal and more with its decomposed state, but I am bustled out of the apartment by Jónína.

Jón waves. 'Goodbye!' he calls. 'Bless bless!'

The wind takes shape among the drying fish

CHAPTER FOUR

Sauðárkrókur

As soon as the tiny plane to Sauðárkrókur takes off, I am seized with an urgent need to sleep. I am vaguely aware of the light on the wing tip blinking into the gloom, of turbulence, but I am held in a strange dream state. I let my body go loose. My stomach flips again and again as the plane drops, recovers, drops again, even as my eyes close and my head lolls onto my chest.

I wake to the sudden interruption of light. We have arrived, and the woman next to me is waiting patiently for me to exit my seat. I do so, slipping out behind the other passengers, feeling light-headed with fatigue and the anticipatory excitement of meeting my host parents. On the snowy tarmac, I peer through the darkness to the illuminated terminal of the Sauðárkrókur airport, examining the few waiting faces. Surely someone has come for me this time.

Entering, I immediately notice a very tall woman watching me with a small smile. She looks elegant, even in a fleece jumper, and a little apprehensive. Next to her stands an even taller man. He has clean-shaven, ruddy cheeks and surprisingly full red lips. He adjusts his glasses and nods at me.

I approach them, teeth clenched to stop my jaw from trembling.

The woman leans down and kisses my cheek. 'Hello. I'm Guðný, and this is Þórir.'

I immediately forget their names in the difficulty of their pronunciation.

'How was your flight?'

'Good, thanks. I slept.'

'You must be tired.'

The bags arrive quickly, the plane being the only one, the passengers so few. Mine is by far the biggest. Þórir insists on picking it up. 'Okay,' he says. 'Let's go.'

In the back seat of my host parents' four-wheel drive, my eyes dart between their profiles and the window. I am desperate to learn who these people are and what they might expect of me, but they do not talk much. The car headlights reveal a stretch of white road, its sides heaped with ploughed snow. The darkness to my left is absolute and to my right I see only a clutch of distant lights.

Þórir gestures towards the window. 'So, this is Sauðárkrókur.'

He may as well be welcoming me to an abyss.

We veer closer to the lights, now recognisable as some kind of township, and as streetlights appear overhead, I see houses of different colours cowering under a weight of snow, but little else. The occasional flash of a reflector strip on a step. A porchlight under an entryway. A parked car, topped with white. A yellow street sign, unreadable, covered with snow.

It all feels very strange.

When Þórir pulls up outside a red-walled, single-storey building I unfasten my seatbelt, but Guðný tells me that we're at a shop, that they just need a few things for dinner. I'd like to go in and explore, but it's clear they want me to wait in the car. Þórir keeps the engine running. A shock of icy air darts across my face as Guðný opens the door. I wait for her husband to say something, but he's quiet. I would start a conversation but for the way I am now fighting a whole-body tremble. I have had six hours sleep in three days of travel and now, finally here, it is not light enough for me to get a sense of where I am. It is not a panic attack – I feel calm – but my body shakes like an animal.

Guðný returns to the car with a plastic bag. She mutters something in Icelandic to Þórir and turns briefly back to me, feathered ends of her cropped hair illuminated in the green glow from the dash.

'Okay,' she says. 'Now we go home.'

Guðný and Þórir's home is the last on a road dotted with houses at a respectably suburban distance from one another. When we pull up I see that their house is the colour of blood and sits next to a deep expanse of darkness. In the far distance I can see the lights of two larger buildings. I have no idea what they are, or what lies closest to the house in all that black. It could be a forest. A lake. It is impossible to know.

As Þórir shuts the boot, my bag in hand, the front door opens and a tall, dark-haired youth steps out in a t-shirt. He looks down at me from the step, arms crossed against the cold. I wave to him. My host brother, I think to myself. He looks about nineteen or twenty, handsome, albeit for a slightly snubbed nose that lends his face a sullen bearing.

'Hæ,' I say.

He takes me in but says nothing.

'This is Garðar,' says Þórir.

Garr-tharr, I repeat to myself. The speed with which these unfamiliar names are uttered makes them difficult to remember.

Garðar nods, then goes back inside the house. It's a cold reception. My eyes dart to Guðný and Þórir, hoping for an explanation as to why my host brother has turned his back on me without a single word of greeting, but they say nothing.

'Can Garðar speak English?' I ask Þórir.

'Yes,' he replies. 'Very well.'

After taking off our shoes in an entryway cramped with hanging coats and snowsuits, I am shown the rest of Guðný and Þórir's home in my socks. Their golden retriever jumps on me in excitement. It's warm inside and I can smell something rich and meaty cooking. To the left of the entryway is a kitchen, the dinner table pushed up against the wall, a bench one side and chairs on the other, and a lamp hanging low over its surface. It has been set for dinner. Beyond the kitchen is a living room with two sofas pointed at a television, a CD tower, a sound system and a pine cabinet displaying photos of Garðar and an older sister at various ages. In the corridor, which extends into the other half of the house, there is a desk and a computer. Beyond that, a bathroom, a shut door I am told is Garðar's bedroom (I can hear him talking to someone within), another belonging to Guðný and Þórir and, finally, a bedroom for me. It is small and cosy, accommodating a single bed with a blue-checked quilt, a wardrobe and a desk and office chair next to a radiator and a window. I am thrilled to see the desk.

'Takk,' I say. 'I really like it.' I point to the radiator. 'How do I turn it on?'

Guðný taps a dial on its upper corner. 'We always leave it on in winter,' she says. 'But you can turn it up or down here.'

She watches as I peek out between the blinds over the window. Darkness.

'Would you like to come and eat?'

The four of us eat roast lamb around the table. The food – the first proper meal I have had in days – is delicious, and I appreciate the effort they have gone to for my arrival. Still, I have to force it down. Everyone is very quiet. Garðar does not speak to me at all, only asks in Icelandic for someone to pass him the potatoes. I cannot help but wonder if I've done something wrong or already offended him in some way. I think of my own family at home, our companionable chatter. I think of the Rotarians I saw briefly in Amsterdam with their hugs and enthusiasm. The thought that perhaps these people do not actually want an exchange student with them turns my stomach. Maybe I am not what they hoped for.

You are tired, I think. You are just very tired.

I offer to wash up after the meal. I want to be useful. I want to be liked. But Guðný encourages me to go to bed. 'You must be sleepy. In the morning, we can show you the town.'

In my new bedroom I massage my jaw until it relaxes. I can hear the muted voice of the television. The clink of plates being placed in the dishwasher. Even in my absence no one seems to be speaking. Perhaps I have arrived during some kind of fight.

I pull at the cord of the blinds until the window is uncovered. I can see only my reflection, so I draw closer until my forehead is pressed against the glass. I expect it to be freezing cold, but it isn't. The panes are triple glazed. This close, there is nothing but a suggestion of white amid the gloom.

I let the blind drop and unpack my bag, aware that I am trying to claim this space as a home for myself. I place my few books on the shelf above the bed, my new Icelandic–English dictionary – gifted to me by Jón – on the desk. Then I pick up my notebook and flip through its opening pages. As if in anticipation of homesickness, I carefully pasted photos of friends and family on its cover alongside handwritten quotes to serve as guiding lights throughout my time away.

The most difficult thing is to know oneself, I read.

I am suddenly embarrassed at my childish collage and the notebook's many empty pages; its hope for a renewed understanding of myself and what my future ought to be.

I have no idea who I am. I have no idea what to do with myself.

I leave the notebook on the desk, undress and crawl into the bed without brushing my teeth. There is no top sheet. The duvet cover smells of unfamiliar laundry powder. Sleep comes with the sensation of falling.

*

It is late when I wake the next morning. Eleven o'clock. A cold light hems the outline of the shuttered blinds and I quickly sit up and pull the cord to reveal the world outside. Finally, I might see where I am.

Snow. Snow billowing against a hedge, heaped against the outer wall of the neighbour's house, piled along the ploughed road. All of it cast in blue. I feel the return and reverberation of the wonder that belonged to me as a child. I want to throw my body against this view. I want to eat that light. It is terribly beautiful.

Unsure of the family's morning routine and unwilling to dosido anyone in a towel, I dress without showering then quietly finish putting my clothes and belongings away to prove I will be a good and tidy presence in this house. Then I tentatively open my bedroom door. I can smell toast and hear the incomprehensible muttering of a radio, the clink of a glass set down in a sink. I pad down the corridor in my socks towards the kitchen and find Guðný pottering about.

'Good morning,' she says, opening the dishwasher. 'How was your sleep?'

I open my mouth to answer but I am suddenly distracted by the kitchen window. In the rising light I can see that the house lies next to a clear field of snow, untouched by footprints. Behind it stands a mountain so close and gargantuan it leaves me breathless. I had never expected mountains like this. The ocean, too – a grey belt taut between snowy caps – is visible from the window. I realise that the curve of ocean I had only seen on maps is a fjord, and that the land on each side of the water is steepled with peaks. The mountains are smoother than the jagged crenellations I have seen in my parents' calendars of European Alps or Canadian Rockies, less triangular, more rounded, heavier. Sauðárkrókur, tucked in this lower corner of the fjord, feels like an anomaly. After so many months of not knowing where I would be living, of anticipation, and then of arriving to unequivocal darkness, finally seeing the small town and discovering it to be wild with mountains and sky and sea is so gratifying I feel a physical rush.

Guðný joins me at the window. 'That is Tindastóll,' she says, pointing to the mountain within view, the one that first pulled my gaze.

I try to pronounce the name as she does, tongue breaking on the final ll's, like the chl of chlorine. An unfamiliar consonant.

'It's so beautiful,' I say.

Guðný gives me a funny smile, then resumes stacking the dishwasher. 'We can go for a walk in a minute, if you like. I'll just finish this.'

Outside, the light is crystalline, the world is still. I glory in the cold air as Guðný adjusts a woollen headband over her ears and then we set off uphill with Kolur the dog. Along the sloping road is the shop we stopped at the previous night. From this height on the hill, I can see that the house where I am staying is on the outskirts of the town.

We make our way off the road into deeper drifts. I pause, delighted at the noise of the snow under my boots.

'It squeaks!' I say in astonishment.

Guðný nods at me, eyebrows raised.

'I haven't seen snow before.'

'Well, now you will see a lot of it.' Guðný smiles. 'You will get sick of it.'

'Never,' I reply quietly. It is all I can do not to throw myself into the snowdrifts. I bend down and scoop a handful of powder into my hand. It is impossibly light.

Guðný throws a stick for Kolur, then points to the building on the far side of the field, multistorey and inexplicably orange. 'That's the high school,' she says, then nods at the other building whose lights I saw last night. 'And that is the hospital.'

From this incline, the view is uninterrupted and panoramic. I take in everything to the horizon. The houses climbing the rise to my left, the orange school and its five flagpoles out front, blue flags limp in the still air, the small hospital and the steam issuing in white plumes from its basement. The suggestion of sea. And Tindastóll, soaring above the fjord. I turn and look inland. Just the mountain line extending as far as I can see on both sides of a wide, flat valley.

'There aren't any trees,' I comment.

'No.'

'It's amazing how far you can see without them. I'm not used to it.'

'We do have some small trees, but … Actually, we have a joke about this,' Guðný says. 'What do you do if you get lost in an Icelandic forest?'

'What?'

'Stand up.'

I smile.

'Do you like horses?' asks Guðný.

'I do.'

'We have some horses,' she says. 'We can take you to the stables tomorrow.'

'Okay, that would be lovely.'

'And after lunch today, we can go for a drive. Show you the rest of the town.'

'Thank you.' I start walking again but Guðný holds out a hand.

'Just wait,' she says. 'I need to take a shit.'

My mouth drops open. Then I realise my host mother has taken a plastic bag from her pocket. She bends down to collect a steaming dog turd.

I eat the cupped snow in my hand to hide my laughter.

Þórir returns home for lunch and we eat a darkly blistered flatbread with cheese and butter. It is a delicious combination. The bread tastes of smoke. Garðar remains in his bedroom.

'I walked around in the snow for the first time,' I tell Þórir.

'Já, that's one thing you will see here. Lots of snjór.'

'Snjór,' I repeat. That will be easy enough to remember.

'There are lots of words for snow here,' Guðný says, sipping her tea.

My smile falters a little.

'Já, perhaps one hundred,' she adds. 'If it's hard or soft. Icy. That type of thing.'

Þórir takes in my expression. 'Snjór is a good place to start.' He clears his throat, looks at Guðný. 'Ókei, förum við?'

Guðný gives me another of her small smiles. 'Let's go.'

*

It takes less than two minutes in the car to reach Skagfirðingabraut, the main road that threads through the heart of Sauðárkrókur. We pass the senior school on its hill, its tangerine walls stark against the white, and a petrol station. Guðný points out the unremarkable building following it. 'That's the biggest shop here. The supermarket.'

I nod, taking it all in. The town is very small. We pass the primary school, an open-air swimming pool, a bank, a post office, a DVD rental store doubling as another small petrol station, all in a matter of seconds. Most buildings are concrete and functional rather than beautiful. There are several clumps of apartment buildings, a choice of housing which seems strange to me given the abundance of space everywhere, as well as close-set single-storey houses like the one I am now living in. I wonder at this puddling of buildings at the foot of Tindastóll, the shops and homes sharing walls, all clustered against the main road. Perhaps, faced with such a vast sky, the daunting mountains, there is an inclination to have everything – and everyone – close to hand.

The further we go down the main road, the older and quainter the architecture becomes. A small, white Lutheran church bears up against the snowy hill behind it. Next to an ugly, grey bar are a clutch of tiny, colourful, steep-roofed houses, and a wood-panelled, red-trimmed 'cafe bar' called Kaffi Krókur. I see few people about, although I glimpse movement in the bakery, and there are lights on in a bright blue building Guðný tells me is a restaurant.

'What kind of food do they serve?' I ask, thinking of my aunt's *Gourmet Traveller* article on cod.

'Pizza.'

Before I know it, we have reached the end of the main road. After conferring with his wife, Þórir turns left, following the wide curve of the fjord. Suddenly, the sea is there, flat and bigger than I'd imagined, lurking beyond a low sea wall made of grey stone. Before me, beyond the reach of Tindastóll and the two islands I can see in the mouth of the fjord, the North Atlantic meets the north sky in a suggestion of oblivion.

Þórir heads towards Tindastóll and the open ocean, and we drive past the harbour and some rust-stained fishing boats bobbing in the dark grey water. There are a few parked trucks. A windowless fish factory. A hardware store. We draw closer to the great bulk of the mountain and its scarification of rock under the snow, and then, at the very end of the township, we are in front of what looks like an expanse of wooden clotheslines bearing hundreds of garlands of strung fish. Þórir pulls up and invites me to get out for a closer look. The smell is so intense, so unexpected, I place a hand on the warm bonnet of the car in a brief swoon.

Þórir points to the racks closest to us, strung only with fish heads. Hundreds of decapitated cod faces stare at me, stacked on top of one another, all wide-eyed and open-mouthed. *What the fuck has happened to me?* they seem to be saying.

'The heads go to Africa,' explains Þórir. 'The rest is for us. And for Europe.'

I feel that this is not the time to tell him I do not like seafood.

'This is what we call harðfiskur.' Þórir points at the swaying flanks of fish.

'Why does it need to be hung like this?' I ask.

'It is drying.'

I watch the fish heads blow and smack against each other as the wind picks up.

'Doesn't it go bad, left outside like this?'

Þórir shakes his head. 'It's too cold.'

We stand and watch the wind take shape among the hundreds of drying fish, before Þórir sniffs and heads back to the car. I notice that the day is dimming. The wind has brought with it that strange blue cast of light. It is closing in on us like an approaching shadow.

I check my watch. It is not yet three o'clock.

I am glad I will have somewhere to retreat to

CHAPTER FIVE

Outsider

When I wake early the next morning I suffer my first wave of homesickness. I knew this was to be expected but the force of it takes me by surprise. There is something about my unfamiliar bedroom with its blank walls and the deep silence both within and without the house that makes me long for the songbirds of my home and the usual noises of my father making breakfast. I have only been away from my family for six days, but Garðar's continued unwillingness to speak to me has made me anxious. Guðný and Þórir have not addressed it, and that makes me wonder if their hospitality has been forced. Perhaps they are hosting an exchange student out of obligation rather than out of interest. It is hard to shake an abiding sense that I am an imposition.

The thought that I may have left my loved ones and travelled vast distances only to be an encumbrance makes me pull the duvet over my head and cry. Then, hiccupping, I tiptoe into the bathroom and wash my face under the hot, sulphuric shower, resolving to do better. I will learn this inexplicable language. I will make this family like me. I will find the joy in this adventure.

When I sit down to breakfast, I smile at Guðný and Þórir and tell them I am determined to learn Icelandic. They tell me that's good, because I will be starting school tomorrow.

'Already?' I had assumed I might be allowed more time to settle in.

Guðný smears butter over her bread. 'What else would you do?'

The phone rings. Þórir gets up to answer it, and after speaking in Icelandic, motions me over and hands me the receiver.

'Hello?'

'Hæ, Hannah, this is Pétur Björnsson. I'm with the Rotary Club here.' His accent is oddly American. 'Welcome to Sauðárkrókur. How do you like Iceland?'

'It's beautiful,' I say. 'I like all the snow.'

Pétur laughs. 'Yeah, well, we got a lot of that. So, Hannah, I'm going to show you Fjölbrautaskóli Norðurlands Vestra today. You know where it is, right? You should be able to walk there.'

I have no idea what he's just said. 'Sorry, what are you going to show me?'

Pétur repeats the Icelandic name for me. 'It's the high school. Do you know where it is?'

'Oh, right. But isn't it a Sunday?'

'It's no problem. The school is open for all the boarders and I work here. I'll meet you out the front at ten.'

'The orange building?'

'That's the one.'

An hour later I am standing at the entrance of the school, having walked through the snow and a rising wind from Guðný and Þórir's place. A few Icelandic teenagers walk past me and stare. I wonder if my nose is running. The wind has blasted my cheeks red. It rattles the wires of the flagpoles above me.

'Góðan daginn.'

I turn and see a man in his thirties smiling at me from the foyer.

'Pétur heiti ég. Gaman að hitta þig, Hannah.'

The Icelandic greeting catches me off guard, but I do my best. 'Hæ, ég heiti Hannah.'

'Hannah, it's nice to have you here. I'm your Rotary counsellor while you're here, okay? Any issues, any problems, you let me know. I'll show you my office and you can come find me when you're at school, or you can call me. I'll give you my cell number.'

Pétur seems too young to be a Rotarian. Up close his face seems boyish and ruddy.

'You have really excellent English.'

'Thanks. I studied in Florida. Me and my wife, Regína, and Gunnar, our eldest son, lived there about ten years ago. I have four children now.'

Pétur shows me the pegs and racks where students leave their jackets and shoes. I had assumed that the Icelandic no-shoes-inside policy was only for private homes, but everyone is walking about in their socks or slides. My own socked feet slip on the heated wooden floors as Pétur takes me through three floors of classrooms and facilities. Everything is very clean and, thanks to the large windows, bright with natural light. The walls, I discover, are just as orange on the inside.

Pétur introduces me to the librarian, who has popped in on her weekend. She shows me the library's collection of fiction in English, about twenty-five novels in total. At a glance, I see Atwood, Hardy, Woolf.

'You can borrow anything, of course. We'll get you a card. You like reading?'

'Very much.' I lift a hand and touch the spines, marking the books for later. Mine. At home I have one tall bookshelf filled with novels I have thrifted from second-hand stores. I miss it. I have already read the books I brought with me and re-read those that I could not bear to leave behind. My worn copy of *Little Women*, one of my favourite books from when I was young, is one of these companions. I feel better for having it with me.

Pétur tells me that I can use the library computers anytime I want. I am relieved to know that I can email friends and family from school. Last night, I connected the computer to the internet to chat to my family on MSN, only for Þórir to walk up and down the corridor with an expectant look on his face. I felt guilty for hogging the telephone line and ended the chat and my family's barrage of questions as soon as I could. Already the library seems a haven, its lighting soft and warm, windows looking out onto the snowy mountains. I am glad I will have somewhere to retreat to.

Pétur gives me a cursory overview of the canteen, which sells snacks and drinks, the central hall where students socialise, the toilets and the classrooms, all of which seem very modern, and then takes me into his office to complete my enrolment. He suggests I take maths, German and Icelandic studies, but I also ask for English and visual art. He prints me out a timetable. Some classes start much earlier than at home, and a few finish very late.

'The school days are long here,' I say.

Pétur shakes his head. 'No, you don't have to come to school unless you have class. Just come and go as you need.'

'Like university.' This place seems to treat students more like adults than kids. Already I have seen groups of students openly smoking outside.

Pétur peers over my shoulder at the timetable. 'You have maths tomorrow. Eight o'clock.'

'I feel nervous,' I admit.

Pétur gives me a kind look. 'Just be yourself.'

That afternoon, Guðný offers to take me to the stables. I dress warmly, having learned how easily the wind slices through clothes on my walk to the school, but despite my thermals and fleece jumper, Guðný gives me a jumpsuit lined with sheepskin. I feel like an astronaut, following her to the car, arms pushed aloft from the thickness of my clothes.

The stables are outside the township, set among snowy expanses of pasture. After we park, I look inland and marvel again at the extraordinary distance one can see without the interruption of trees. The ghost of the glacier that once gouged out this valley is apparent in the space between the mountains and in the land's seaward groove. The last of the day's light catches the shallow waterways that thread along the valley floor.

When I turn and look the other way, northwards, the land looks like cupped hands held in offering to the sea.

Guðný hands me a rake and, as we muck out the stalls, she tells me that Skagafjörður, this district around the fjord, is famous for its horses.

'We have many horseriding competitions,' she says.

'In the snow?'

'No, we have an indoor arena.'

The Icelandic horses Guðný brings in from the yard are small enough to be ponies, their bodies solid and very hairy. I run my gloved hands over their icy coats and marvel at the length of their hair. They are unlike any other horses I have seen.

'These horses are descendants of those the Vikings brought with them,' Guðný says.

I believe it. It does not stretch the imagination to think of these creatures capable of holding fast through blizzards. I lift a hand to the nostrils of the horse closest to me. He breathes an exquisite warmth over my fingers.

I am reminded, then, of my aunt Gaynor, one of my mother's sisters. I never met her. She died after falling from a horse on her twenty-third birthday. Growing up, my other aunts often told me that I resembled Gaynor not just in looks but also in my nature and sensitivity. Sometimes I yearn so much to meet her, this aunt I have never known and yet love so deeply, I feel bereft. When Papa died, my grandmother gave me Gaynor's books of writing. I hadn't known she was a poet until then. Reading her words was the closest I'd felt to her since I was a small child, when I dreamed she held my hand. Thinking of her now bolsters me against my homesickness.

'Do you know what makes these horses so special?' asks Guðný.

This is the most she has spoken since my arrival.

'Their size?'

'No, it is because they have two extra …' She hesitates, searching for the word in English. 'Gaits? Yes, two extra gaits. So walking, trotting, galloping. But they also have tölt and skeið. Tölt is fast, but a rider can tölt and hold a full glass without spilling a drop.'

I cannot picture it until later, when we pause on our way to the car to watch a rider take her horse out into the snow.

'There,' says Guðný. 'That is tölt.'

It is extraordinary. The horse is flying, yet the rider is strangely still in the saddle. When I turn back to Guðný she is smiling broadly.

'You know, Hannah, if an Icelandic horse leaves the country, it can never come home again.'

I wait for Guðný to explain further, but she is already walking away.

The next day I walk to school in the dark, stomach swimming with nerves. It snowed again during the night and the crunch of my boots as I walk across the field is loud. At one point my step is met with a sudden cracking, and it takes me several moments before I realise that I am walking upon a body of water and that the ice is giving way under my weight. I lurch sideways until I am sure I am on solid ground again. There is no semblance of a path in front of me, just snow. I have no idea what lies underneath it. It might not be a field at all. I am guided only by the lights in the distance.

Entering the school, I hang up my coat and undo my shoes, casting surreptitious looks at the other students. Guðný and Þórir are so quiet, this is the first time I have heard an abundance of Icelandic. I spent the hour before bed last night diligently practising 'Hvað segirðu gott?' or 'How are you?', but the language I hear sounds vastly different to my own pitiful attempts. Regardless, I promise myself I will try to engage at least one person in conversation today.

I find the maths classroom and sit down in a spare seat. Everyone is staring at me. A girl seated nearby offers a polite smile when I introduce myself and tells me her own name, but it is so foreign to my ears that I struggle to repeat it back to her. 'Gwitherin?'

She fights a laugh. 'Sure. Something like that.'

The maths teacher begins taking roll call. He hesitates over my name, then offers a 'Velkomin' once he catches my eye, but makes no attempt to introduce me to the other students. The class begins. I have no idea what is going on. I don't have any textbooks, but even after 'Gwitherin' pushes her book between us so that I might share, I see that the text is entirely in Icelandic. It has been two years since I last took a maths class. Not even the sums make sense to me.

My next class is German, which I have never studied before. After five minutes I realise I cannot tell German and Icelandic apart, and by the end of the hour I am exhausted from attempting to understand two unfamiliar languages. I am not used to appearing so stupid to others. By the time I find my Icelandic studies classroom I am disheartened. Every lesson is filled with students who gape at me, but no one seems interested in talking.

'Excuse me? Hannah?'

I turn in the doorway of the classroom to see a girl beaming at me.

'Yes?'

'Hi! It's nice to meet you. You can call me Nok. I'm the other exchange student here in Sauðárkókur. From the AFS program in Thailand. Geirlaugur said you should sit with me so I can teach you the days of the week.'

'Oh, thanks. Who is Geirlaugur?'

'Our teacher.' She gestures to the desk at the front where a tall man is taking his seat. 'Everyone calls teachers by their first names here. Everyone calls everyone by their first name.'

I follow Nok to a desk up the back and she walks me through some basic vocabulary while Geirlaugur takes the class. At one point I look out the window and notice that it has finally grown light outside, the sky peach against the white of Tindastóll.

'How long are you staying for?' asks Nok as we pack up our books at the end of the hour.

'A year.'

'I'm going home soon,' Nok says.

My heart sinks.

Nok gives me a sympathetic smile. 'It's hard when you don't know anyone,' she says.

'Is it just me,' I ask, 'or does everyone here stare all the time?'

'Yes, they stare, because they do not know you. I'll try to introduce you to my friend Mæja. She's really nice.'

*

Nok takes me to her house at lunchtime so she can give me her *Learn Icelandic* CD-ROM. The light turns sallow and snow begins falling as we walk. I am grateful to Nok for her help and quietly thrilled to be out in such a thick snowfall, but when Nok drops me at Guðný and Þórir's house I feel homesickness crash against me like a wave. By the time I set out in the afternoon for more incomprehensible classes, the day has already collapsed back into darkness.

Afraid of accidentally walking over whatever it was that cracked beneath me, I take a longer route this time, following the road and its streetlights past the hospital. I am hunched into my coat and scarf, bent against the wind and snow, but after a few minutes I am aware of a car driving slowly alongside me. When I speed up, it does too. Alarm flares. It is dark and I am being followed. I wonder whether I need to make a run for it. Then the front and rear windows of the car wind down and three faces peer out at me.

I stare back at them. I have no idea what is going on.

'Já, þetta er hún. Hannah, frá Ástralíu.'

I catch my name and the word for Australia, and then 'skiptinemi' or 'exchange student'. Word has travelled fast. These locals want to get a good look at the stranger in town. I stop walking, anticipating some kind of conversation, but the car's occupants, now satisfied that I am indeed the exchange student from Australia, roll their windows back up. The car drives off.

The cold is deep within my bones

CHAPTER SIX

Midwinter

My first weeks pass. Winter tightens. The dark comes in like high tide.

One night I arrive home from a late class to a bustle in the kitchen. Guðný tells me that we are going to have the traditional food of Þorrablót, the midwinter feast of Þór.

There are hrútsprungar, lambs' testicles, pressed into a loaf bound with something clear and gelatinous. There is also sviðasulta, which is the boiled meat of a sheep head that has been pressed into a mould. It, too, is jellied, and as I cut a slice I am told that the eyes and tongue are included in the mix. I glance at my plate, half expecting to find the steady, clouded gaze of a boiled eye. Alongside these dishes are blood pudding, blóðmör, dark red and granular, and liver sausage, lifrarpylsa.

I dutifully take a sample of each of the traditional meat and offal dishes, all of which are served cold or at room temperature, and then I pile my plate with more palatable vegetables. When Guðný points out that I have only a small serving of dinner, I add flatbread and hangikjöt, thin slices of strong-smelling smoked lamb, which I have tried before and like, as well as the dried fish, which, though I like it less, seems innocuous compared to the platters of glistening organs in aspic.

'Skál,' says Þórir, raising his bottle of beer.

'Skál.'

There is nothing for it. I power through the food on my plate. I am here to experience the culture, I tell myself, as I force down the sviðasulta and blóðmör, washing them both down with beer. The smell of both reminds me of wet dog food, and I chew quickly and efficiently, my tongue coiled to the roof of my mouth to protect as many of my tastebuds as possible. The pale pink spheres of testicle have a surprisingly mild flavour, however the texture is unnerving. The rye bread tastes sweet by comparison, the many sips of beer are a necessity, although the combination of its yeasty malt with the organ meat is an unpleasant surprise. Still, I need liquid to swill the coagulated blood from my tongue.

For a fleeting instant I think of the four exchange students from my district who went to France.

Arseholes.

Just as I think I have done as good a job as anyone could expect of me, Þórir rises and goes to the fridge, returning with two sealed plastic tubs. I watch warily as he removes the lid of one and skewers a square of something white and fishy-smelling with a toothpick.

'What is it?' I ask.

'Súr hvalur,' he replies.

Guðný translates. 'Preserved whale.'

I take it.

It's not until I bite into the piece of whale that I realise this offering is not meat but blubber. It's appallingly soft between my teeth, heavy and waxy, and it tastes both sour and intensely of fish. I swallow it without chewing.

'What do you think?' asks Guðný.

I drain my beer then take a moment to see if it has washed the taste away. It hasn't. I will taste blubber until the end of my days. 'It's like …' I hesitate. 'Like biting into a lipstick. Made of fish.'

Þórir then reaches for the second container. I try to read the label but the Icelandic makes no sense to me and all I can see is another pile of small, off-white cubes. As soon as he cracks the lid, however, I am reminded of Jón Ásgeir and his revolting breath.

'Hákarl,' Þórir says. Again, he skewers a segment with a toothpick and hands it to me.

I'm aware that the family has stopped eating and is looking on with amused anticipation.

'Is this the rotten shark?'

Þórir nods.

The smell is overpowering. It is not so much fishy as unquestionably putrid.

'You don't have to eat it,' says Guðný.

'It's okay,' I say. Maybe it tastes better than it smells, I think.

I open my mouth and drop the shark onto my tongue. Immediately, my body rejects it. I retch and, without conscious thought, sprint out of the kitchen to the bathroom. It is only after I spit the shark into the small bin on the countertop that I regain some semblance of control over myself. Even as I gulp water from the bathroom tap and reach for the toothpaste, my body continues to shudder.

When I return to the kitchen, even Garðar is laughing. I notice that the tub of hákarl has been put away, though its smell still hangs over the table with dreadful potency.

Guðný hands me a glass of water. 'I don't like it either,' she says to me.

Now that it is midwinter, the wind becomes alarmingly strong. The absence of trees means that the wind is unimpeded in its force. It also means that it is difficult to guess at its speed when looking out the window. I learn to brace for the possibility of a shove sideways when I step outside.

One night, walking home from school in the dark, the wind is so fierce that I must lean into it with the full weight of my body to move forward. Icy snow blown up off the road peppers my face with a sharpness that makes me panic. I am exhausted by the time I reach the house and fumble my way indoors, eyes and nose streaming, my ears ringing and aching as if from blows to the head. The cold is so deep within my bones I may as well have been walking naked. Guðný makes me a cup of tea and as I sit at the kitchen table, slowly thawing, she tells me that once, when Garðar was small and she went to pick him up from preschool, the wind was so strong that he was lifted into the air.

She managed to snatch the cuff of his snowsuit before he blew into the road. Then she had to commando-crawl back along the ground, holding him under her arm, to the safety of their car.

I know she is not exaggerating; I have heard of cars being blown off the road.

On gusting nights, I lie in bed and feel the wind hitting the house. I begin to think of it not in terms of weather but of spirit. Not in terms of speed but of outrage. The wind here moans and wails and howls, but it also uses a tongue inflected with a tone that sometimes sounds like a question, sometimes a greeting, sometimes a curse. I lie in the dark, and as the gales buffet the walls and gust against the three panes of glass in my bedroom window, I feel a deep respect for its power and, within that, an acknowledgement of the wind here as a sentient being.

It wakes me up, sometimes, with its urgency.

Sometimes I dream of crying women.

Sometimes I wake up to find myself crying. On these days I go and sit on the tiles in the shower and sob until I have muted my longing for home and family to a more tolerable thrum. The twenty hours of darkness each day is not helping my feelings of alienation in this small community, nor the new heaviness that has come over me. Sometimes it takes all my energy just to rise out of bed in the morning.

I tell myself that every negative emotion is being compounded by the claustrophobic winter gloom and the near constant confinement indoors. I remind myself of my beautiful family at home and the love that has buoyed me my entire life, and I remind myself that I will see them again in time, that I carry their love with me. I tell myself that things will get better. I must do everything in my power to engage in the culture, to make friends, to learn the language.

Every day I sit at the desk in my bedroom and study Icelandic. I am diligent. There is a lot to learn. The Icelandic alphabet, while mostly familiar to me, omits some letters (c, w, q and z), has a handful of accents that change pronunciation (á, é, í, ó, ú, ý), two more vowels (ö and æ), and two runic-looking letters, ð and þ, both of which are pronounced as 'th', one hard (as in 'the') and one soft (as in 'thing'). I sit on my bed and practise contorting my tongue into positions that better let me turn my hard rolled r's into softer, breathless ones: a gentle, single trill. The hardest sound to correctly say is 'au', which is one of several unfamiliar vowel sounds. My guidebook says it is comparable to the French 'oeill', but that is not quite right either. My mouth is stubborn. It has committed its shape to the vowels of my mother tongue. I repeat the unfamiliar vowels over and over, and I wonder whether my host family can hear me and if they think I'm crying again. Ohye, ohye.

If they're aware of my homesickness, of my weeping in the shower, they do not mention it.

Alongside Nok's CD-ROM, I have also bought another dictionary and a *Learning Icelandic* textbook from Skagfirðingabúð, which is not just a supermarket, as it turns out, but a one-stop shop for electronics, whitegoods, clothes, toys and anything else people in the district might want, including books. My Icelandic teacher, the gruff Geirlaugur, has also given me some photocopied sheets of simple phrases and exercises. The exchange committee in Australia told us that we would have access to language classes in our host towns, but Jón Ásgeir has emailed to say that, while the Rotary students placed around Reykjavík are learning together, there are no formal Icelandic classes available in Sauðárkrókur. I must just get on as best as I can.

Before I arrived in Iceland I thought that learning a language would essentially involve memorising a vocabulary list. Find out the Icelandic word for 'horse' and say that instead. It has been dispiriting to learn that language, particularly Icelandic, is so much more complex, that it demands so much more of me. Icelandic is a dialect of Old Norse, a tongue once common across Scandinavia, and I have learned that Iceland's geographical isolation peat-bogged the language from the twelfth century on, while elsewhere it evolved into Swedish, Danish and Norwegian. This means that it has (devastatingly) retained a lot of its twelfth-century inflections, highly irregular conjugation patterns and full-body embrace of compound words. When I ask Þórir about how the word for horse, 'hestur', might be inflected, he tells me it might be hest, hestinn, hestar, hesta, hesti, hestum, hestinum, hests, hestarnir, hestunum, hestana, hestanna or hestsins depending on the context.

I decide I do not like inflections. Even my own name is subject to them. After correcting a few people who refer to me as something like 'Her-noo', I am told that Hannah is sometimes 'Hönnu'. 'From Hannah', for example, is 'frá Hönnu'. Even when not warped by grammatical quirks, my name is pronounced differently here. Emphasis falls on its first syllable, the second an afterthought almost expunged by breathy exhalation. The 'a' is softened into an 'uh', the consonant held so long it sometimes carries a pause. Huhnn-na. The Icelandic spelling for Hannah lacks the final h, too – Hanna – and I am weirded out by this amputation, my own name unfamiliar on paper.

I have discovered that Icelanders sometimes speak on the in-breath, especially when in agreement. They literally do not stop talking to take a breath. I didn't know it was possible to do this. I have never attempted to speak while inhaling, but now I practise it in my bedroom so that one day I might sound like a local. Instead of projecting my voice into the world, I inhale words from the air, as though they were always there, suspended around me, and only needed breath to form. It is a curious sensation, to finish speaking with my lungs full.

It is hard to keep my spirits up, doggedly trying to untangle Icelandic alone like this. I do not know if I will ever be able to master it. I want to. It has a charming, whispered quality, all aspiration and voiceless sonorants. But my first attempts at initiating conversation in Icelandic have been atrocious. I realise I not only speak at the pace of a snail, but I also pronounce everything phonetically – I have no sense of slang or the way words are abbreviated in everyday speech, which letters are commonly left off or which syllables are pushed into the next. Students who can speak English default to it when I ask them questions. Those who only speak Icelandic shrug their shoulders at me. Everyone is polite, no one is unkind, but I am frustrated by my inability to express myself.

The good news is that my attempts at Icelandic are attracting gestures of inclusion at school. 'Gwitherin' from maths class (whose name, I learn, is spelled Guðrún) gives me a lollipop called Tyrkisk Peber from the school canteen. It tastes of licorice and is bewilderingly spicy. Nok introduces me to her friend Mæja, who is softly-spoken and very pale, with long, blonde hair. I cannot tell if she is shy or someone who simply prefers to do her own thing. Nok invites me over to Mæja's house one afternoon to eat the Thai instant noodles her family has sent her. After that, we eat harðfiskur, which Mæja likes. She insists we coat it with butter. The first hour is a little awkward – not so much friends hanging out as ambassadors engaged in a formal cross-cultural tasting exercise – but when the conversation veers to music, we all relax. Guðný has let me borrow her acoustic guitar at home, and Mæja shows me her electric guitar, tells me about her great love for Pink Floyd. We promise to make each other some mix CDs, and when I leave, I feel happy in a way I have not felt since I arrived. Another group of girls approach me one morning with questions about the television show *Neighbours*, then invite me out to Kaffi Krókur that night. I am excited when they pull into Guðný and Þórir's house and beep for me, and the night spent drinking coffee around a table in the cafe proves an interesting introduction to the hobbies of the local teens. I mention to Hjördís, the one who first spoke to me, that I have been surprised by how mature the students my age seem here. Hjördís tells me that it's not uncommon for people to have babies young.

When I ask her if young mothers have a hard time of it, she frowns, confused. 'But children are wonderful. Maybe you have your babies, then you go study afterwards. No one cares.'

Her friend, Birna, smiles at me. 'It's different here from, you know, America. England. Maybe Australia. Here, it is much more common to have children before you are married. Lots of people don't get married and it's fine. Everyone loves babies!'

'We are familiar with love,' Hjördís agrees.

*

I am grateful for these small interactions. It's hard to build on them, though. Pétur, catching me sitting alone at school, has told me to keep trying, that he's happy to introduce me to some lovely people, but I tell him I find it difficult to enter social circles when everyone already knows each other and they have been friends since preschool. I had assumed my Australian-ness might be exotic enough to lure friends, but once it has been established that I have never lived on Ramsay Street, the interest in my cultural difference is minimal. As one girl tells me in art class, disappointment in her voice: 'You look like us. We thought you might be super tanned. You know, like a surfer.'

I laugh when I relate this anecdote, but Pétur seems concerned. 'How is everything going with Guðný and Þórir?'

'Good,' I lie.

He waits for me to continue.

I tell him that Garðar now speaks to me occasionally, although his conversation is generally limited to telling me that dinner is ready. My host parents, when not working, spend a lot of time at the stables.

'Do you go with them?'

'Sometimes. I help them shovel the manure, but often they've already left when I get back from school. It's okay. I don't mind being home alone.'

I don't tell Pétur that the reserved, quasi-formal relationship we have is not for a lack of time spent together. I keep waiting for something to click, for Guðný and Þórir to give me a hug or ask me how things are going. They do not share much of their lives. In fact, they hardly speak.

'How is the homesickness, Hannah?'

'Fine,' I say. There is a split second when my chin trembles, but I quickly break into a smile. I assure myself Pétur hasn't seen it.

The homesickness is not fine. I try to spare my parents from it, but it becomes harder and harder not to write long emails home, all of them tinged with upset. Outside of the occasional afternoon of social promise, my only solace is the English-language bookshelf in the school library. I borrow *Jude the Obscure* and Margaret Atwood's *Alias Grace* and *To the Lighthouse*. The latter I read one evening when I am alone in the house, the wind howling outside. There is something revelatory about Woolf's words; her articulation of rich inner lives existing beneath a surface of trivialities, and the way she presents the problem of perception, the difficulty of knowing others, is so acute that I break out in goosebumps while reading. The hair lifts from my neck and I feel as though a molten liquid is being poured over my skull. When I have finished it, I am dazed.

The calibre of books on the library shelf is high, and I find myself not only soothed but inspired by them. My reading habits have been fairly scattered across genres, but those I'm reading here are all literary. They make me think of my own aspirations to write, and I begin to fill my notebook with poems and philosophical ramblings.

I do not want to know the answers, I write. *I want to know and question the questions.*

When I am writing I am lifted out of my sadness. I am above it, observing it, making sense of it in a way I cannot when I am consumed by depth of feeling. When I write, I am a wiser self. The relief of this is exquisite.

One morning I am so absorbed in composing a poem during Icelandic studies that I don't notice Geirlaugur standing in front of me until he clears his throat. He frowns and taps the page of my neglected exercises.

'What is so important that it stops you from working, Hannah?' He picks up my notebook and squints at my scribbles. 'Poetry?'

I nod.

'Hmm.' He puts the notebook back on the desk and gives me a dark look before returning to his chair.

I am deeply embarrassed. The whole class has been interrupted. I avoid Nok's look of sympathy.

I have Icelandic again the next day. After giving the class their assignment, Geirlaugur summons me to his desk. I think I am in for it again, but to my surprise he hands me a book.

'This is for you,' he says.

Cold was that Beauty. It is an anthology of Icelandic poems, translated into English.

I open the cover and see that he has inscribed the title page.

To Hannah,
From one poet to another.
Geirlaugur

Geirlaugur nods at me. 'You will get some of your work published one day.'

I feel as though my heart might burst. 'I hope so.'

'I know it,' he responds.

That night I write a poem about the physical rush I sometimes feel when writing. As though embers are sparking down my spine, as though my veins are filled with fire. I send it to my sister.

I have rediscovered my passion for writing, I tell her. I mention Geirlaugur, how I suddenly feel as though writing is a calling. *I feel that I must pursue it.*

She writes back within the hour. *I believe you*, she says.

Geirlaugur Magnússon, voice carved out with smoking, continues to let me write poetry from that day on. Icelandic becomes my favourite class. I sit at my desk and rub my socked feet together, smell the usual classroom odour of coffee and old cigarette smoke clinging to washed hair, and let the soft Icelandic consonants of my classmates flow around me like water, until I feel suspended and loose in body and mind. Then I write. Each line is a muscled stroke hauling me to some distant shore of meaning.

And when I look up, Geirlaugur is there, nodding at me in silent encouragement.

Something of the dreamscape

CHAPTER SEVEN

Blood

One evening I am interrupted in my writing by a knock on my bedroom door. It is Þórir.

'Hæ, Hannah. So, I'm going to take you downtown in five minutes.'

I don't recall any plans, but I assume I've unknowingly agreed to attend some kind of event.

It is dark outside. Snow on the ground. Þórir has already started the car and is waiting in the driver's seat, wearing his usual leather jacket. We head towards the town, lights from the houses brilliant against the darkness. It is only when he pulls off the main street to take the road by the sea, filled with industrial buildings empty of light, that I begin to wonder where we are going.

'So. You like theatre?' Þórir asks.

I recall I'd listed drama as an interest in my Rotary application. I nod, confused.

Þórir reaches inside his jacket for a packet of nicotine gum. He pops out a piece, bites it in half, and places the remainder back inside the blister packet. He says nothing more.

The car pulls up outside an ominous two-storey cement building, headlights illuminating a pile of hard rubbish rimmed with snow next to a wooden door. The place looks closed. Derelict. I haven't been here before.

'Okay. We're here.'

He cuts the engine and I fight a sudden wave of apprehension – is he going to kill me? Þórir has already started walking towards the door, hunched against the cold. I follow him.

The smell of coffee and cigarette smoke hits me as soon as I step into the entryway. Þórir shuts the door behind us and nods at a wooden staircase to my left, his face impassive. 'Go on,' he says.

Reassured by the light filtering down and the suggestion of voices, I decide I am unlikely to die and start climbing the stairs. They lead to a closed door. Þórir reaches from behind me and opens it.

In a plain, wooden-floored room, twelve or so people stop whatever it is they're doing and stare at us. Þórir says something in Icelandic and then heads back down the stairs. 'Okay, see you in a few hours,' he calls to me over his shoulder, and then he is gone.

My face flushes as I stand in the doorway. I have no idea what is going on. The people in the room exchange glances.

One of them, a kind-eyed, red-haired woman with pronounced cheekbones, asks me a question in Icelandic. I apologise, ask her if she speaks English.

'Oh, you're the exchange student,' she replies.

'Yes. I'm Hannah.'

'I'm Embla,' she says.

We look at each other, as if waiting for clarification.

'Sorry …' I feel as though I might just let myself fall backwards down the stairs to end the excruciating awkwardness. 'Can you tell me where I am?'

'Oh,' Embla says. 'He didn't tell you?'

'No.'

'We're the theatre company. Leikfélag Sauðárkróks.'

Someone mutters something to Embla and she looks back at me, eyebrow quirked. 'He thought you could be in our next play. But …' She frowns. 'You don't speak Icelandic?'

'Not yet. I'm learning …'

'The play is in Icelandic.'

'Oh.'

'Well, come in,' she says. She closes the door behind me and gestures to an ancient coffee pot gurgling its last upon a stained hot plate. 'Have some coffee. We'll find something for you to do.'

I sip the very strong coffee from a chipped mug as the company gather for some whispered conferral. I recognise one or two of them from school, but there is a wide assortment of ages. Eventually they break off their conversation and one of the younger men hands Embla a photocopied script. She passes it to me, smiling. 'Welcome.'

I look down at it. *Ertu Hálfdán?* it reads. *Are You* something something? I translate.

'You can paint the stage and scenes and make props,' an older man with dark bags under his eyes tells me as he lights a cigarette.

'Yes, you can be …' Embla searches for the right word. 'Like, our slave.'

I feel enormously grateful. The prospect of sitting in this room for another few hours stewing in my uselessness would have been too much to bear.

'I can do that,' I say. 'Takk.'

'It's no problem,' Embla replies.

An unsmiling blonde girl contributes something in Icelandic. Another man translates. 'You can put up the posters in the town.'

I nod. 'Sure.'

'And you can mop up the blood.'

I stare at them. 'Blood?'

'Yes, that would be good.' A short woman with a long plait and nicotine stains on her teeth nods.

'I'm sorry … blood?'

The stiffness in the room dissolves a little then, as the Icelanders notice my wide eyes and start laughing. Through stilted English, hand gestures and some miming, they collectively tell me that *Ertu Hálfdán?* is a comedy in which every character dies a violent death – requiring, by way of hidden tubing, a lot of exaggerated bleeding. I am tasked with cleaning up the syrupy mess left onstage and, it turns out, with firing gunshots, setting off arrows and releasing nooses.

'Is that something you think you can do?' asks Embla. 'Help us with the blood and the murders?'

'Yes,' I say. 'Yes, I can do that.'

I assume, as I head home several hours later, that most of my responsibilities as a newly minted member of the community's amateur theatre group will not require any spoken Icelandic. I am right, but in the coming weeks I realise that I will, at the very least, be required to identify *their* spoken Icelandic in tandem with the written script. How else will I fire a starter gun at the precise moment a character needs to be shot in the head?

The play is going to show in a month at Bifröst, the town's cinema and sometime theatre. I have four weeks to, if not completely understand the script, at least decipher it well enough to contribute to the murder of the six characters according to verbal cues.

I begin to translate the script, word by word, with my Icelandic–English dictionary. I am working away at it in the school library one lunchtime when Mæja stops by to see what I am doing, and after I explain my predicament, she offers to help. With her pronunciation, I slowly learn how to differentiate words within a stream of Icelandic and understand the correlation between how it is written and how it is pronounced.

Blóð. Blothe. Blood.

Dáinn. Da-winn. Dead.

Morð. Morth. Murder.

Draugur. Droh-ger. Ghost.

Að vera reimt. Ath vera raymt. To be haunted.

I learn Icelandic from the grave up.

In March, Guðný and Þórir take me with them to visit Þórir's parents in Reykjavík.

The hours lift into light as we drive south, travelling around the coast on the Ring Road, the single-lane 'highway' of Iceland that encircles the larger mass of the country. Even though it is a main road, we are often the only car. The views from my backseat window are extraordinary. I lose myself in thought, watching the mountains and valleys and hills undulate as we curve around them, the shining ribbons of river capturing all available light and carrying it out to the sea. The sudden endlessness to my vision makes my mind feel as though it is unfurling, as though there is room enough within me now to hold more. More beauty, more feeling. The earth seems an offering to the higher power of the sky, and I wonder whether this country is more light than anything else. It wraps around the horizon.

The mountains stand together in broad and spectacular ranges extending inland, the valleys between them sweeping and concave. In the distance I see low cloud, a swathe of rainfall beneath and its grey concealment of the farmhouse behind. I see it move in real time, then dissipate, clarity restored. I have never seen water act on air like this; I am hypnotised and skin-struck. The same feeling that sounded through my childhood returns to me and I gaze out, heart on the cusp of some deep and wild understanding.

I am in this reverie when the car veers around the staunch shoulder of a mountain and I see a sudden strangeness. Instead of the snow-flecked expanse of a valley floor, the land before us is interrupted with a vast and densely clustered mass of rounded hillocks, each circular and smooth-sided. There could be hundreds of them. Thousands, perhaps. There is something weird about it all, something of the dreamscape.

My curiosity is high enough for me to broach the silence in the car.

'Are these Viking burial mounds?' I lean forward and point out the windscreen.

Guðný shakes her head. 'No. They're not anything like that.' She looks at Þórir. 'Snjóflóð?'

Þórir clears his throat. 'Yes, they were caused by an avalanche. A long time ago.'

'Yes, but you see there …' Guðný points to the right side of the road, where the hills are fewer. 'Those three there together are called Þrístapar.'

My eyes follow her extended finger and I see a gathering of three, their pale grass snow-smacked.

'This is where we had the last execution in Iceland.'

A shiver runs through me. I wind down the window and stare at the hills as we pass. The wind is cold. It buffets against my ears and they immediately ache from the assault, but I wait until we've driven past before winding the window back up. I swivel in my seat and see that the sky behind us has darkened into low cloud. There is something very lonely about the sight of the hills melting into the vastness of the valley against such a failing of light.

'What happened?' I ask, turning back around.

'It was a woman, actually,' Þórir says. 'They cut off her head with an axe.'

'What did she do?'

'A murder. Another man was executed too.'

'Já, Friðrik.' Guðný nods to herself.

'Já, Agnes og Friðrik.'

'Her name was Agnes?'

'Já.'

'Who did she kill?'

Þórir and Guðný glance at each other, frowning a little.

'I know this, but I can't remember right now. You know, it's a famous story here –'

'Natan Ketilsson,' Guðný interrupts. 'That was his name.'

'Já, það var hann.'

'This happened a long time ago, you know,' Guðný continues. Raindrops begin to land on the windscreen. 'It was the old days.'

Þórir glances back at me with a smile. 'We don't do that anymore.'

'No.' I return his smile, but when he turns, I twist back, trying for one last glimpse of the hills in their eerie multitude. But the road has sworn to the rise of the next mountain and behind us the sky has claimed all distance in rainfall.

The rest of the journey is one of shadow and cloud upon the wilder road of the highlands, where the road is squeezed between steep inclines of shale and rock, and old, dense snow lies in ditches long untouched by sun. I watch it all pass, suddenly weary, my mind's eye moving from the wintered landscape before me to a glinting imagination of those dark historical details. Low cloud. Rock. Snowfall in the cloistered height of the mountains.

A trinity of hills.

Axe fall.

Later that month there is an opportunity to see a little more of the country. In a brief reprieve from school and the silence of my host family, Jón Ásgeir and the seven other Rotary exchange students collect me for a short holiday to visit Rotary Clubs in the north. As soon as I get on the bus, I am overwhelmed by the students' cheerful calls of welcome. It has been a long time since I have been met with such friendliness and warmth. Roman is there, already friends with the three Brazilians – Diego, Marcia and Paloma – and Clara, from Columbia.

That night we stay in a cabin outside of Ólafsfjörður. As the snow falls outside, we drink hot chocolate and play cards. Marcia suddenly grips my ear.

'What's wrong with you!' She shows the others my attached earlobes. 'Hannah, are you an elf? A witch?'

When I laugh, she takes the cards from everyone's hands and passes them to me. 'Tell my fortune.'

'No.'

'Please!'

I roll my eyes, ask her to select three cards from the deck and then improvise predictions.

She grows pale. 'You are a witch,' she says.

'Do me,' says Clara.

The South Americans crowd around, crowing as I make this or that observation.

'You know I'm just making this up,' I tell them.

'No, this is very accurate,' Marcia says.

'It's really not.'

'But this is my life. It's true.'

'Can you read hands?' ventures Diego.

'Palms?'

'Yes, palms!'

The Brazilians shove their upturned hands in front of me, arguing in Portuguese and then breaking into laughter and nudging each other out of the way. I realise, as I examine the lines upon their palms, that this is the first time I have touched another person in over three months. I had not realised how starved I have been for physical contact. Such a small thing, to hold someone's hand in mine, and yet I feel that I am almost vibrating, like a struck bell, for the joy of it.

With their fortunes all inexpertly told, the South Americans accept me as one of their own. They pull me back onto the couch with them, and I realise that I have been feeling like a ghost since arriving in Iceland. Untouched and unaddressed and always prickling with the sensation that others are talking about me. Now, in the press of shoulders and knees against mine, I am reminded of my own body.

The next day, after presenting at the local club meeting, we drive through a pristine whiteness back west towards Akureyri. In this northern city, we visit Listasafnið á Akureyri, or the Akureyri Art Museum.

The first room contains brightly coloured, backlit photographs of food. I wander around for a good ten minutes before I realise that every photograph has a sliding board behind it that can be pulled out. On these boards are the mug shots, names and crimes of people executed within the American justice system. The foods pictured, I realise, are last meals requested by the prisoners.

The other Rotary students move on to the next exhibition, but I stay, studying each photo and reading about the men and women who died by electric chair and lethal injection after requesting a hamburger, a plate of spaghetti, ribs and sides. One of the last images I come to is of a birthday cake. It is one of the saddest things I have ever seen and when I pull out the photo and look into the eyes of the young man who requested it, my breath hitches in my throat until I can bear it no longer and cry, silently, in the darkest corner of the gallery. Eventually I pull myself together and walk out to the foyer to buy a guide. It is called 'Aftökur og útrýmingar', or 'Executions and Exterminations'. The work that made me weep is by German artist Barbara Caveng and called *Hinstu máltíðir* in Icelandic, *Finalmeals* in English. I feel utterly altered by it, as though I have been made to witness the deaths of these people who asked for green apples, a single strawberry. The artwork's emphasis on their humanity reframes their deaths by capital punishment as unbearably cruel. I am reminded of the distress of Björk's character in *Dancer in the Dark* as a noose is placed around her head. Then I think of Agnes, that woman beheaded by axe. Since passing through those hills, I have asked some friends what they know of her and have learned that Agnes Magnúsdóttir was Natan Ketilsson's maid. She stabbed him to death while he slept, although no one has been able to tell me why.

A violent shiver runs through me and I fight a new upswell of tears. The woman at the front desk gives me a strange look.

'Are you all right?' she asks in English.

I hold up the guidebook. 'It's a powerful exhibition.'

She nods. When she speaks again, her voice is gentle. 'Why don't you go outside and sit in the sun for a little bit? I'll tell your friends where to find you.'

That afternoon we all go to a cafe. Icelanders like to pause at around four o'clock for kaffi, which is a break for coffee and often something to eat. It is one of the many little observations about Icelanders I have recorded in my notebook. Others include their widespread enthusiasm for pizza and caffeine, and the way people often leave their cars unlocked, motors running, when they go into the shops.

Jón Ásgeir buys us slices of cheesecake and hot chocolates, and between the richness of the dessert and the warmth of the cafe I feel queasy. I keep thinking of the last meals, the terrible sadness of them. Then, lethal injections. Beheadings. I excuse myself.

In the bathroom I vomit violently into a toilet. The restroom is cool, unheated, and I stay there until my blood is no longer swimming in my cheeks, my forehead pressed against the tiled walls.

We are billeted out to families in Akureyri that night. I am taken in by a young couple who have a four-year-old. Their boy keeps charging me with his foam sword, but Rakel and Siggi are warm and welcoming, and as we have dinner together I am struck by how easy it is to talk with them, how I have already laughed more in one night than during all the dinners with Guðný and Þórir combined. As I listen to Rakel speak about how she likes looking at the bodies of male athletes, I realise that Guðný and Þórir's enduring silence may not necessarily be cultural.

'But don't you look at the boobies?' Rakel asks when Siggi protests.

'No, I don't,' Siggi says.

Rakel considers this. 'If I was a man, I think I would look at the boobies.' She winks at me, grinning, as Siggi rolls his eyes.

When Siggi takes their son to bed, Rakel asks me how I am finding Icelandic. I tell her I have learned a lot through the translation of *Ertu Hálfdán?* Our conversation turns to ghosts then, and Rakel becomes thoughtful.

'There are many stories of ghosts within Icelandic culture. Tourists like to make a lot of the elves and huldufólk, but lots of us also believe in ghosts. And you know, Icelandic ghosts are different. They aren't, you know, just puffs of air. They act as though they are alive. Some can move their bodies around.'

A few weeks earlier, I'd been to the indoor horse arena with Guðný and Þórir to see a local rider re-enact 'Djákninn á Myrká', or 'The Deacon of Dark River', one of Iceland's most well-known ghost stories. I had already encountered the folktale in Icelandic studies. Many years ago, a deacon was courting a girl called Guðrún, who lived on a farm over the river Hörgá. One day he rode his horse Faxi to the farm to invite Guðrún to a Christmas feast at Myrká. He told her he would return on Christmas Eve to collect her. As he returned home, however, the ice on the river cracked, and the deacon fell into the roiling water and died. His body was found, and he was buried a week before Christmas, but no word of his death reached Guðrún. On Christmas Eve she was getting ready to meet him when there was a knock at the door. She had only one arm in the sleeve of her coat, but when she looked out into the dark she saw Faxi, so she hurried over. She assumed the man he carried was the deacon, even though he wore a hat that hid his face. She climbed up behind him and they set off. As they rode, the horse stumbled, the rider's hat tipped forward, and Guðrún suddenly saw the deacon's skull shining in the moonlight.

'The moon fades, death rides,' the deacon then said. 'Don't you see a white spot on the back of my head, Garún, Garún?'

Guðrún, knowing that ghosts cannot pronounce the name of God, which is Guð, replied: 'I see, as is.'

They rode on, and when they arrived at Myrká, they dismounted and the deacon said, 'Wait here, Garún, Garún, while I move Faxi, Faxi.'

Ghosts often speak in verse, repeating the last word of each line.

At this moment, Guðrún saw an open grave in the churchyard of Myrká and, at the same time, felt the deacon pulling her towards it. Luckily, she was still only wearing one sleeve of her coat. The coat ripped, Guðrún escaped and ran to the church bell, tolling it until people came out to see what was happening. At this, the deacon returned to his grave with Guðrún's sleeve. The grave filled back up with earth.

'Djákninn á Myrká', performed with real horses in the darkness of the arena, had spooked me. There was something strange about it, something unnerving. The story does not end with the deacon fleeing back to his grave, either. He continued to haunt Guðrún until finally an exorcist was summoned. In every telling of the story, it is said that she was never the same again.

I tell Rakel that I can understand why ghosts have a strong presence in Iceland. Even in my few months of living here, I have seen how the wind moves the snow along the ground at night, like a spirit looking for rest. How sometimes the mountains seem to possess faces, and how the wind can sound like a crying child. Iceland feels like a place where ghosts abide. There is another air here. The boundaries feel permeable somehow.

Rakel nods. 'Well, maybe our eyes are only made for some things in this world. But there are others. Some people here, they can see these other things. I believe there are people who have been given the eyes for such things. Special people.' She reaches for my coffee cup and gives my hand a pat. 'This, I believe.'

This place is breathing

CHAPTER EIGHT

Kin

Somehow, spring arrives. The sun finally rises above the height of the mountains and its return feels miraculous, like the sighting of someone I long believed dead. The valley is now pale yellow, the snow on the mountains melting to show grey-brown rock beneath. The rivers and streams in the valley run gold. There is little green and yet, under this new and wheaten light, everything seems on the cusp of revival. The trees in Litli skógur, Little Forest, shudder with the roar of snowmelt that now tumbles through it, the birch suddenly in bud. Set deep within a steep gorge on the higher slopes of the town, the park is the only place in the village with trees. I take the path to the wooden bridge that spans its river and watch the ravens circle above. The sky lifts. Everything is drawing breath.

*

On the morning of my birthday, I am gifted with a beam of sun that slices past my blinds and throws warmth into the room. I am lying in bed, watching it move across the wall, when Þórir knocks on my door to tell me that my parents are on the phone. I sprint down the corridor. It has been a long time since I have heard their voices. The line is good – they sound as though they could be in the next room – and my chest swoops at their outpouring of love.

At school, my English class sings 'Happy Birthday' to me in English, then again in Icelandic, and finally in Danish for good measure. I am learning, from the many small concerts at school, the numerous choirs in the district and the inevitable acoustic guitar sessions that conclude a lot of social gatherings, that Icelanders love to sing.

'Til hamingju með afmælið!' Classmates come up and hug me and some of them give me cards and presents, and I realise that I am making friends.

That night I sit up until midnight writing in my notebook. It seems astonishing to me that I am eighteen, that I have already lived so many years.

The great wonder of existing at all.

Maybe life is a river, I write. *And death is the ocean.* Ocean as end and as beginning. Ocean as source of life. All rivers moving beyond their boundaries into physical reunion.

Two weeks later, on Páskadagur, Guðný and Þórir give me an Easter egg. Guðný explains that, in Iceland, Easter eggs have proverbs inside of them. I crack mine open and take out the scroll of paper.

'Sjaldan verður ósinn eins og uppsprettuna dreymir,' I read aloud.

Þórir explains the adage to me. 'It is saying, no matter what you think of the future, it will most likely be different.' He hands the scroll back to me, smiling. 'No one knows what will happen.'

Later that day, I sticky-tape the proverb into my notebook. I get out my dictionary and write the literal translation beneath it.

Seldom is the estuary what the river source dreams of.

At the end of May, Pétur finds me in the school library, where I am studying for upcoming exams.

'Hannah, I have some news. You're moving host families.'

My stomach drops. 'I thought I wasn't going to move for at least a few more months?'

Pétur nods. 'We-ell, you're actually going to live with me. You okay with that?'

I leap out of my chair. 'When?'

He laughs. 'Let me speak with Regína. It will probably be in a week or two.' He turns to go, then hesitates, turns back to face me. 'Hey, Hannah? We're really happy to have you.'

I have met Regína, Pétur's wife. Leikfélag Sauðárkróks' production of *Ertu Hálfdán?* is now in dress rehearsal and Regína has volunteered to do hair and make-up. Together with her sister, Sylvía Dögg, she applies the grisly wounds and bruises to the actors and transforms them into ghosts. They both greet me with kind smiles each time I arrive at the theatre, and between my broken Icelandic, some English, and occasional translation by

Begga with the long plait, we have got to know one another. The prospect of living with Regína and Pétur and their four young children is a wonderful one. I have had enough of sitting alone in a silent house.

The weekend before I leave, Guðný asks me if I would like to see a glacier.

'The weather is so much better now,' she says. 'The roads will be good.'

We drive inland, turning off onto a gravel road outside Steinsstaðir. The landscape shifts from the swell and cleft of mountain valleys to something harder. There is a shift in energy. We have left the places of settlement and breached the central Icelandic highlands. No one lives here.

'There,' says Guðný, pointing through the dusty windscreen to a great expanse of light listing above a horizon of rock. 'That is Langjökull.'

The glacier rises as we draw closer. It is so white under the force of the unclouded sun, I squint. The sky cuts a raw blue behind its mass.

How far I am from home, I think. The glistering, ancient force of ice, the rock and earth extending in a rising intensity of mineral reds and browns, is unlike anything I have seen before. Steam lifts from the ground. Here, I think, is true wilderness.

'This is Hveravellir,' says Guðný. We pull up at an expanse of steaming pools. A wooden boardwalk has been provided for visitors, and we follow it between wells of bubbling water, their sides turquoise from mineral deposits. I stop and watch the ribboning upswell of gases before they reach the surface. Steam wafts over our faces, damp and hot. This place is breathing. Even the ground seems porous, issues lifting clouds of vapours.

'Hofsjökull,' Guðný tells me, pointing to another glacier within view.

I cannot fathom how a place of boiling heat and rupture is held between such gargantuan squats of ice. It feels elemental, as though I am watching the earth create itself.

'I packed some swimmers for you to borrow,' Guðný says.

I look apprehensively at the pools blistering with heat.

'Come on,' she says.

Thankfully, the hot spring Guðný takes me to does not peel the skin from my flesh. The milky, mineral blue water is hot, but not agonisingly so. Guðný rests her head against the pool's rocky side to bask in the sun and I join her.

I look up at the glaciers and then across to Guðný. It is lovely to be here together, and I wonder why it has taken so long for us to spend some time like this. It occurs to me that I have very little idea of who Guðný is and how she is feeling, and whether she is happy. I have spent so many months wondering whether I am okay that I have not stopped to think about her. She looks happy now. The sun on our faces is a warm benediction and I am content not to talk in this moment. The silence between us is finally an easy one.

Walking back to the car, I look at a monument beside the boardwalk. It is a powerful statue, a cage of bars between two heavy, rough-cut rocks, imprisoning two smoother stones. Guðný tells me it is a memorial to the outlaws of Iceland. The plaque tells of Fjalla-Eyvindur, or Eyvindur of the mountains, who lived in the wilderness for twenty years in the late 1700s. His wife, Halla, chose to live with him as an outlaw.

When we are in the car, driving home, I ask Guðný how outlaws like Fjalla-Eyvindur survived.

'The warmth of places like Hveravellir helped them survive. There are also some caves near the glaciers. They probably stole some sheep.' Guðný gazes out at the road ahead. 'But it was a bad thing, to be made an outlaw. Many died.'

I am quiet then, thinking about this place and about exclusion within it. I want to understand why Iceland is so close-knit, why it has been so difficult to weave myself into its fabric. Hearing stories like these helps me. There is survival in insularity, I understand. It is not a place where it is easy to prosper alone.

Arriving at Pétur and Regína's home is very different to my first night at Guðný and Þórir's. Regína is holding their one-year-old daughter, Birgitta Björt, and shifts the baby to one hip so she can hug me. Two boys, blond heads shorn in identical haircuts, are introduced.

'This is Gunnar Stefán,' Regína says, putting her arm around the eldest, who is blue-eyed and serious-looking. 'Gunnar is learning English in school.'

Pétur has already asked me if I would encourage Gunnar in his studies.

Gunnar hesitates, then says in a quiet voice: 'Welcome to our home.'

The younger boy asks Regína a question in Icelandic. I don't catch it.

'Hvað heitir þú?' I ask him.

'Óli Björn,' he says immediately. His voice is a little raspy. 'Komdu.' He takes my arm and directs me to a staircase by the kitchen.

'Óli Björn, bíddu aðeins …' Regína lifts Birgitta higher on her hip.

'Ég er að sýna henni herbergið hennar,' he replies.

I understand what he is saying, but Gunnar Stefán takes on the role of translator.

'We show you' – he hesitates, apprehension on his face before he remembers the word in English – 'your bedroom.'

The boys take me down to the lower floor. Óli Björn chatters away, showing me Gunnar's bedroom, a playroom scattered with toys, an office with a desk and computer, a large laundry with two washing machines and a large chest freezer, and a small ensuite in the process of being renovated.

'Og hér,' Óli Björn continues, urging me through a door, 'er herbergið þitt.' He looks up at me and grins, one front tooth missing. 'Sjáðu, sjónvarp.' He points to the television sitting on a shelf.

Regína pokes her head in the bedroom door. 'Is okay?'

I look at the room, with its window facing onto a small back lawn, yellow curtains covered in cartoon bees, the double bed with patchwork quilt.

'Já, takk,' I say. 'Það er frábært.' It's great.

Another blond boy, younger again, pushes past Regína and stares up at me.

'This is Jón Arnar,' Regína says. 'He is three years old.'

Jón Arnar gives me an appraising look then follows Regína to the laundry.

'Hvað ertu gamall?' I ask Óli Björn. How old are you?

'Sex ára,' he says. Six years old. Chattering away in Icelandic, he picks up the TV remote and shows me every channel I can watch on the television. He leaves momentarily, before returning in a skeleton costume, carrying a CD player.

'Þetta er mitt en þú getur fengið það lánað.'

I look at Gunnar Stefán for help.

'He is give you this.'

I smile at Óli, and he beams back up at me.

The two older boys hang around as I bring my suitcase downstairs, suggesting drawers and cupboards where I might put my clothes and examining all the items I place on my shelves. Regína tells them both to give me some time alone. Five minutes later, they return.

'Hannah! Matur!' Óli Björn announces.

Gunnar nods solemnly. 'It is food,' he says.

Óli Björn insists I sit next to him and asks if he can pour me a drink.

Pétur comes through the front door as Regína is sliding Birgitta into her highchair.

'Welcome,' says Pétur. 'You settling in okay?'

'Yes, thanks.'

Regína puts a spread of chicken and chips on the table. 'Gjörðu svo vel.'

I feel a warmth spread through me during dinner. The noise of this house is comforting. There are plastic cups and spills and children crawling under the table and interruption and laughter.

'I'm going to see if my friend Jón can give you some work, so you have something to do when school finishes for the summer break in June,' Pétur says. 'Then you'll also have some more money.'

'I thought Rotary didn't want me to work?'

'Don't worry about that,' he says, waving a dismissive hand. 'All the other kids from school, everyone is going to have a summer job. School won't begin again until the end of August. I think it will be better for you to work for a few months.' Pétur tells me to come and go as I please, to have friends over, whatever I like. Then he stands up and plants a kiss on Regína's head. 'Takk fyrir mig.'

'Verði þér að góðu.'

Pétur carries his plate into the kitchen and then turns to me. 'I have to go back to work right now, but if you need anything, just call or ask Regína. Okay? It's no problem. This is your home now.'

The next morning, I am woken at six o'clock by Jón Arnar shouting outside my door. It takes me a while to understand what he is saying.

'Má ég fá ís? Mamma? Má ég fá ís?'

I laugh when I figure it out.

Can I have an ice cream?

I hear Regína come and close the chest freezer before ushering him back upstairs.

It's already day outside – my yellow curtains are brilliant with sun. Even though the weather is still bad sometimes, I feel the relief of light in every cell of my body. I push the window open to let in the fresh air and hear birds singing. They are all returning to the island for the summer.

At the table I offer to feed Birgitta her breakfast of súrmjólk, a thick, fermented milk. She looks at me with her big brown eyes and I worry she will cry, but she simply takes my measure and then allows me to spoon food into her open mouth.

'Talar hún mikið?' I ask Regína. Is she talking much?

'Já, hún talar smá. Mamma, pabbi, sjáðu … Hún talar slatta.' Yes, she speaks a little. Mum, Dad, look … She speaks a fair bit.

'Jæja,' I say to Birgitta. 'Kannski við lærum að sama tíma.' My Icelandic is not perfect, I know, but I want to be able to speak to these children.

Regína laughs. 'Yes, maybe you learn together.'

I email Mum and Dad and tell them I love the chaos of the house, the kids following me around, endlessly asking, 'Hvað ert þú að gera?' What are you doing?

'Má ég fá ís?' becomes an alarm clock – Jón Arnar is surprisingly regular with his pleading – and I get in the habit of rising earlier. It does not take long before Birgitta calls for me by name and asks to sit on my lap while I eat breakfast. Every time she masters a new word, I repeat it with her. I carry her around the house, and occasionally rescue her when Óli Björn, an affectionate brother, tries to do the same.

Each day now brings the assurance of biscuit crumbs in my bed, pieces of shrubbery poked through my open window, the scattering of my art supplies across the floor. I hang the pictures the kids scribble for me on my wall and become used to rumpled bedding from them jumping on it. There might have been a time when the lack of privacy would have irritated me, but I am grateful to no longer feel isolated. I don't mind retrieving my quilt from the playroom, or finding my stuff sticky from discarded ice-cream wrappers. I love these kids. They embrace me in a way that is pure and generous. I am now continually hugged and climbed on, and not only by Óli Björn and Birgitta, but by other kids who drift in and out of the place. Pétur and Regína keep an open door, and the house is often full of children who have wandered over to play. I knew Sauðárkrókur was safe, but in this home I witness just how far the trust of this community extends.

I start to hear my name being called when I make my way down to Mæja's house or the supermarket, or to the theatre for the performances of *Ertu Hálfdán?* Anna Jóna, a five-year-old cousin of the kids, holds a 'tea party' at Pétur and Regína's with a friend and invites me along. The two girls shoot some imaginary birds with a toy gun, place the carcasses on the table and then dig in with glee. After this distinctly Icelandic tea party, I realise I have understood everything the children said.

At Pétur and Regína's request, I speak English to Gunnar Stefán, peppering it with Icelandic when necessary, and he does the same to me. But the other children, and the neighbouring kids, only speak Icelandic. When I don't understand, they take it upon themselves to teach me. They point at things and repeat words and phrases, and shriek with laughter when I mess up. I feel my grasp of the language growing through the simplicity of their conversation and my desire to be able to speak with them.

My vocabulary also expands in new directions as I am introduced to a lexicon of emotion and endearment. Here, children are not cutie pies but cutie buns. They are not sweeties but little raisins.

Some expressions of tenderness catch me unawares. When I first hear Hera, Regína's cousin, call Birgitta 'svo mikið rassgat' I believe I have misheard.

Did she just call the one-year-old 'such a little arsehole'?

I slip away to look up the word in my dictionary. I see that, yes, 'farðu í rassgat' means go fuck yourself, but 'hún er óttalegt rassgat' means something along the lines of 'she's such a sweet little thing'. As does, I discover, 'rúsínurassgat': raisin arsehole.

The many relatives of Pétur and Regína all seem to live in Sauðárkrókur, and there is a steady stream of adults visiting the house. They are introduced to me as Pétur or Regína's frændi or frænka, but as these words are used for uncle/nephew, or aunt/niece, and for cousins of all degrees, I often have no idea how everyone is related, knowing only that they are kin. The patronymic naming system, whereby last names are created by adding 'son' or 'dóttir' to the father's first name, does not help. Every member of a family might have a different last name. Women don't change their names after marriage.

I notice that Pétur and Regína introduce me to everyone who comes over. Everyone probably knows who I am, but these introductions make a big difference. People seem friendlier, more inclusive, and I realise it has not been enough for me to live here.

In this very family-oriented culture, they need to know how I am connected to *them*. Pétur and Regína name me in relation to their family, and I am suddenly accommodated.

One day I hear Pétur call me 'Hannah okkar', or 'our Hannah'.

I have been claimed.

Hólar, the oldest stone church in Iceland

CHAPTER NINE

Midnight Sun

After a successful run of *Ertu Hálfdán?* I am promoted. Icelandic National Day – þjóðhátíðardagur Íslands – falls on 17 June and commemorates Iceland's independence from Denmark in 1944. Sauðárkrókur is going to celebrate with musical performances on the main street and Leikfélag Sauðárkróks has been tasked with providing entertainment.

'We would like you to be a monkey,' Embla says.

After more conversation, I learn that Elva – a very funny member of the theatre company with an incredible capacity to chain-smoke – is going to be Lína Langsokkur, or Pippi Longstocking. I am to be Herra Níels, her monkey.

I am assured that I will not have to deliver lines in Icelandic, but I will have to perform the song 'Hér sérðu Línu Langsokk', which – thanks to the children I live with – I already know intimately. There is choreography to be learned, and by the time the day arrives and I am in Níels's overalls, Sylvía painting my face, I am a bit nervous. It is only when Elva asks me if her bright orange plaits cover the hickey on her neck and whether the pack of cigarettes in her pinafore pocket is showing that I start to relax. Elva winks at me.

Together we walk over to the primary school, where a group of children with balloons and Icelandic flags crowd around us.

A little boy soon spots the bulge in Pippi's pinafore. 'Nammi!' he cries. Lollies! The sugar-hungry kids push their hands into her pocket.

'Nei, nei,' Pippi says. 'Nei, þetta er sígarettur!' These are cigarettes!

A stage has been set up on the back of a truck in the main street, and when we step down after our performance, sweaty from dancing in costume, I am patted on the back by parents.

'Þú stóðst þig vel,' they tell me. You did a good job.

Pétur gets me some casual work, as promised, and when school finishes I begin shifts at Kaffi Krókur. I spend most of my time operating the dishwasher and listening to the banter between the chef and waitresses. My Icelandic, which has improved dramatically, allows me to appreciate the insults they let fly between them, and when they hear me snickering, they welcome me into the fold. Together we crack jokes and, when there are no customers, practise tae bo.

Pétur was right. Everyone from school has at least one summer job. I wonder whether this strong work ethic stems from those 'centuries of long cold winters and a struggle for survival against a hostile environment' mentioned in my guidebook. If there was survival in insularity, surely there was survival, too, in working hard. They keep busy.

Perhaps it is because I am now involved in the community in ways I wasn't before, or because my understanding of Icelandic has improved, or because summer is now upon us, but my impression of Icelanders shifts. What I had initially thought of as coldness towards strangers I recognise now as a reservedness that comes from a respect for people's right to privacy, and maybe also a cultural distaste for friendliness without grounds – anything which might be read as insincere or fake. It is true, I think, that the Icelanders in this town are slow to warm up, but I am learning that when they do, they are friendly and funny and generous.

Hera is my age, and after getting to know her at Pétur and Regína's, she asks me over to watch Iceland's Birgitta Haukdal sing 'Open Your Heart' in the Eurovision Song Contest with her friends. I am amused at how seriously everyone is invested in this competition. The entire town empties before the final in a collectively held breath. Soon after this, Hera asks me if I'd like to hang out with her 'saumaklúbbur', or sewing club.

Many people have hobbies here in a way that seems more pronounced than at home. People belong to choirs, play in bands, write poetry and novels, paint, play team sports. I am surprised at how widely accepted it is for young people – men included – to knit. Crafts are popular and there is a shop on Skagfirðingabraut which sells yarn and needles and patterns, as well as some other art and hobby supplies. I'm tempted to go down and buy some materials before I meet with Hera's sewing club, but I've never actually been taught to sew, and it's been a long time since I knitted anything. I decide not to embarrass myself at the first meeting.

When I arrive with Hera, everyone is sitting around and chatting, and I can tell that this group of friends is close. There is an ease between them that has probably come from knowing each other since preschool. Most friendship groups start then, I've learned.

During a lull in the conversation, I ask them what they're all sewing.

The girls burst out laughing.

'Neeeiii,' says Lóa. 'Saumaklúbbur is just what we call it when you hang out with your girlfriends. It's, like, our group.'

'Mostly we eat,' adds Ósk.

Hera laughs. 'Yes, we go to one another's houses and eat. That is saumaklúbbur.'

I like Hera a lot. She has a very expressive face and an inner warmth that adds to her beauty, and since I moved to Pétur and Regína's house I feel her taking me under her wing. One night, as we're waiting in line for entry into a dance, a boy grabs my hips and starts dry-humping me. Before I can react, Hera unleashes a torrent of furious Icelandic on him and he runs away to some friends at the back of the queue.

'Are you all right?' she asks me. 'That boy is such an idiot. I'm sorry he did that.'

'I'm fine,' I say. 'He was probably just drunk.'

Hera puts an arm around me. 'That's not an excuse,' she says.

These dances – or 'balls', as they are called – are being held all the time now. Many of them begin at midnight, and yet the bars and dance venues are often darker inside than out, and it is a curious feeling to stumble home at three or four in the morning in what feels like broad daylight.

One night I go out with some new friends I have met at these dances. We drive to the foot of Tindastóll, where the mountain meets the water, and sit on the grass of the promontory to watch the sun complete its circle. It is a deep gold orb, but as it lowers itself over the water, just kissing the ocean before rising again, it turns red and sets the sky aflame. We watch it skim the islands where the puffins have begun to flock. The sea, which is calm, holds the pink brilliance of its light. I have never seen the world so full of colour.

Everything becomes abundantly green. The mountain streams pour cold water through the gullies, so clean it can be drunk with a cupped hand. I spend a lot of time walking and marvelling at the wildflowers that now grow where, a few months ago, there was only snow and howling wind. Purple arctic lupins foam among the grass and the valley is full of lambs and foals. It is almost a parody of summer. It is the promised land illustrated in rhapsodic technicolour in a religious pamphlet. On the clearest days, the blue of the sky hollows me out with its vastness. I feel cleansed by it and, at the same time, subsumed by its enormity. I cannot fit it in. I cannot wrap my mind around it.

I walk every day and am astounded. I walk every day to break my heart with beauty.

When the enduring sunlight prevents me from sleeping, I try to distil this nirvana of light into poetry. I am falling in love with Iceland, and I need to articulate the hold it has over me. My writing, once a balm for solitude and loneliness, takes on a euphoric urgency. Writing now feels like prayer. When I tell my friends what I am doing, they do not ask me if I will be a writer, they tell me I am one.

I think I should apply to study creative writing at uni, I email Mum.

Mum writes back advising that most available courses admit students on the strength of a creative portfolio and curriculum vitae.

You'll need twenty pages of your best work to include in an application. Do you have that?

I tell her I am writing every day and promise to try to polish a selection of pieces for a portfolio.

If you want to pursue writing as a career, you might not be able to make a living from it, but that's no reason not to try, replies Mum. *Remember that you must always write for yourself and for the love of it. That is what writing with integrity is all about.*

As the summer reaches its zenith, Pétur asks me if I would like to work at a farm further out in Skagafjörður.

I am interested to see what Icelandic farm life is like. Other than a few trips down to Reykjavík, and to neighbouring towns like Hofsós and Varmahlíð, I have not spent much time in the country. Moving to a farm for summer is also a particularly Icelandic rite of passage for many young people here.

Pétur tells me that the family's English is limited but he thinks I am now speaking well enough for this not to be a problem. It is true that I have a lot more confidence after living with the children, and I am keen to test my ability in a place where I will not have the option of my mother tongue.

The farm where Pétur drops me one clear August morning is called Syðri-Hofdalir. It is in a valley, between the many intertwining rivers threading their way north and the mountain of Hofstaðafjall to the east. Hofstaðafjall and its neighbours are almost clear of snow, and loom purple now, the green of the valley creeping upwards until rock and shale take over.

The family are warm and welcoming, and although I try to follow the explanation of how everyone in the house is related to one another and to other people I may know in town, I am lost after the mother of the house tells me she has eleven siblings. After Pétur leaves, saying that he'll pick me up again in a week or so, they tell me I don't really need to do anything on the farm, but if I would like to help, then they'd be glad of it.

'Ég vil hjálpa.' I reassure them that I want to help, and that day I start scouring a barn with Sara, an Icelandic girl of about thirteen – a frænka staying with them for the summer – and Regula, a Swiss woman who is working at Syðri-Hofdalir in exchange for board and the opportunity to work with their Icelandic horses. After ten hours of scraping old paint from the wood and replacing it with a deep forest green, my arms burn and I am worn out and happy and starving.

Regula, Sara and I eat a hearty meal together with the family after we've cleaned up. I learn afterwards that the meat was horse. Noticing my stricken face, the family try to put me at ease by explaining that they do not eat the horses they ride. There are horses bred for meat in Iceland, and they are not named or broken in. A little reassured, I go upstairs to the bedroom I have been given. It has a sloped ceiling, a window that looks out onto the farm's home field, the tún, where the best hay is grown and cut to nourish the animals in the winter time, and an entire wall of books. Behind the home field soars the impressive height of the mountain. I feel that I am in a storybook.

When I come downstairs to the kitchen the next morning, ravenous and sore-muscled after sleeping like the dead, there is a woman I have not yet met standing at the stove. She beams at me from beneath a halo of white hair and tells me she does not speak English.

'What is your name?' I ask her in Icelandic.

She tells me to call her Amma, which means Grandma, and nods at me to sit down by the little table next to the window. It is covered in a lace cloth, and outside I can see the cows being driven back out to pasture.

Amma sets a bowl of porridge before me, and a jug of milk, yellow with cream.

'It is from the morning's milking,' she tells me.

It is one of the best things I have ever tasted.

*

Besides dairy cows, the farm has sheep, although they are currently roaming in the highlands as all Icelandic sheep do in summer. When I am not helping paint the barn, I feed the bulls, or the chickens in the hen shed, or I help Regula round up the horses. There is always something to be done, but there is time, too, for me to play with the kittens in the hay loft, work on my writing portfolio or chat to Amma in the kitchen. We sit at the table and dip homemade kleinur, cardamom-scented Icelandic donuts, into coffee, and in my conversation with Amma and the wider family I find a new fluency. I begin dreaming in Icelandic.

At night, I lie on my bed and read *Independent People* by Halldór Laxness. Reading about early 1900s Icelandic farmers while on an Icelandic farm is to have the story imprinted on me in a way that feels life-changing. I read, *books are the nation's most precious possession, books have preserved the nation's life through monopoly, pestilence and volcanic eruption*, and look up from the page to see my bedroom lined with such books, as though they are insulation against the *tons of snow that have lain over the country's widely scattered homesteads for the major part of every one of its thousand years.*

Living here, reading Laxness, is to feel the history of this country pushing close against me.

On Sunday I go to church with the family from the farm. Other than an Easter visit to Hólar, the oldest stone church in Iceland, I have not had much experience with Icelandic religious life. So far it seems that the primary role of the Lutheran church here is to facilitate christenings, confirmations, weddings and funerals, rather than weekly religious instruction. Still, people seem to feel warmly towards it, even if they are not devout. At the church I am surprised to see that the priest is a woman. She wears a clerical collar but ordinary clothes and spectacular knee-length leather boots. We all walk halfway up the mountain behind the church to pick bláber, bilberries, then come back down again for the service. The priest reappears in a long black gown and starched white frill and leads us through the singing of two hymns, a prayer and a short service from a pulpit built in 1729. I notice that she keeps her leather boots on under the robe.

That night, just as I am about to go to bed, Regula offers to take me horseriding. She shows me where the saddles and tack are kept, and picks out a black horse for me to ride. His name is Vörður, which I think means 'guard' or 'warden' in Icelandic.

We ride down the heart of the valley towards the midnight sun, hanging low at this late hour like a red lantern over the sea. Vörður wants to go, and I let him. He is strong and beautiful and we ride as fast as I have ever gone on horseback before. There is hardly a breath of wind, and the only thing I can hear is the sound of Vörður's hooves meeting the soil and the exchange of our breath with the cool evening air. It is exhilarating.

In time we slow to a walk. The grass is filled with white butterflies. Everything smells of cut hay and wildflowers.

When we reach the shore the sun is melting into the sea, streaking liquid gold against the islands in the fjord. The year has already turned. Soon summer will wane and winter will come again.

On one of my last days at Syðri-Hofdalir, a friend of the family takes me on a trek up through the mountain valleys with Sara and some other friends. In the narrow, grassy corridors between the peaks we find horses with their foals left to roam the lush highland grasses. We also find great fields of blueberries and bilberries, and in the late hours' bright unhurry we sit among the sprawling shrubs and eat our fill.

At midnight the valley before me is still held in deep colour. When I look down at my hands, my skin is blushed red. And I feel, suddenly, that I will be forever standing in this hidden place, out of time; that the world has slung from orbit and is now unspinning, unspun, content to rest forever in such tender light.

We drive the sheep across the
face of the mountainside

CHAPTER TEN

Réttir

You will find me changed, I write to my parents. *Iceland has acted like a breath in my life. In pausing I have rediscovered what I love and what is important to me.*

I tell them I went to Iceland with the hope of knowing myself a little better. I now know that is impossible.

> *Everything that lives exists in flux. Let me hold the possibility of change. Let me surprise myself. Everyone is complex. All I can do is what I think is right at the time. To act on my intuition and heart and have faith that it will be okay. Þetta reddast. Everything turns out.*

School begins again at the end of August, and I enrol in French (my favourite class, because Mæja also takes it), German, English,

Icelandic and sport, where the teacher plays Men At Work's 'Down Under' over the gym sound system in my honour.

I also join a motley volleyball team of older Icelandic women, Russian and Polish abattoir and fish factory workers, and a Lithuanian au pair who looks after twin babies. Audra and I start to spend time together when she's not working, and when another au pair arrives, Audra introduces us. Emma is Danish and cares for a child out in the country. She has white-blonde hair and a snaggle-tooth and enjoys complaining about the food she is fed by the farmer's wife. I have never met anyone so blunt in my life. We like each other immediately. Emma starts coming over to my place to hang out in the evening, and Audra often joins us. Other nights we go out to drink beer and dance and take snuff (which the Icelanders call snus) with the locals in the bar.

My days are filled now. Between school and friends and the warmth of Pétur and Regína and the kids, I have finally nestled into a life in Iceland that feels as natural to me as the one I left in Australia.

I have a home here, I write in my journal. *A family. I feel I now belong in a way I did not think would be possible.*

In early September Pétur tells me my third host family is now expecting me. Gísli and Steinnun live in the countryside on a farm called Stað, five kilometres from Sauðárkrókur. Their daughter, Sólveig, is my age and has just started working at Kaffi Krókur. Gísli is the president of the Rotary Club and manager of a local bank.

The news comes as a shock. When leaving Þórir and Guðný I felt ready. Now, moving feels a lot like being uprooted.

As I pack my stuff, Pétur tells me that I can keep the room as my own. 'Hannah, this house is always open to you. Just come and go whenever you need.'

I fight tears. I want to hug him.

He tells me I should drop in any time – for lunch, for a sleep, to use their excellent internet. 'You don't have to ask,' he tells me again and again. 'This is still your home. We'd keep you here if we could.'

Stað is set back from the road, a little isolated, but lovely. My bedroom is on the second floor, next to the kitchen and living room, and I have wonderful views of Skagafjörður valley and the mountains beyond. Sólveig has a bedroom and bathroom on the ground floor. As well as two cats, a dog and several horses, the farm also has sheep and a greenhouse where the family grows grapes and tomatoes.

When I first arrive, Sólveig comes upstairs to say hello and introduce me to her boyfriend, who is visiting from France, but after making small talk for a few minutes they disappear again. After a few days I understand that I won't be seeing a lot of my host sister. She and her boyfriend cloister themselves downstairs, and when he returns home, Sólveig spends all her time talking to him on MSN. Our paths rarely cross.

Gísli and Steinnun are older than Pétur and Regína. They have grandchildren and their house and home life is fastidious and ordered. Everything feels settled in place; I feel that if I were to adjust the angle of a photo frame, switch the cushions on the couch or raise the volume of the television, the house would crumble in outrage. Instead of the burgers and fries and cereal and súrmjólk of Pétur and Regína's house, the food here is traditional. Every Saturday, we sit down to rice porridge for lunch, and Steinnun slices pieces of blood sausage into her bowl to eat with it. The division of labour is more gendered here than in other homes I've visited. Steinnun cooks and cleans. Gísli goes to work. In the evenings they sit in their separate armchairs and watch the football or news on the television, while Steinnun knits for their grandchildren and Gísli does the crossword. They are warm to me, but quiet, and when I sit with them in the living room during the first few evenings, they seem surprised. Eventually Gísli reminds me that there is a television in my bedroom. I take the hint and retreat.

At Pétur and Regína's I was a short walk away from everything. Now I am dependent on my new host family for lifts to Sauðárkrókur and back. Both Gísli and Sólveig have cars, but after a few days it becomes clear that they would prefer not to give me a ride unless they are going into town themselves.

On Thursday evening, I ask Gísli how I might make my eight o'clock class the next morning.

'I leave at nine o'clock,' he says.

I wait for him to continue. He doesn't.

'What about Sólveig?' I ask.

'She doesn't have classes until midday.'

I don't really know what to say. 'Is there another way I can get to school on time?'

Gísli looks a little irritated. 'Við skulum sjá.' We will see.

The next morning, I get ready while the rest of the house sleeps. Just as I am thinking I might have to skip school, Gísli comes out of his bedroom in a dressing-gown.

'There's a school bus leaving in a few minutes,' he tells me on his way to the bathroom.

He doesn't offer any more details, such as where to meet it or if I will need to pay, so I decide to wait by the main road and see what happens.

After a minute or two a van approaches. As buses in Sauðárkrókur are invariably minivans, I wait for it to slow, but it passes me by. A few more cars drive past, and then finally, as I'm swinging my arms around in an effort to keep warm in the frigid morning air, a white van pulls up next to me. In the back I see a couple of younger kids. It makes sense that the bus also does the rounds of the primary school.

Still, I want to be sure, so I ask the driver if she goes to the high school.

'Já,' she says. 'Hop in.'

I sit in the front passenger seat and the woman continues towards Sauðárkrókur, asking me how long I've been in Iceland and chatting a bit before returning to companionable silence.

When she pulls up at the high school I get out and offer a brief thanks.

'Það var ekkert,' she replies. It was nothing. Then, before I close the door, I hear one of the kids in the back seat call the driver 'Mamma'. As the van pulls away, I realise it was not the bus at all. I just accidentally hitchhiked my way into town.

September is the season of the réttir in Iceland, when all the sheep and horses that have spent summer growing fat on the lush grasses and berries of the highlands are rounded up and brought back down. Beginning with horseriders and dogs who search for and gather the animals in the uplands, a process which can take days, it ends with a final herding that involves the local community. Everyone comes together to move the sheep or horses down the mountainside and into the réttir, a large, circular pen. The animals are then sorted into farms and moved into separate sections which radiate out from the inner circle.

Emma, Audra and I go to a local réttir one Saturday, eager to see what happens. There we find a large crowd of Icelanders wearing traditional woollen lopapeysur and carrying flasks of whisky, vodka and cognac in their pockets. When we strike up conversation with them we discover that this réttir is for horses. Sure enough, after half an hour we hear a deep thundering, and then cries from riders on horseback as they guide the herd down from the mountains towards where we are standing. The pounding of the hooves reverberates in my teeth. I did not realise there would be so many. Audra, Emma and I scramble up onto a stone wall to avoid being trampled and then look at each other, wide-eyed and grinning, as hundreds of horses jostle and rear beneath us in a stream of chestnut, bay and grey bodies. By the time the last of the horses has been caught and led into the corral, we are laughing from the surge of adrenaline.

The next day I am picked up by Pétur, Regína and the kids, and we go to a different réttir situated in the more isolated reaches of the north country. This one is for sheep, and I am determined to do my part. I wear a traditional lopapeysa with its circular patterned yoke, and climb the mountain with some of the men instead of waiting down in the valley. It is cold and windy, and trudging up the steep incline I feel the history of the land drawing close to me in the same way it did on Syðri-Hofdalir. A mist descends. My ears ache in the wind as we wait for the mountain riders to bring the sheep from the uplands. The damp settles on my lopapeysa. Eventually, the horsemen appear, silhouetted through the mist at the top of the range. They call out in greeting, and then hundreds of sheep pour down before them.

Together, we drive the sheep across the face of the mountainside towards the corral on the valley floor. Arms wide, I copy the shouts and whistles of the Icelanders, and herd sheep through bogs and outcrops of rock, trying not to slide through patches of loose gravel and shale. Others join me as I reach the lower expanses, greeting me with a friendly, 'Hæ, Hannah,' before helping me bring my corner of the flock towards the pen. We finally make the journey down the mountainside without any escaped sheep, and everyone goes back to a nearby farm to revive themselves with smoked lamb, boiled potatoes, beans and soðið brauð, deep-fried bread slathered with butter.

We go back to the pen for the sorting after the meal. Gunnar Stefán shows me how it is done. He climbs into the corral and grabs a sheep by the horns with both hands. I watch as he swings his leg over its body, checks the tag, and then walks it to the correct section. These sheep are daintier than my own family's flock of wethers back in Australia, their fleece much finer. Still, I am surprised by their strength and how difficult it is to walk a bucking sheep to its pen. The mist does not abate and the skies are ominously dark, but everyone is in high spirits, and we all laugh when someone is bested by a sheep and left lying in the mud. It isn't long before my legs are sore from being stuck by so many horns, my hands aching from a constant grip. I cannot wipe the smile off my face.

After the sheep have been sorted, we return to the farmstead for a traditional kaffi. There are kleinur and biscuits, milk and coffee and great saucepans of hot chocolate. By seven o'clock we are stuffed full, and Birgitta and Jón Arnar are yawning. Muddy and damp, we pile back into the car. During the long drive home, I watch the dark skies brood over the mountain tops and imagine I can hear again the riders' cries of greeting emerging from the mist, the calls travelling down the valley, before rising back up in echo.

Christmas arrives overnight

CHAPTER ELEVEN

Northern Lights

Snow returns after the réttir. I wake one morning to the sound of a gentle tapping and see snow flinging itself at my window. The wind is howling. The previous day was bright and fine, and I went to sleep with the mountains across the valley in green and brown. There was no hint of cold in the weather. To wake and find the mountains wholly white is a humbling reminder of nature's power here.

The following weekend, sleet flies sideways in winds going over one hundred kilometres an hour. By late October the sea has turned violent, and freezing, blustery rain squalls across its surface. Everyone retreats indoors. I close my curtains to northern lights billowing green across the mountain range and open them to frosts pinking in late sunrise. The days drop into night more quickly with each passing week, and I sleep longer and deeper in accordance. It feels restorative. Summer's profusion of light was almost too exhilarating and the late autumn's glut and colour was heady, its sense of urgency heightened by the need to complete my portfolio. Sending in my application to study creative writing coincided with the arrival of snow, and I feel a need to lie fallow now, to rest. To wait and see what happens. Reading in bed while the farm withstands whistling onslaughts of wind and sleet feels cosy rather than claustrophobic. It fills me with a renewed sense of gratitude for underfloor heating, the insulation of triple-paned glass, a watertight roof. Electric light. When the wind whips hailstones at the panes with the volume of a snare drum, I think of the Icelanders who lived here a hundred years ago. What difficulties they must have faced.

By November, daylight does not arrive until nine o'clock, and a gloom has already settled over the town when I arrive at Bifröst for *Galdrakarlinn í Oz* rehearsals after school. Inside, the theatre is warm and familiar with its smell of cigarette smoke and brewing coffee. It feels good to have finally earned the right to act onstage, even if it is only as a freckle-faced munchkin and a moustachioed man from Smaragðaborg, the Emerald City. Travel between Stað and Sauðárkrókur being dependent on the unpredictable availability of my host family, I end up hanging about Bifröst even when I don't have to rehearse my scenes. This, and the excitement and mild stress of impending performances, consolidates my friendships there.

One evening I approach Begga in the theatre stairwell. The backstage door is cracked open and her cigarette end glows against the blue. It's our last dress rehearsal and she's in costume as Norðannornin, Glinda the Good Witch, tiara a little askew on her golden braid.

'Hæ, Begga. Hvað segir þú?'

'Allt gott bara.' Begga lifts her cigarette to her painted mouth and then points it at me. 'I was thinking about you.'

'Oh?'

'I think you need to speak more Icelandic. You know. Only Icelandic.'

'You're probably right.'

'Já.' She takes a deep drag and blows smoke out of her nose. 'I am right.' She smiles, flicks ash off Glinda's satin corset and grinds out her cigarette in the ashtray. 'Ég segi öllum að tala bara íslensku við þig.' I'll tell everyone to only speak Icelandic with you.

From that night on, the theatre group refuses to speak English to me. I add stage directions and the low-slung banter of amateur actors standing around in wig nets and underwear to my vocabulary, alongside every song from *The Wizard of Oz* in Icelandic.

When the last performance of *Galdrakarlinn* is over, we share a cake backstage and toast our success. I am forking in a mouthful of cornflake-studded meringue, the ubiquitous kornflexmarens that appears at every Icelandic celebration, when Gubbi the Lion, traces of make-up still in the crinkles of his eyes, mentions me by name.

'I also want to thank Hannah, who has joined us for the last three plays. It's been great to have you here, Hannah. We're sad that this was your last show with us.'

Everyone claps and I suddenly feel incredibly sad. I have not been thinking of leaving. All thoughts of returning to Australia have centred around my hope to continue writing. I have not allowed myself thoughts of loss, of what and who I will be leaving. But in this moment, I understand that my life here will end. I will need to let this place go.

The next morning, I wake late. When I open my curtains white snowdrifts are sparkling in soft light. The mountain creek has frozen over and icicles shine where they hang from the rock, water stilled in plummet. I dress quickly and set off up the mountainside. I let Mollý, the dog, lead the way. She intuits where pools and ice may lie under snowfall much better than I can.

After an hour's walk, we rest on an outcrop and look out over the valley. Our breath rises in mist before us. The hush is exquisite. Light catches every glinting speck of ice. I want to thank this north country for its beauty, for the gift of my being here. I want to offer it something in return.

When we come back to the farm, Mollý and I are completely dusted in white. I let the dog into the laundry, knock snow off my boots and clothes, then climb the stairs to the kitchen. I am greeted by a delicious smell. Steinnun, wearing an apron, is busy at the counter. Gísli has told me proudly that she is an excellent caterer and her ability – and the massive oven in the kitchen – testifies to this.

I greet her while I put the kettle on.

'Hvað ertu að gera?' I ask her. What are you doing?

'Ég er að baka.' Baking, she tells me. 'Jólasmákökur.' Christmas cookies.

Soon I am helping, pressing out circles with an upturned glass, filling the dough with prune jam and sealing the edges with a fork. There are hundreds to be made. Steinnun gives me a crash course in Icelandic festive baking and stresses the need for many different kinds of biscuits to ensure satisfaction. I sense that producing vast quantities and varieties of cookies is also something that Steinnun prides herself on: Christmas baking as domestic swagger. She tells me she will also make piparkökur, gingerbread, and chocolate-dipped sörur, or Sarah Bernhardt cookies, as well as at least three other types.

The following weekend is also devoted to Christmas baking, only this time it is laufabrauð, or leaf bread, a very thin, decorated flatbread. Gísli and Sólveig show me how to take the thinly rolled circles of dough and, using a knife or a specially made laufabrauðsjárn (iron leaf-bread cutter), make triangular incisions that are then folded to create patterns. It's fiddly work, and we share a companionable morning at the table, chatting and fussing over the laufabrauð while Steinnun deep-fries the completed rounds in hot sheep tallow.

I have started to pay attention to the foods that seem to me distinctly Icelandic. I want to be able to recreate Regína's waffles with rhubarb jam, the lamb soup and cod at Stað, the various rye breads and snúðar (cinnamon scrolls), and the delicious travesty that is brúnaðar kartöflur, boiled potatoes finished in caramel. I want to remember the Icelandic fish stew and the savoury brauðterta, or 'bread cakes', which look like cake but comprise layers of sandwich bread filled with ham or prawn or fish, glued together with extravagant amounts of mayonnaise and cream. I write what I remember of Amma's recipes and ask Steinnun and my friends for theirs too. I will be grateful to have an abundance of fresh fruit and vegetables when I am back in Australia, but I will miss the Icelandic food. I doubt it is something I will find readily at home.

Christmas arrives overnight. In late November I walk to Skaffó, the supermarket, to buy nammi – having succumbed to the Icelandic addiction to licorice – and see that the whole shop has been transformed into a festive wonderland. Kids are selling homemade cakes opposite the checkouts, wreaths and baubles hang from the ceiling, and people have gathered to celebrate. A girl hands out gingerbread and coffee, and in the generously stocked sweets section, half-a-dozen kids fill bags with festive glee.

Outside, illuminated stars and snowflakes and candles have been put up everywhere, and a crane lifts a tall fir tree into place next to the post office. I watch until it starts to snow, and then continue downtown to join Emma at the outdoor swimming pool. It has taken me all year to brave the nude communal shower required for admittance, and as we sit in the hot tub, snow settling on our hair and eyelashes, I kick myself for being so bashful. Emma agrees that I am ridiculous, tells me that no one gives a fuck about nudity in Denmark or Iceland, and blames my self-consciousness on Australia's colonising British. Sitting in the steaming waters with the snow coming down and Christmas lights shining in the darkness around us is divine.

*

I mention the Christmas celebrations to Gísli and Steinnun that night, and they tell me that today is the first Sunday of Advent, the time when many families put up their decorations.

They glance at each other.

'Hannah, I wanted to tell you … we will have family flying home for Christmas.'

'Okay.'

'They are coming from Sweden and America, and while you are welcome to have Christmas with us' – Gísli clears his throat – 'we will need your bedroom.'

'Ekki málið,' I say. Not a problem. 'Where should I sleep?'

'Maybe somewhere in Sauðárkrókur?' Gísli suggests.

I must look taken aback, because he hurriedly follows with: 'I could ask my son and his wife if they'd have you?'

'Have I met them before?'

'Nei,' Gísli says. 'Maybe you could ask a friend?'

I mention that I need to find a place to sleep over Christmas to Regína and Sylvía the next time I visit. They give each other a look, then immediately invite me to spend Christmas with them.

Pétur calls me later that day.

'You're moving back in with us,' he says. 'I've already spoken to Gísli.'

That night, as I am packing my things, I notice the northern lights outside my window are particularly intense. Gísli, Steinnun and Sólveig are all out, and so the house is dark. I turn off my lamp and press my face to the window. The sky is more brilliant than I have seen all year.

Filled with excitement, I dress and head up the mountainside until my view is completely unimpeded. Then I lie down on my back and turn my face to the aurora.

I have always yearned for euphoric sublimation to beauty. Lying in the snow with the creep of cold against my neck, the great and living wash of light pouring down upon me, so thick as to occlude the stars behind, so bright as to throw the mountains surrounding the valley into such silhouette they lose mass and become merely a corrugated horizon of darkness, I feel it. I feel dissolution into the world and the rapture of my own insignificance.

Who am I, to see such things?

To lie under a rippling ecstasy of colour is a moment beyond articulation. Still, I long to fit these swerving arcs of brilliant green and violet and red into language.

In my brief breath of life, might I find a way to fit light to paper?

I return to Pétur and Regína's at the beginning of December and am immediately glad to be experiencing an Icelandic Christmas with a family of young children. Óli Björn and Gunnar Stefán are eager to tell me about the jólasveinar, or the yule lads, who will start arriving on the twelfth of December. In Iceland, there is no Father Christmas. Rather, the yule lads are the thirteen sons of Grýla, a gruesome ogress, and Leppalúði, her feckless husband. Each day a yule lad, named after his preferred prank, comes down from the mountains to make mischief. My favourites are

Hurðaskellir (Door Slammer), Gluggagægir (Window Peeper), Skyrgámur (Skyr Gobbler) and Christmas Eve's Kertasníkir (Candle Beggar). The bearded yule lads have an air of gleeful misbehaviour, but their mother, the formidable Grýla, is much more sinister. She leaves her cave at Christmas time to stalk the towns for disobedient children, whom she eats with monstrous appetite. Her pet, jólakötturinn, or the yule cat, is just as ravenous, killing and devouring anyone who does not receive new clothes before Christmas Eve.

Despite this folkloric menace, the children are delighted when December twelfth approaches, and with it Stekkjastaur (Sheep Worrier), who comes to harass the sheep. Óli Björn, noticing I have not put a shoe out for Stekkjastaur, fetches me one of his own and places it on the windowsill.

'He'll put nammi or presents in it,' he explains. 'Unless you are naughty.'

'What happens if I am naughty?' I ask him. 'Will Grýla eat me?'

'Maybe.' Óli Björn nods, considering. 'Or you might get a potato.'

The next few days are cold and clear and icy. The number of lights and decorations throughout the town increases, and everywhere I go I am fed vast quantities of jólakökur and konfekt, chocolates filled with soft centres or marzipan. My volleyball team wins our competition in Akureyri and we celebrate with a house party. Olga, our Russian coach, hands out liquor with the same draconian insistence she used when announcing team push-ups.

I spend a lot of time taking the kids out into the snow to play. We go sledding, make snow angels and have snowball fights.

I drag Birgitta around in her red bucket sleigh while she joyfully and inexplicably tells everyone we meet that 'hún bíta mig' – that I have bitten her. One day, while watching *Winnie the Pooh* dubbed in Icelandic, there is a knock at the door and I open it to find three men in bright red suits and hats, their faces almost entirely covered by shaggy beards of sheep fleece.

'Jólasveinarnir eru komnir!' cries Jón Arnar, and the kids rush outside to accept sweets from the visiting lads.

Later that night we all go down to the town's Christmas tree and sing songs with a choir and several more jólasveinar. Everyone is in high spirits. The snow glimmers under the twinkling lights.

Darkness closes out the days with astonishing rapidity, until there are only three hours of light each day. The Christmas decorations stave off winter's melancholia, however. My favourites are the triangular frames of seven candles in the window of every house. Advent lights, glowing welcome in the dark.

Sauðárkrókur is my home now. Walking down the main street in the cold, my gloved hands pushed as far into my pockets as possible, I feel a visceral attachment to the place. I walk past the swimming pool, which is full, then past the service station, the hairdressers, Bifröst, then over the road to the bakery, where I talk to Begga and eat something delicious and full of cinnamon. The loose snow on the ground whips around my feet as a wind blows in. I let it push me up the incline behind the church that leads to the churchyard. Set up high on the hill overlooking the town, the Icelanders have placed lights in among the gravestones, either flickering candles in glass lanterns or colourful bulbs that lend the cemetery a festive air. I look out to the town below, glittering in the darkness, then the soaring mountains behind me. My bones have knitted with this place. There is a quiet exchange of marrow between us now.

I wonder if I will ever come back.

Jól begins at six o'clock on Christmas Eve in Iceland, when the church bells are rung to bring in the Yule. Gísli and Steinnun have asked me to have Christmas dinner with them, perhaps in apology, and we are all dressed in our best clothes, the table set with candles and bowls of towering laufabrauð and spiced red cabbage, and glasses of a Christmas drink called 'malt og appelsín', orange soda stirred with a carbonated malt extract that reminds me of the shandies my grandparents poured. Sólveig's siblings and their partners have arrived home for jól, and the house is warm as we exchange greetings of 'Gleðileg jól' and sit at the table to eat hamborgarhryggur (smoked, glazed pork) with caramel potatoes and gravy. For dessert there is coffee and cake and ice cream.

The family exchanges presents after dinner, many of them receiving books. I had not known books were such popular Christmas gifts in Iceland until a few weeks ago, when a book catalogue titled Bókatiðindi arrived at the house. I had been impressed that so many books were being published in a nation of only 250,000 people. Pétur had told me that most books in Iceland are published in the six weeks leading up to Christmas.

'We call it the jólabókaflóðið.' The Christmas book flood.

I already know that, per capita, Iceland publishes more books than any other country and that books hold a special place in Icelandic culture. The Íslendingasögur, or Sagas of the Icelanders, and the *Poetic Edda*, yes, but also contemporary literature. Books are venerated here, and I know this because I am sensitive to this reverence. I share it. And I have been finding validation and significance in every house lined with bookshelves, every teacher who has encouraged me to write, every sign on an out-of-the-way country road referring to Saga events which occurred in the area. Books are built into the Icelandic identity. They matter here in a way that is central not just to cultural life, but to life. And now, I understand, to Christmas.

Earlier this morning I received an email from my dad, letting me know that I have been accepted into the creative writing course. I have been in a state of elation all day.

Pétur picks me up from Stað after dinner, and when we arrive home I emerge from the car into the most beautiful snowfall of my entire time in Iceland. Large snowflakes float slowly to the ground. The night is perfectly still. Pétur and I stand in it for a moment.

He smiles at me. 'Do you know the name for this kind of snow, Hannah?'

I shake my head.

'Jólasnjó. Christmas snow.'

Inside, Pétur and Regína give me a necklace.

'So you can wear it and remember us all,' Regína explains.

I cry then, for the first time in ages.

Time pours through my fingers. My ticket home to Australia arrives and I email Jón Ásgeir asking if Rotary will be coordinating a flight for me from Sauðárkrókur to Reykjavík, or if I should find a lift.

Hannah! Jón writes back. *I thought you had already gone!*

He tells me that everyone else, except Roman, departed at the end of the summer holidays. For some reason, he thought I'd gone too.

No, I've been here all this time, I write back.

He tells me he'll arrange the flight.

Guðný and Þórir invite me for dinner once news of my impending departure spreads. I speak Icelandic with them, and even manage a conversation with Garðar. Afterwards they give me a small present.

I wonder what has changed to make them so friendly, when they had been so silent before.

I decide it is my Icelandic. Communication is crucial, of course, but something else was unlocked in learning Icelandic. To know a language is to also know a culture, and a history. So much is held in language. So much is explained.

I spend áramót, New Year's Eve, with Emma. We join the rest of the town at an enormous bonfire that has been lit well away from the houses. The fire grows and grows as people continually throw pallets of wood onto it, until we are standing in puddles of water from all the melting snow. At midnight, everyone in Sauðárkrókur returns to the streets of the town to light fireworks. I have only ever seen official public pyrotechnic displays, and watching six-year-olds lighting their own crackers and fireworks in snowbanks takes some getting used to. The explosions go on for hours, until a thick layer of smoke and airborne residue settles over the town. Coughing, Emma and I escape to the bar, bringing in the new year by dancing with our friends.

The week before I leave, my dreams darken. Each night brings a nightmare filled with potency and meaning.

I have murdered someone and I must walk out into the North Sea to kill myself.

I am standing in the snow, my body freezing cold and my hands bound.

My hands are bloodied and I am exiled into the mountains, and I do not know my way.

After these dreams I do not easily return to sleep. They make me think of the execution of Agnes Magnúsdóttir at Þrístapar. They make me think of death and irrevocable endings.

I tell myself that I am having dreams of finality because I am so deeply sad to leave. I am worried that I am not making the most of my days, despite the goodbyes and last dinners and meet-ups. I am afraid that I will forget everything that has happened to me here. Who will I speak Icelandic with at home? People at school and in the town have unexpectedly started saying they will miss me. I don't know if I'm going to see any of them again. No wonder I dream of points beyond return.

On my last morning in Sauðárkrókur I wake to the fury of the wind. I get up, wrapping my blanket about me, and step outside into the fray. Loose snow is sweeping and winding along the dark streets, like a company of ghosts, towards the dark and stormy sea.

When I go inside, I pick up my notebook. On its final page, I write down my thoughts.

Iceland, I don't know how to let you go.

Crisp, golden brown kleinur

Landamæri
Boundaries

2021

In June 2021 I receive an email from Stella Soffía, the director of Bókmenntahátið, inviting me to the Reykjavík International Literary Festival this coming September. My heart lifts in excitement then plummets just as quickly. New laws have bound me to Australia.

I respond expressing gratitude and disappointment.

Under normal circumstances I would love to attend. As you may know, the Australian government has an international travel ban in place for all citizens. It is my hope that it will lift next year, but we shall see. Please keep me in mind for future events. I would love to take part one day!

I tell Heidi that I am gutted at not being able to return to Iceland. I mean that in its most visceral sense; I am hollowed out. I would love to attend the literary festival, of course, but I also want to see the mountains again. I want the white ribbons of waterfalls streaming from the heights, the expanses of lava softened by pelts of moss, the black sands of the north. I even miss the wind – I want to fight with it again.

And I want to see my family.

So much has happened to the people I love in Iceland since I first went on exchange eighteen years ago. It took me four years before I could return to Sauðárkrókur, but since then I have gone back to Iceland another four times. Six trips in total. It seems I cannot allow more than three years to pass without heeding Iceland's summons and returning to see everyone, to meet the new babies born to my friends, to mourn those who have passed. Distance amplifies the precarious, fleeting nature of life.

The impetus to go back has become stronger since Pétur and Regína's children have become parents themselves. When Gunnar Stefán had a baby girl with his partner, Rannveig, Pétur had sent me pictures and told me I had become an aunt.

Þú ert orðinn frænka.

Five months later Óli Björn became a dad, too. Then Pétur's mother passed away. Helga was a wonderful woman, a strong woman, and much beloved by her family. The distance between Australia and Iceland felt great when I heard the news, and I was reminded of when Pétur had called me six years earlier to tell me that Anna Jóna, the little girl who had loved tea parties, his niece, had died tragically in a car accident. It is hard to grieve at a distance. It is hard to be away from those who are grieving.

I want to pay my respects. I want to meet my new niece and nephew.

I want to go home.

The night after I turn down Stella Soffía's invitation, I dream I am walking the streets of Sauðárkrókur, speaking Icelandic to everyone I meet there. When I wake my tongue is sore, as it was when I first returned home to Adelaide. I had never known that languages favour their own muscles, that fluency requires physical alteration. For weeks English felt like a strain, and I would go to bed with my tongue aching. Now I wake up with my dream of speaking Icelandic manifest in a tender mouth.

That day I have a yearning to make kleinur, the cardamom doughnuts, from scratch. After an hour of rustling around in our shed I find my notebook of Icelandic recipes. Flipping through the pages is to transport myself in time. I am embarrassed to realise I have forgotten some of the Icelandic words. My younger self talks to me in a language I no longer fully understand. But now I have Google Translate. Now the internet is bigger, the world is smaller, and Iceland is no longer the little-visited island it used to be. There are ways of deciphering it – and its language – beyond a dubious travel guide. Now Icelandic can be learned on YouTube. There are blogs devoted to its cultural quirks. Gordon Ramsay has visited to try hákarl, the rotten shark.

I find a translation of my own Icelandic.

Flipping through the notebook, I decide to use Amma's recipe from Syðri-Hofdalir. I go slowly, my mind dancing between the recipe and memories of watching Amma cutting the dough into diamonds, looping one end through a slit in the middle. I feel a great tenderness towards her as I make them. I wonder if Amma is still alive. I have met Icelanders who cling to the years with a great and dignified tenacity. Perhaps she is still there, sitting at her table with the lace cloth, watching as the cows are driven to pasture.

I invoke her in my own kitchen, in this southern hemisphere, in this time of plague.

The kleinur are crisp, golden brown. Rory gums one with enthusiasm. Anouk nibbles on hers then takes great delight in crumbling it to pieces upon the floor, where they are snuffled up by our dog.

Heidi and I sit down with a cup of coffee.

'Yum,' she says. 'I like them.'

'They don't taste like I remember,' I say, disappointed. I look over to the pot of oil cooling on the stove. 'I think she made hers with sheep tallow. It must have given them a certain flavour.'

'I don't think you'll find sheep tallow here, Han,' Heidi says, reaching for another. 'They taste pretty good to me.'

A few days later I make snúðar, the cinnamon scrolls topped with chocolate icing that Regína would bring home from the bakery. Then on Sunday morning I make vöfflur, Icelandic waffles. I serve them with homemade rababarasulta, rhubarb jam.

I have submitted my third novel now. *Devotion* was written through a vigilant keeping of kvöldvökur, evenings of wakefulness and storytelling when the rest of my family were in bed.

No longer under the pressure of its deadlines, I rest my mind by making Icelandic food. Throughout the wet and gloomy August, in between interviews and some early press ahead of *Devotion*'s release, I make rye bread and sörur cookies and pönnukökur. One of the last things I had bought at Skaffó, all those years ago, was a pönnukökupanna, an Icelandic pancake pan. My friends had laughed at me – a weird souvenir – but it is now the most precious item in my kitchen.

I give the bread and biscuits and pancakes I make to friends and family, pre-emptively laughing at my behaviour before anyone else can. But the truth is that all this cooking is an act of grief. I am engaging in ritual, locating a place and people I miss deeply, trying to create a little of the culture I miss. There is looking at a doughnut as a doughnut, then there is looking at a kleina as a cultural object that embodies both Denmark's colonisation of Iceland and its self-determination, that symbolises rare luxury and generosity in a place of historically little prosperity, that reminds me of people I miss and their hospitality, of places I cannot access. Ritual, memory, culture.

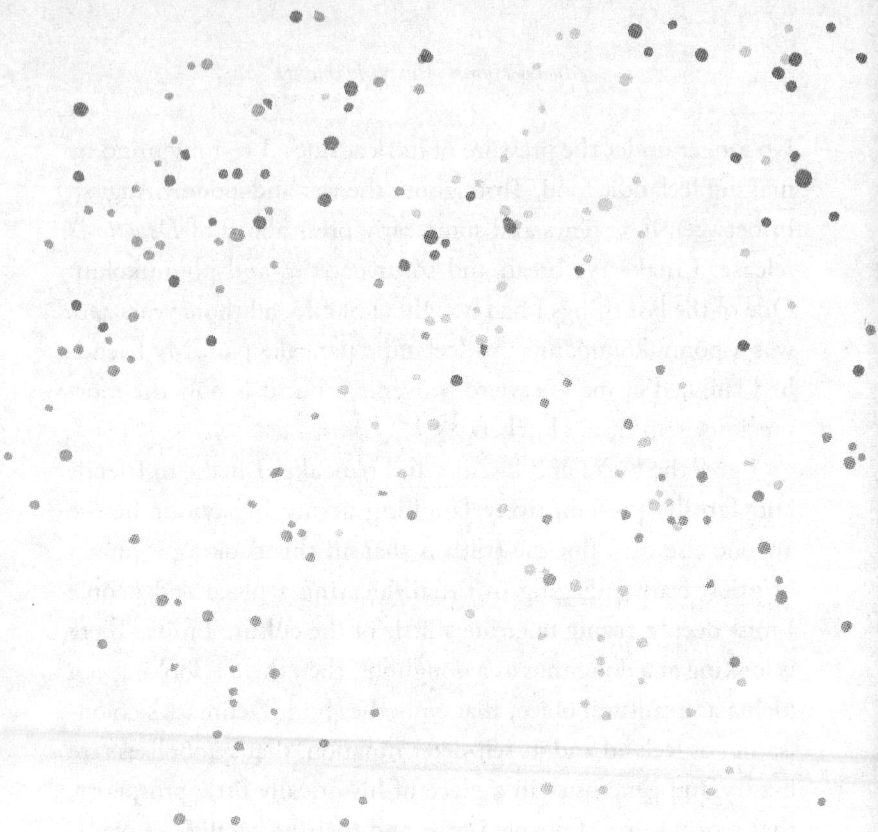

PART II

Hugfangin
Enthralled / Captive of the Mind

2007–2011

Glaumbaer, a preserved traditional turf dwelling

CHAPTER TWELVE

They Bury Rocks in the Rain

2007

When I see the dark shores of the island appear on the descent into Keflavík, my heart hammers with such force I feel its reverberation throughout my body. It continues as I am waved through customs by a bored official, pick up my hire car and begin driving north to Sauðárkrókur. The sight of the landscape is so familiar to me I feel physical relief. When I pass through the highlands and round up into the north, passing through the hills of Vatnsdalshólar, a weight I did not know I was carrying lifts from my mind.

When I pull up at Pétur and Regína's house, I am trembling. I have been thinking of this moment ever since my journey back to Australia in early 2004. We had all cried in the tiny airport. My last view from the plane window had been Regína, arms waving, blowing kisses, eyes red. Here I was, hand raised to the painted door, about to see them again.

I notice the curtain in the window by the door twitch, and as soon as my hand touches the door, it opens.

'Nei, Hannah! Gott að sjá þig!' Regína is there, children crowded around her, Pétur grinning at me over their heads.

My family, I think as I hug them tight. My family.

It has taken me longer than expected to make my way back to Sauðárkrókur.

After returning from my exchange, I spent three years studying alongside ten other writers in a university creative writing program. Their ambitions had helped me hone my own. We were mostly of a similar ilk: talented, quirky, in love with books. As readers, we found ourselves citizens of the same country. The exacting standards of our tutors, most of whom were writers themselves, gifted us with improvement and a sobering understanding that writing takes a teeth-gritting resilience above all else. Many of my friends, sustained by their momentum of study, decided to complete an Honours year. I wanted to do this too. But I also wanted to return to Iceland. I needed to see the people I loved there, but I also felt another voice calling me back.

Since my exchange I have been dreaming of Agnes Magnúsdóttir, the woman beheaded at Þrístapar, with such frequency that I have started recording them in a journal.

Thoughts of Agnes are haunting me, pinning me down. I can almost see her face flickering in the darkness of the room, at the edge of my vision, like a moth suddenly lit by some wayward light, before disappearing into the night again …

During my degree, the dreams – dark, sorrowful, brimming with heightened emotion – would occasionally push me into the university library to find out what I could about her life. Between lectures and essays and tutorials, I would find myself seated at a library computer, entering search terms like 'Iceland execution' and 'Agnes Magnúsdóttir' and 'Agnes morðingi'. Most of what I unearthed was in Icelandic. Translating these articles soon became a way of mitigating my homesickness for that north-skied country.

I'm finding the facts slowly, I wrote in my journal. *I am brushing away the dirt with my feeble translation, speck by speck, revealing the old bones of this story.*

By the time I finished my studies, I had unearthed the more-or-less agreed upon account of the events that led to Agnes's beheading:

In the early hours of 14 March 1828, the people living at Stapakot farm in the north of Iceland were woken up by Agnes Magnúsdóttir, a thirty-two-year-old servant from Illugastaðir, a neighbouring farm. She told them that Illugastaðir 'stood in bright flames' and that the farmer and master of the house, Natan Ketilsson, and another man, Pétur Jónsson, a guest, were still trapped inside.

The family at Stapakot returned to Illugastaðir with Agnes, and when the fire was extinguished the badly burned bodies of

Natan and Pétur were discovered in their beds. It was thought to be a tragic accident. But when day broke, blood was found on remnants of unburnt clothing, and a closer examination of the corpses revealed stab wounds.

Agnes and sixteen-year-old Sigríður, the other maidservant at Illugastaðir, were brought before the district commissioner and bailiff, Björn Blöndal. They were questioned separately, and although both denied stabbing the men, they confessed that both men had been murdered and said that Friðrik Sigurðsson, a seventeen-year-old farmer's son from Katadalur, had killed them. While he denied his involvement for a long time, Friðrik eventually acknowledged his guilt after being counselled by a priest. He wanted Natan's money, he said, and confessed that he had come to Illugastaðir and hidden in the cow shed until both men were asleep. Then he and Agnes went into the baðstofa where the men were sleeping, and Friðrik killed them both with a knife. Then they set the farm on fire. Friðrik was arrested. Despite his confession, many believed that Agnes, the eldest of the three and known to be intelligent, orchestrated the murders and turned the trio into 'a gang'. It was rumoured that Agnes had been spurned by Natan and, seeking revenge, took advantage of Friðrik's existing ill will towards him, it being well-known that the boy was avaricious. Pétur Jónsson was simply in the wrong place at the wrong time. It was Natan the three had wanted to kill.

Agnes, Sigríður and Friðrik were all charged with double murder and arson. The judicial trial for the defendants was comprehensive and extensive, lasting from July 1828 to 25 June 1829. It resulted in death sentences for all three, although Sigríður, who was widely believed to be simple-minded, had her sentence commuted to life imprisonment in a Copenhagen labour prison. Agnes and Friðrik were beheaded by broadaxe on 12 January 1830 at Þrístapar in Vatnsdalshólar on a platform built for the purpose from stones, peat and red cloth. Both the condemned had been given time with priests and it was formally reported that both had repented and walked 'respectfully and contentedly towards their fates'. But other sources say that Agnes had seemed visibly depressed. One hundred and fifty men watched Friðrik then Agnes die. Their severed heads were set on stakes and their bodies were buried in the vicinity of the execution site 'like dogs' – without ritual or ceremony, in plain coffins and without anything to mark the site of their graves. The next day, the heads had disappeared. And eventually, years and years later, Agnes and Friðrik's bones were reburied in the churchyard of Tjörn.

I had hoped learning about the events surrounding Agnes Magnúsdóttir's death would have sated my curiosity, but the opposite has been true. Each translated article, while offering insight into the executions and the murders that preceded them, mention Agnes only in her capacity as a murderess. Most are primarily concerned with the life of Natan Ketilsson. I understand why. He seems to have been a man of great mystery, complexity and charisma: a womaniser, a quack doctor, a great healer, a thief, a poet. Agnes is represented as a peripheral monster, relevant only as the instrument of Natan's death. I have learned nothing of her life or, really, her character. She is only an 'inhumane witch, stirring up murder'.

*

My plan had always been to go back to Iceland as soon as I graduated. I would see Pétur and Regína, and exorcise my preoccupation with Agnes. But in my final year of studies I was called as a witness in a court case, and the legal team asked me to remain close to Australia in case a date for the trial was set suddenly. My cousin, fluent in Thai, suggested I qualify in TESOL and come teach English.

Iceland – and Agnes – must wait, I told myself.

I had thought, initially, that I might fall in love with Thailand in the same way I loved Iceland. When I first moved to Phra Nakhon Si Ayutthaya, eighty kilometres north of Bangkok, I was intoxicated by the ruined splendour of the ancient historic city, the carved sandstone buddha face encircled by the trunk of a bodhi tree, the night market with its utes heaped with durian and stalls of kanom gui chai. I loved the way the pavements cracked open with plants and tree roots, the force with which things grew in the heat and humidity. Each morning, I took a motorbike taxi to Chomsurang Upatham School and revelled in the vitality of the city. As the motorbike veered around dogs and open water channels with their stink of rotting vegetation, I'd take in the roadside vendors with their bags of soup, the smell of frying pa tong ko, and the light coming down through a gauze of smoke and steam and air pollution, and feel the same euphoric headiness that had enervated me at the sight of Iceland's mountains.

But over time, teaching English to over 1500 students in

stultifying routine and sweltering heat left me depleted. By the end of each day, back in my apartment, my body laminated in layers of sweat, chalk dust and ink from worksheets, I could do little more than lie on the tiles under the ceiling fan and fight a bewildering fug of loneliness.

Writing left me in my exhaustion. Instead, I spent weekends cutting out words from English-language newspapers and arranging them on the floor, my throat closing in a prelude to tears. Making poems like this did not feel intentional but compulsive. It felt like automatic writing, like a call for a spirit to join me, a means of communication. It was trance-work: I treated my cuttings like bone runes, throwing them up into the air so that I might divine a way out of my stupor.

One afternoon, an arrangement of clippings on the tiles offered a sudden dip of clarity. I looked down at the poem that emerged from the cut strips of paper.

The North skies collide
over
the black coast country
    saga lurks like cancer
    centuries old
the trees cannot grow
little country
    keeper of giants
        they bury rocks in the rain.

There was a quickening within this poem. A reaching out. I knew immediately whose voice this was.

Agnes Magnúsdóttir.

I sat and stared at the clippings, and suddenly I was back, Þrístapar before me, the three hills standing under a sky full of bad promise.

It was a seed rather than a poem. A feeling. Evidence of the continued, humming hold this woman had on me. It was like finding a heartbeat under my fingertips.

When my contract ended, and the lawyers confirmed I would not be needed in court for at least three months, I declined the option of extending my teaching and booked my tickets north. The prospect of returning to Iceland filled me with a deep and soaking calm.

Nothing embodies passing time like a growing child. Gunnar Stefán is now a teenager, Óli Björn is ten and Jón Arnar is seven and nothing like the ice-cream-demanding toddler I remember. Birgitta is four, with long blonde hair. No longer a baby at all. She is shy with me at first but tells Pétur and Regína she remembers me. There is also now a fifth child, Fannar Orri. Despite being a family of seven, Pétur and Regína have insisted I stay with them. I am folded into their home once more.

Sauðárkrókur has not changed. It is autumn and the mountains are powdered white with snow, although the floor of the valley bears the green of recent harvest as well as longer, yellowing grass that holds the shape of the wind. I walk through the town, noticing which shops have changed, then go up to the churchyard for the view of the fjord. On my way back down the path I tuck a silver one krona coin under a loose stone.

So I can look for it when I come back again, I think to myself. To make sure I do come back.

My return to Sauðárkrókur falls within a normal working week, but the family try to spend as much time with me as possible around school and work. Regína's mother invites me to her house for a special meal of roast lamb. The three oldest boys take me to the beach of black sand. I look after Fannar and hang out with Regína. I make a pavlova for the family. We watch football together. I drop into Kaffi Krókur to surprise my old boss and see Hera and Sylvía again. Coming back is better than I had hoped. It feels as though I never left.

One morning, Pétur takes me for a drive and we end up at Flugmýri, the farm whose destruction by arson was famously described in the Saga of the Icelanders. We talk of the many farms intentionally set alight in Icelandic history, the particular violence of it. The doors blocked, the people within unable to escape the flames and smoke.

'Except this man, Gissur,' says Pétur, pointing to the sign marking where the farm used to lie. 'He survived by hiding in a barrel of whey in the pantry.'

'Shame about the other twenty-five people who burned alive,' I add, reading the next line.

Later that day I drive out to Glaumbær, a preserved traditional turf dwelling in Skagafjörður. The last and only time I went to

Glaumbær, I was with the other Rotary students, and it had been closed for repair. We had marvelled at the outside – the slabs of turf fitted in herringbone slant, the roof of grass – but I wanted to look inside. It does not escape me that Glaumbær is similar to the dwellings Agnes Magnúsdóttir lived in. Similar to the farm at Illugastaðir she was accused of setting on fire.

I am unprepared for the smell inside. It is of damp and dirt and must, and so strong as to make me pause. The dank and stale air is the first thing that triggers my imagination. Time dissolves. I see how dark it is. How my eyes must adjust from even the low October light outside. The sound of my footsteps are absorbed by the packed earthen floor. It is like living underground. Strands of dead grass hang down in the gaps between the boards of the sloped roof like women's hair. What must it have been like to live in such a home? In the eighteenth, nineteenth centuries?

The rooms of the farmhouse are connected by narrow thoroughfares, and as I make my way through them I run my hands over the walls. I want to imprint this place upon my body.

The kitchen is all rocked wall and hearth, giant iron cauldrons hanging from rough-cut timber beams. The baðstofa is the only room with floorboards, three bunks fitted lengthways against each wall, a sign alerting visitors to the fact that most people slept two to a bed, despite each bunk being narrower than a conventional single. I wonder at the forced proximity of so many bodies in such a small space.

I am the only visitor in the museum, and so I take my time examining every detail. I memorise the carved bones upon the shelves, the decorated bed boards, the painted chests, the wool crafts in progress, the bone needles, the colour of the yarn, the carved wooden askur that Icelanders ate their meals from. The sheepskins, scythes and rakes. I take hundreds of photographs. I feel compelled to record everything.

I try to imagine enduring a bad winter in such close and claustrophobic quarters. I know what the winters are like in this country.

I wonder at what would drive a person to kill another after such a winter. I wonder at what it would take to burn one down.

That night I keep thinking of a poem I learned in Icelandic class during my exchange, 'Draughenda' by Ari Jósefsson. My hours of reflection on the old Icelandic farmhouses and the violence and vengeance inflicted within them reminds me of its terrifying premise.

> I come tonight
> while the people in the house sleep
>
> They conjured me
> they invoked and performed witchcraft
> and the sorcerer boiled his potion over his fire of hate
>
> I rose up from the earth
> I, murderer, terror, death
> my axe was blunt and rusty
> but I have whet it on gravestones

I come tonight
tonight I will begin
I will cut you all
and the blood will flood the floor
and the walls echo with distorted anguish

They conjured me
they invoked and performed witchcraft
and now I am coming and night is coming
and the people in the house sleep

The people in the house sleep.

I think of Guðrún, forever changed by her encounter with the undead ghost of the deacon of Myrká. I think of all the ghost stories I have gathered from this country.

And I think of Agnes.

Which Icelander finally agreed
to swing the axe?

CHAPTER THIRTEEN

Speculative Biography

2008–2010

Back in Australia, I begin my Honours in Creative Writing. With my friends already engaged in postgraduate research or diverted into the workforce, my studies are winnowed of social distraction and take on a new primacy. Returning to Iceland has sharpened my intent: I have a story I want to tell.

The university term begins with compulsory attendance at Adelaide Writers' Week and, devoted, I go every day. The program is star-studded: Ian McEwan, Hazel Rowley, Robert Manne, Margo Lanagan, Georgia Blain, Inga Clendinnen, Paul Auster, Siri Hustvedt. I read every biography in the program and circle sessions and stages like I'm going to a music festival.

On the first day my bus arrives too late for me to find a seat under the marquees. Every stretch of shade is packed with people.

The Adelaide heat is intense and inescapable, and by the time the final session finishes I am sunburned and in a foul mood. The next day I catch a lift into town with Dad so that I might arrive early enough to snare a seat. The West Tent is entirely empty at seven thirty in the morning.

I take out my notebook to pass the time. Soon enough a wide-brimmed sunhat clips me in the face. I look up to find an older woman smiling in apology. She takes off the offending hat.

'Is this seat taken?' she asks.

I shake my head and close my notebook.

There is a buzz of preparatory activity on the stage now. Microphone checks. The pouring of water into waiting glasses. The chatter from the gathering audience is loud.

The woman sits down with relief and then gestures to the notebook on my lap. 'Are you a student?'

'Yes.'

'What are you studying?'

'Creative arts.'

The woman fans herself with her program. 'Do you want to be a writer?' she asks after a moment's consideration.

Something in me cringes, bracing for condescension. But she is genuinely curious.

'I would like to be,' I say.

The woman regards me for a moment and then offers me her Writers' Week program. 'Write your name down there,' she says. 'That way I'll remember you when you come to this festival as a writer one day.'

I do so, embarrassed, but also grateful for the seriousness with which she has met my aspiration. As I hand it back to her, the poet Dorothy Porter and a moderator climb onto the stage and take their seats amid applause.

'Thank you, Hannah,' the woman next to me whispers, reading my scrawled name.

'Thank *you*,' I whisper back.

A feeling of inward expansiveness comes over me as I listen to Dorothy speak. She is here to discuss her most recent verse novel, *El Dorado*, but the discussion soon encompasses poetry and passion and nature and desire. Dorothy is funny and intelligent, and later that day, when I see her browsing titles alone in the book tent, I muster my courage and approach her.

'Dorothy Porter?'

She looks at me from under her spectacularly expressive eyebrows. 'Yes?'

Her eyes are boring into my skull. I back off slightly.

'I just wanted to let you know that I loved your session earlier. And I love your books. Your poetry.'

She regards me, frowning a little. 'Oh, come here,' she says, and suddenly pulls me into a hug.

Held by her, the thought occurs to me. If Dorothy can write a verse novel about a serial killer, then maybe I can write a verse novel about Agnes Magnúsdóttir.

By the time of my first meeting with my supervisor, I have made up my mind.

'I'm going to write a verse novel about the last woman to be executed in Iceland.'

Ruth Starke leans back in her chair. My stomach drops as I see she is fighting a smile.

'A verse novel?'

'That's what I was thinking.'

'Hm. Why a verse novel?'

'Because I've already written some poems. I've been reading a lot of verse novels – Tim Sinclair, Dorothy Porter, *The Golden Gate* – and I think that it's a good form for the voice of Agnes Magnúsdóttir, the woman I want to write about.'

I pause, trying to gauge Ruth's thoughts. She gives nothing away.

'Basically, I believe Agnes was a woman who was denied any form of self-representation, and who couldn't argue back against any misrepresentation by others. She was silenced, both in the sense that she was never permitted to tell her side of the story, but also in the sense that she was killed by the state. In writing her voice, I want to position her outside language. I want her voice to be poetic.' I'm on a roll now. 'I want to lean on Hélène Cixous' theories of écriture féminine, and –'

'Hang on, hang on,' Ruth interrupts me. 'Ignore form for now. Ignore … Cixous. Just tell me what happened. Why was this woman executed?'

I tell her the story insofar as I have been able to piece it together and then I admit to Ruth that I haven't been able to stop thinking about Agnes. I do not say that I dream about her, but I mention that I have translated enough articles to have grown frustrated with the unequivocal representation of her as monstrous.

'There seems to be so much absent from the story,' I tell her. 'The crime has been documented, but something is missing. When I look to find Agnes, there is only a stock character. You know, the vengeful whore. I want to learn about what her life was like before the murders. I want to write something that will contextualise her crime.'

'You are looking for her innocence?' Ruth asks.

I shake my head. 'No, I am looking for her humanity. I am looking for her life story.'

Ruth nods. 'When did all this happen again? The execution?'

'She was beheaded in 1830.'

Ruth inclines her head and gives me a searching smile. 'Okay. You want to write a verse novel about a woman who died in 1830s Iceland, which subverts previous representations of her character and is biographical in nature? You think you can do all of that in a verse novel?'

I hesitate. My face is suddenly hot.

'Verse novel aside, it's a very ambitious project, Hannah.'

'Maybe.' I have not thought of this as an ambitious project. I have not thought of it as a project, or even a choice. It feels like a haunting.

Ruth swivels her chair back to her desk. 'Do you have some poems already written?'

'Yes.'

'Send them through.'

I submit thirteen pages of poems. Ruth responds quickly.

The voice is good, she says in an email. *But I really think you should consider writing this story as a novel. Write the first 10,000 words and submit it as an extract for your thesis.*

I thank Ruth for her advice but admit that I am anxious about writing long-form prose.

Later that day she accosts me in a university corridor. 'What's wrong with novels?'

'Nothing. I just haven't written one before. I don't know how.'

'Hannah ...' Ruth sighs. 'That's a terrible reason not to do something.'

A month after I commence my novel, I realise with some embarrassment that Ruth is right. My project is ambitious. I had thought that my familiarity with modern Iceland would be enough for me to write my way into its nineteenth-century history. The truth is that, when I try to write prose, I cannot see anything in my head beyond the landscape. I need to know Agnes's world in all its small, domestic detail. I need to understand the social, political and economic forces turning around her, shaping her as I am shaped by those of my time. If I am to contest the representation of her as monstrous, I will need to make my narrative plausible and capture the tissues and textures of life in Iceland more than two hundred years ago. I know that people lived in turf houses, but were they lit with candles or lamps? And if lamps were used, was seal or fish oil burned? Was everyone literate? If porridge made from Icelandic moss was consumed, how was it prepared?

Being completely unskilled in historical research, I throw a wide net. If there is any likelihood that a source might have a bearing on my understanding of Agnes's life, I read it. I return to Halldór Laxness and Icelandic folktales. I consult journal articles on childhood in nineteenth-century Iceland, statistics regarding Nordic family patterns and class systems, maps of Scandinavian bird migrations and botanical illustrations of Arctic plants.

Early on in my research I stumble across a 'journal of residence' in Iceland during the years 1814 and 1815 by a Scottish Anglican pastor, Ebenezer Henderson. It is not only blessedly written in English, but his observations about the customs, manners and character of Icelanders are highly relevant to the time of Agnes's life – she would have been nineteen during Henderson's sojourn. I make a note of his comment that:

> at present, fines, imprisonment and whipping are the only punishments inflicted in Iceland. Such as are capitally conflicted, it is necessary to send over to Copenhagen to be beheaded; it being a curious fact, that, for some time past, there was no person on the island who would execute the law.

What changed? I write in my notebook. *Why was Agnes beheaded in Iceland rather than Copenhagen? Which Icelander finally agreed to swing the axe?*

I note Henderson's repeated wonder at the literacy of the population, the boys and girls as young as eight who could read and write with ease despite their destitution.

> Every clergyman in Iceland keeps what is called a register of souls, which contains an accurate statement of the age, situation, conduct, abilities and proficiency of each individual in his parish. The books in the possession of the family are also entered on this list.

It is useful to have an outsider's eye, I realise. Someone on the periphery has an excellent view of the centre.

Research into rural life in Iceland's early 1800s soon becomes easier than my inquiry into Agnes's own life. Only a few secondary sources are available to me in Australia, and these imply that her death was the result of her behaving outside norms of feminine behaviour. One source refers to her as a 'loose' woman and implies that her promiscuity justifies her execution. This same source refers to Natan Ketilsson as a 'womaniser' but does not suggest it justified *his* death.

I had assumed from Guðný and Þórir's vague summary of Þrístapar's history that the case was not well known in Iceland, but it is famous enough to have warranted several creative representations. There is a pop song by Bubbi Morthens titled 'Agnes and Friðrik', a Danish play called *The Death of Natan Ketilsson* (in which Agnes frequently 'smiles like a devil') and *Agnes*, an Icelandic film from 1995. I am excited by my discovery of the latter, especially when the English language trailer suggests it is sympathetic to Agnes, a 'spirited woman driven by hope of a better life'. But the film disappoints me. I admire the electrifying performance of María Ellingsen, who plays Agnes with deep emotion, but the facts of the case have been wildly stretched and I find fault in the filmmakers' decision to saint Agnes. The film frustrates me in its reinforcement of a binary understanding of women as one or the other, angels or devils.

I do not want either. I want a human.

At the end of the year I submit 10,000 words of a novel-in-progress titled *Agnes*. In its accompanying exegesis I talk of the novelist's attraction to what is unsaid and describe my (incomplete) novel as an attempt to fill the silences surrounding Agnes Magnúsdóttir.

I ask Ruth if she'll support me in my application for a PhD scholarship to complete the project. She agrees, and the next year I continue what I am now calling a 'speculative biography'.

Speculative is right. After twelve months of research I have only a meagre amount of reliable information about the murders and absolutely no reliable information about Agnes beyond the date of her death, her age and her name.

I decide to use Margaret Atwood's methodology for balancing fact and fiction as described in the afterword of *Alias Grace*:

> I have not changed any known facts, although the written accounts are so contradictory that few facts emerge as unequivocally 'known'. [...] When in doubt, I have tried to choose the most likely possibility, while accommodating all possibilities wherever feasible. Where mere hints and outright gaps exist in the records, I have felt free to invent.

With so few 'known facts' about Agnes's life, I lean into my research into nineteenth-century Iceland to find fictional likelihoods.

A scholarly article on high infant mortality leads to my supposition that Agnes had a sibling who died. An 1816 diary describing the prevalence of poverty in Iceland suggests to me that Agnes would have been destitute. Census information on child labour tells me that Agnes, a vinnukona (servant) at the time of her conviction, might have started work at five or six. Maps, journals, academic articles, song lyrics, photographs and even tourist brochures begin to feed into my fictional construction of Agnes's early life.

I buy a notebook and paste in detailed colour maps of northern Iceland as endpapers. It is not a document I intend to share with anyone and so I let it be the strange cauldron of poetry, musings and research it wants to be. In the first few pages I write:

> *All stories are ghost stories. All stories deal with things that are absent, things that perhaps once were, or would have been, but are no longer there for us to touch or know. Looking for a story is ghost hunting. I am reaching into the dark, hoping to touch that which haunts me.*

On the front cover I paste an illustration of a hand driving a razor through the cover of a book, blood seeping from where it has been cut.

This is what I want, I think to myself every time I open my notebook. I want my pages to bleed.

I compose a fictionalised timeline of Agnes's life, beginning with her birth in 1795 and ending with the date of her death. It is a combination of informed speculation and a few singular intuitive guesses that have little basis in research. I can't shake the feeling that Agnes would have grown up without a mother. I sketch out scenes in which she describes a younger brother, an impoverished childhood. I make her a foster child.

It is a vulnerable methodology, and while it allows me to draft 40,000 words I have little confidence in my work. Without primary sources, I feel like a trespasser. I am an outsider writing about a time I did not live in, a country that is not my own.

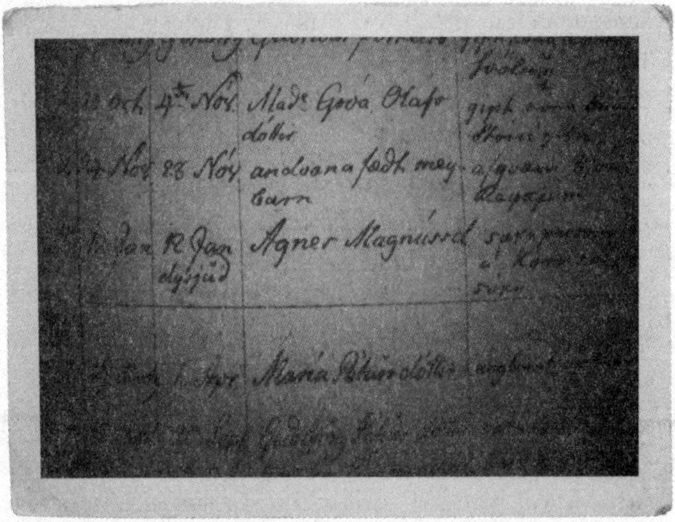

I feel the dowsing rod swing again

CHAPTER FOURTEEN

Return

2010

I am thirsty and tired to the point of dizziness. My feet and shins ache, my mouth tastes of raw onion from the Bæjarins Beztu hot dog I ate after dropping my bag at the hostel, but I am determined to walk for as long as possible. Reykjavík is obscured with a misting rain, but I have taken myself out into it, walking down Laugavegur to stave off my jet lag and lessen the swelling of my legs from two days of flights. I am not the only one out in the weather. Tourists, easy to spot in their coloured anoraks, are everywhere. I do not remember ever seeing so many. At Tjörnin, the city pond, I stop and watch the ducks – and the foreigners with their bread and cameras – until the sea fog that has been obscuring the mountains around Reykjavík clears to reveal recognisable shoulders of purple around the horizon. There is no snow to be seen. It is August, after all.

Finally, after two and a half years of frustrated research, I have received funding for an eight-week study trip to access primary sources. By now I am deeply familiar with 1800s Iceland, but Agnes remains elusive. I am here to find her in the National Archives, in the censuses and parish and soul registers available only on microfilm. I am here to find the books written by amateur Icelandic historians and folklorists that might offer anecdotal flavour. One book in particular has beckoned me here: *Enginn má undan líta* by Guðlaugur Guðmundsson. In the nationwide library catalogue of Iceland, I can see that it is one of the few full-length books concerning itself with the murders. It also promises an entire chapter on the early life of Agnes Magnúsdóttir.

I had not intended to go to the National Museum today, but after the rain clears I find myself standing outside its doors. I decide to have a quick look.

I pay the student fee of five hundred krona and go up the stairs to the permanent exhibition, but it is not until I see a sign pointing towards a display of artefacts from 1600–1900 that I remember that the axe and wooden block used in Agnes's beheading is in this museum. Fatigue evaporated, heart suddenly pounding, I head towards a banner reading 'Punishment'. There is an information placard, a display case showing an old door taken from a prison and a pair of vicious-looking handcuffs. Then I look to my right and see, on the floor by my feet, the block and the axe.

Something like alarm trills down my spine. To discover myself in such close and unexpected proximity to these objects is startling. I am not prepared.

The blade is a fearsome thing, dark red from the rust that has corroded it and visibly thin. I can almost feel its terrible weight. The block of untreated oak is grey, roughly cut and holds the curve of the tree it was taken from. There is a chunk of wood missing in a semicircle on one edge. I realise this is a groove for the chin, placed in such a way as to ensure the neck is arched over the wood, away from the shoulders. I glance around the empty gallery, then sink to my knees for a closer look. Stomach dropping, I see horizontal markings in the wood. This is where the axe bit.

I suddenly feel horribly aware that Agnes died upon this slab of oak not two inches from my hand. Her chin was pushed into that hewn space. Her blood spilled here. How unnerving to know that this woman whose voice I am trying to capture lay upon this block. How awful to think that this oak, so close to my own body, was the last thing that held her.

It takes me some time to move away and explore the rest of the exhibition, but when I do, many of the research questions I have brought with me from Australia are answered. Yes, it is likely Agnes would have eaten out of a wooden bowl like this one. This is how they made candles. These brass buttons are what would have shone on Björn Blöndal's coat as he pronounced sentence on Agnes. These are the kinds of spinning wheels, shoes, needles, plates, knives, scales, barrels, butter churns, blankets, reins, ropes, kettles, stockings, wool combs, fishhooks and slaughter spikes used by Agnes and the people in her life. Here is a recreation of a baðstofa. These are the small, ordinary things – hymn books, snuff boxes, quills, lamps, children's toy knuckles – that will make my book as real as possible.

I spend three hours in this single section of the total exhibition and take over four hundred photos. By the time I make my way back down the stairs at closing time, I am exhilarated to the point of deliriousness. I have not yet been in Iceland for twenty-four hours and already my novel is filling with blood.

I fall asleep with my clothes on that afternoon, and doze fitfully during the night until light creeps into the hostel dorm shortly after four am. Over breakfast, I look through the photos I took at the museum. Every discovery branches out into further lines of inquiry. Was Agnes kept in the prison in Reykjavík, and if so, were women in a separate section? What clothes would she have worn while imprisoned? Was she allowed possessions? Where did people defecate, especially during bad weather?

By the time I have written a list of new questions, the day has progressed. I use the wi-fi in the foyer to Skype with Hera. Her voice, when she answers, fills me with joy.

'Hannah! You're here! Are you planning on coming to Sauðárkrókur?'

'I think I might come up this weekend for Regína and Pétur's birthday party. There's a bus I can take.'

Hera laughs. I have missed her brightness. It pours through her like sunshine. 'Neeeeiiii, Hannah! Ekki strætó! Not a bus! Donni and the baby and I are in Sauðárkrókur now, but we are coming down to Reykjavík on Wednesday before going north again on Friday. We can bring you with us.'

'Oh, really? Thanks!'

'Auðvitað. Of course. Where are you staying now?'

'In a hostel downtown.'

'Hannah!' Hera's voice whips into reprimand. 'A hostel! Oh my god. You have to stay at our apartment!'

'What? Nei, Hera, you have a newborn!'

'Hannah mín, you are staying at our place.'

'I don't want to put you to any trouble.'

'Okay, good, you are staying with us. Ring me tomorrow. I'm so happy you're here!'

We hang up. I am suffused with love for these good people, and my luck in knowing them.

The next day, I walk to Eymundsson bookshop to buy some maps. Nothing in Australia has been detailed enough: I need one that lists farm names, mountain paths, churches. I pick up *101 Ísland: Destinations Off the Beaten Track*, and there I find two pages on the Illugastaðir murder. The article contains anecdotes related by witnesses at the execution. One man said that Agnes had to be held by the hair before she could be beheaded. Several others were recorded as saying that they thought she was 'fallið í ómegin'. I don't understand this, so I ask the man at the counter what it means.

He reads it, frowning. 'I don't know it. Do you want to look it up?'

I follow him to a massive dictionary elsewhere in the store.

'We would say meðvitunderlaus now,' he tells me in English. 'It is like unconscious.'

I show him the page in the book. 'Do they mean she had fainted when they cut off her head?'

'Probably something like that,' he agrees.

The bookshop is a restful one to browse in. I find a massive atlas of northern Iceland and use the nail on my little finger to measure the distance between Illugastaðir and Stapakot, the farm Agnes ran to after the murders. Two and a half kilometres. What must it have been like to run that distance in the dark?

I find an encyclopedia that covers the years 1800–1899, and when I open it the pages fall open to 1830. In the centre of the page is an article about the execution. It has names and dates. It is precise. My heart starts beating very fast as I read that Guðmundur Ketilsson, Natan's brother, was asked to execute Friðrik and Agnes. As Friðrik approached the block, he asked Guðmundur if he was doing it for revenge, and Guðmundur said no, he was serving justice. Then Friðrik asked to see the axe and said: 'This is a blessed branch of justice which I have defiled with my sins. God be praised for it.'

After Friðrik's head had been cut off, the axe was so firmly stuck in the block that two men were required to pull it out again. Agnes, it is reported, had a priest by her side to comfort her.

There is no mention of her being dragged by her hair. No mention of her fainting.

Hera is as good as her word. She calls and tells me that Lóa, one of the girls I knew at high school back in 2003, lives in Reykjavík now, and she will pick me up from the hostel and drop me off at the apartment. 'I think it will be too much for you to try to find it by yourself,' she says.

I haven't seen Lóa for seven years but I recognise her immediately. She gets out of the car and kisses me on the cheek. 'Do we speak Icelandic or English?' she asks, beaming at me.

'Icelandic,' I say. 'I have to practise.'

I manage to understand almost everything Lóa says and reply without having to think which words to use. My grammar and syntax are atrocious, but it is a relief to know the vocabulary is still there. By the time Lóa drops me off at Donni and Hera's apartment, my Icelandic cogs, although rusty, are nonetheless turning.

The apartment is small, but new and comfortable. I'm thrilled at the prospect of working at a kitchen table, and the luxury of privacy. Researching on a lower bunk in the hostel dorm was not ideal.

From the apartment's balcony, Reykjavík is beautiful, cold and still. The only movement comes from a large gull flying overhead. When I fall asleep at eleven o'clock, the sky outside is still filled with light.

The next day I set out for Borgabókasafnið Kringlunni, one of Reykjavík's eight city libraries. As I wait at an intersection for the lights to change, a lady in her thirties walks up. I feel her looking at me in the direct way Icelanders do. After a moment, she asks me a question.

'Fyrirgefðu,' I apologise. 'Ég tala bara smá íslensku. Geturðu spurt mig aftur?' I only speak a little Icelandic. Can you ask me again?

'What are you doing in Iceland?' she asks in English, curious.

'Ég er að læra,' I say. Studying.

She switches to Icelandic. 'Hvað ertu að læra?'

'Ég er að skrifa bók um Agnesi Magnúsdóttur, sem var síðasta aftakan.' I am writing a book about Agnes Magnúsdóttir, the last execution here.

The woman smiles at me as the lights change. 'Gangi þér vel,' she says, before peeling off in another direction. It is a strange interaction. It leaves me tingling.

Gangi þér vel is a phrase I have always loved. Not necessarily for its meaning, which is 'good luck', but for its literal translation: walk you well. In English, luck is wished upon a person, a hope that things will turn out all right. The Icelandic phrase, literally translated, places your fate within your own feet. I like the implication that it is not luck that is being wished for but sure steps. May you go where you have decided to go. May you watch where you put your feet.

With a small, warm flame in my belly, I tell myself that this is what I shall do. I will walk well. I will make my own path.

When I arrive at the library, the first thing I do is look for its copy of *Enginn má undan líta*. It's not on the shelf. When I go to the counter with my query, the librarian tells me that I am mistaken – they have no such book.

Disappointed, I console myself by flipping through collections of historical Icelandic photography. I have already resigned myself to the impossibility of finding any photos of Agnes – photography only arrived in Iceland in the second half of the nineteenth century – but I want to build a visual store of reference of Iceland's past. I am soon engrossed, spotting the same kinds of seal and fish skin slippers on display in the National Museum, the woollen shawls and tasselled caps worn by women that are so often mentioned in the journals of foreigners. Here they are, inhabited.

I notice a predominance of high cheekbones and blue eyes, all unnervingly light against the dark exposure. Faces are prematurely lined from harsh lives and poor diets. Women have thick-looking arms from multiple layers of clothing. Fishing shacks are filled with dirt and misery. People bend from the waist to wash their clothes in hot springs, children's clothing carefully laid out to dry on the ground. Doorways are small. The mountains are a constant, dark backdrop to these glimpsed lives.

One photo of a farming family outside a turf house makes a particular impression on me. There are two girls of a similar age in the photo, but one stands apart from the family, her clothes not as nice. The caption says she was a foster child.

Was this Agnes's life? I wonder. Could she have been that girl?

My next few days are spent at the Árni Magnússon Institute for Icelandic Studies, where I access the manntal (literally, 'men count') or censuses recorded during Agnes's lifetime. Iceland is unusually diligent in its record-keeping. Landnámabók, the Book of Settlements, compiled in the thirteenth century, names over three thousand settlers and their descendants and their connection to place. Iceland's 1703 manntal was the world's first-ever census of an entire country. Ten other Iceland-wide censuses were compiled in the nineteenth century. I hope to find Agnes within them.

I begin with the census of 1816, when Agnes was twenty-one. The data is organised by district and, not knowing where Agnes was living, I must trawl through the census citizen by citizen. It is like trying to find someone in an unalphabetised phone book.

After a few hours pass without success, I try my luck with the manntal of 1801, when Agnes was six years old. It is written in Danish. After five hours of searching, my eyes swimming, I find her. Agnes is listed as living with her mother, Ingveldur Rafnsdóttir, on a farm called Brekkukot. It is not their farm. Ingveldur is a live-in vinnukona to the farmer, his wife and two children. Ingveldur also has another child, one-year-old Jóas Illugason, a half-brother to Agnes.

Then I read 'begge fosterborn'. Both foster children.

Agnes *was* a foster child.

I suddenly feel like crying. I did not think my speculation would come so close.

I think of the photo I saw yesterday at the library, of the foster daughter standing apart. While Iceland has a long history of fostering children, particularly in the medieval period as a means of cementing family alliances, in the nineteenth century the practice expanded to include the 'fostering' or 'taking-in' of pauper children for agreed periods of time. There were no institutions for families in need of poor relief back then. Instead, families were forcibly split up. This prevented more children from being born and pushed the adults into service. Families were also dissolved when the man of the house died, mothers separated from their children: working women who came with extra mouths to feed were not attractive hires. Some foster children were cared for and loved, especially when fostered by relatives, but others were not wanted and the exploitation and maltreatment of many is well documented. I remember reading about one young foster child who, when asked if he was treated with kindness, responded dryly: 'Everyone's been good to me. Especially the dogs.'

I wonder if the farmer agreeing to foster Agnes and Jóas while employing their mother as a servant was an unusual act of kindness. There was no husband living with Ingveldur. I am glad that, at six, Agnes was still with her mother, but her formal designation as a foster child, and the possibility of her illegitimacy, bodes ill.

With confirmed dates, names and locations to work from, I return to the 1816 census and find Agnes as a twenty-one-year-old servant working at a northern farm called Guðrúnarstaðir. The census offers her place of birth as the farm of Flaga in Vatnsdalur. It is the same valley that opens out onto Vatndalshólar, the site of her execution.

The next day I take the bus into town and walk to the National Archives of Iceland. As I round the corner, my heart stops.

This is where I spent my first night in Iceland.

I must be wrong. This is a public building. No random exchange student spends their first night in a national archive.

And yet. Standing there before the entrance gate I remember sitting in the front seat of Jón Ásgeir's car, the shine of his headlights illuminating those same words on the white wall in front of me now: *Þjóðskalasafn Íslands.*

I am seventeen again. On the precipice of my future.

Perhaps I am imagining it. Everything has become so intimate. Even my research feels personal. I shake it off and go inside.

The Reading Room of the National Archives has a pleasant, seventies aesthetic of wood-panelled walls, red tiles and grey carpet. I am surprised to find many Icelanders already seated at the wooden desks by the windows or at the readers, faces lit up by the projected microfilm. I remind myself that this is a country curious about ancestry and genealogy, where belonging is celebrated through the excavation of blood lines extending deep into the past.

Alongside Iceland's history of census survey is an equally diligent tradition of parish records. The prestsþjónustubækur, or pastoral books, include standard information on marriages, deaths, births, baptisms and confirmations. The sálnaregistur, or soul registers, differ in that they are a record of the priest's yearly visit to all households within his parish and include information on every individual, including their behaviour and literacy.

When I load up a roll of microfilm, the first thing that strikes me is how human the records are. After years of reading only typeset print, these records bear the movement of a hand. The writing is cramped in places, expressive in others. I can see where ink has smudged, where an entry has been rushed.

My eyes are ill-accustomed to reading such old-fashioned cursive, let alone in Icelandic, but after a few minutes of scrolling I find the record of Agnes's birth.

On October 27 [1795] Agnes was born to Magnús Magnússon and Ingveldr (Ingveldur) Rafnsdótt. At Flaga. She was named the same day. She was an illegitimate child (parents are not married). Under comments: *Nothing. Her father lives at Stóridalur.*

An illegitimate foster child.

Illegitimacy was a fineable offence in early 1800s Iceland, but a common one. Icelandic servants were usually unmarried since marriage prospects were severely restricted for those without land. Over ten per cent of children in Agnes's time were illegitimate, most born to 'servants of scant means'. It was unusual for a servant to be allowed to bring her illegitimate children into the household where she served. Most children, particularly those who were too young to work, became paupers.

I locate the record of Agnes's confirmation at fourteen, but do not recognise half of the words used by the priest to describe the 'ferming' of the six children. I find a kind-looking archivist and ask if he can assist me.

He puts down his coffee and follows me back to the microfilm reader, pulling up a chair next to mine. He squints at the screen and tells me that Agnes is listed as 'rétt sennilega' in her knowledge of psalms.

'What does that mean?'

The archivist responds in English. 'It means she probably knew some, but not all. But her reading, here …' He points to the crabbed scrawl on the screen. '"Í betra lagi" is "better than average". She was one of the only children who memorised the larger texts.'

'Was she smart?'

'Já.' The archivist smiles at me. 'I'm Jón Torfason. What's your name?'

I introduce myself in Icelandic and give Jón my email address when he asks for it. He tells me that he will write if he thinks of anything I might be interested in. 'How long are you in Iceland for? Is it okay if I speak and write to you in Icelandic?'

'Yes, of course.'

'Okay, I will try to help you.'

'Takk fyrir. Actually,' I say, 'I have something you might be able to help me with now.'

He lifts his eyebrows. 'Yes?'

'I have a memory of staying here, at the archives, as an exchange student. I think I spent my first night in Iceland in this building.' I shrug my shoulders. 'Could that have happened?'

Jón frowns at me. 'No, people do not stay here.'

'Oh.'

'Were you by yourself?'

'No. I stayed with a man called Jón Ásgeir and his wife.'

Jón breaks into a sudden smile. 'Then yes, maybe. Jón Ásgeir worked here for many years. He was an archivist. I think there might have been one or two apartments on site back then.'

By the end of the day, I have more facts about Agnes than I managed to collect over two years of research in Australia. A foster child with three half-siblings. One dead in infancy, another half-sister dead at twelve from 'a sickness on the inside'. ('Cancer,' Jón speculated, peering over my shoulder.) All were, like Agnes, illegitimate.

Significantly, I have also now found Agnes's death notice (handwriting rushed, painfully casual), and learned that she was never held in the Reykjavík prison but at a farm called Kornsá.

On the bus home, my mind is whirring.

Agnes was not imprisoned. She was essentially billeted with a local family.

I feel the dowsing rod swing again.

What would it have been like to spend the last six months with a family?

It is not the same, but I know a little of what it is like to be alone among others. I know a little of what it feels like to be placed with strangers.

When I return to the apartment, Hera and her mother are there. Hera and I burst into delighted laughter and hug, and then I am introduced to her new daughter, only one month old. She is tiny and perfect and not yet named. Icelanders have up to six months to name their children. She is, for now, referred to as 'Elskan'. Darling.

I am astonished at how light she feels in my arms.

'Here,' Hera says, once I've passed the baby back to Hrafnhildur, Hera's mother. 'Pétur got you this.' She hands me a mobile phone.

'He bought this for me?'

'Yes,' Hera replies. 'So you can call him if you get into trouble!'

I'm overwhelmed by Pétur's fatherly concern. Hera seems amused by it. I call him immediately to thank him.

'Hannah, it's no problem. You know that.' Just hearing Pétur's voice on the line makes me feel emotional.

'You're so good to me.'

He laughs. 'Call me if you need anything, okay? I have a lot of friends in Iceland, so I can always call around to sort things out for you.'

'Takk kærlega fyrir, Pétur.'

'You're still my daughter, you know. I have to look after you.'

'Við sjáumst bráðum.'

'Já, við sjáumst.' See you soon.

Árbaer Open Air Museum

CHAPTER FIFTEEN

Family

When I arrive at the archives the next day, Jón Torfason the archivist is there. He looks up as I enter.

'Hannah! Komdu hingað.' He beckons me into the staff room and hands me a pile of paper. Glancing through it, I see that he has photocopied some articles about Illugastaðir for me. His name is listed as an author.

'You wrote this?' I ask him.

Jón smiles and tells me that he is a historian and researcher. One of his specialties is the original turf farm at Illugastaðir.

I gape at him, and then we both start laughing at the coincidence of our meeting.

'You should look at these,' he says, tapping the papers in my hand. 'I think they will help you write your book.'

I notice they include a floorplan of the now-destroyed turf farm.

'I can show you, if you like.' Jón shuffles back. 'Here.' He takes some large steps around the room, turning sharply to indicate four corners. He puts his hands on his hips. 'That is how big the baðstofa was.'

The baðstofa. The living quarters of the farm where so much happened. I look at the narrow rectangle he has marched into the room and my mind superimposes a version of the baðstofa I saw recreated in the National Museum. This one is much smaller.

'You should also know that Agnes's true father was thought to be Jón Bjarnason. He was married, lived at Brekkukot.' Jón hands me a pile of papers filled with cursive script. 'These are from a friend. He did some research a while ago.'

The papers summarise the births, deaths and places of residence of Agnes, her mother and the two men who may or may not have been her father. I see that, in the thirty-two years before she was charged with murder, Agnes moved between fourteen different farms.

Ingveldur, her mother, disappeared at the time of the murders.

Jón, reading over my shoulder, nods. 'Yes, like she has "gone into the blue". Disappeared into nowhere. She died a few months after Agnes.' He offers a sad shrug, then turns to an archival box sitting on the desk. 'I found these for you too.'

'What are they?' I peer inside.

'Letters. You can take them out.'

'Do I need gloves or something?'

Jón shakes his head.

Overwhelmed, I thank Jón profusely and carry the box out to a table by the window in the Reading Room. I feel electrified. Slowly, reverently, I take out the letters, noting the stamped red wax seals, the bluish green paper, the mottled squares of yellow. The ink is a soft brown. I recognise the signed names of the officials, judges and priests involved in the sentencing, imprisonment and execution of Agnes and Friðrik. My heart sinks when I unfold one and see the small handwriting, knowing how slow the process of deciphering it will be. I am desperate to know what these letters say. But it feels miraculous to hold paper once held by the people I am writing about. And I am suddenly, acutely aware of how we are outlasted by the words we write.

The rest of the day is spent in painstaking translation. At one point Jón comes over to see how I am going. He pulls out a blue paper from the pile. It is a list of Agnes's possessions at the time she was brought into custody. We transcribe the items one by one. A woman's shawl of blue wool. An old blue skirt. Two long black skirts. A striped apron of Icelandic weaving. The list goes on: eighteen humble items. I am taken by the description of 'a white sack with useless odds and ends'. Childhood keepsakes?

When we finish, Jón looks over the letter again. We are quiet.

'Hún var mjög fátæk,' he says eventually.

She was very poor.

Hera and Donni take me up to Sauðárkrókur as promised. When we pass Þrístapar, Hera tells me there are three things in

Iceland that cannot be counted. The hills of Vatnsdalshólar are one of them.

I recognise farms signposted off the main road. There is Brekkukot, where Agnes lived as a six-year-old. Kringla, where her little sister was born and died. The sky the blue of infinity, the grass green and scattered with cut and baled hay wrapped in white plastic. Horses cluster against the wire fences, watching us pass.

Pétur and Regína have erected a marquee that occupies the entirety of their backyard. A huge container normally used to hold fish is filled with ice and over three hundred cans of Carlsberg. Half the town will be coming to the party.

When I ask Pétur what I can bring, he laughs at me. The Australian bring-your-own culture does not apply here.

'We are hosting,' he tells me. 'We provide the food and drink.'

Jón, my old boss from Kaffi Krókur, arrives to cook. He is baffled, then delighted, to see me. 'Nei, Hannah?!'

I help Jón bring in trays of salad and meat and tell him I was sorry to hear that Kaffi Krókur burned down. Shortly after I arrived yesterday, seventeen-year-old Gunnar Stefán and I went on a rúntur, an Icelandic mainy, and he pointed out the newly rebuilt cafe. The changes to the bakery. The post office no longer a post office. It was strange to see the work of seven years upon a place, but it is still the same old Sauðárkrókur, still the same old mountains.

Jón and Pétur don tall chef's hats and aprons and fire up barbecues. People arrive, bearing gifts and dressed in their best, and I realise that Pétur has intentionally not told anyone I have returned. Several people do double takes, then stare at Pétur for confirmation. He grins.

'Hannah?! Nei, hvað ert þú að gera hér?!' Hannah?! No way, what are you doing here?

I laugh and hug them and try out my patchy Icelandic. 'I'm sorry,' I say. 'I've forgotten so much!'

'No, no, it's great! Your Icelandic is really good.'

Soon the backyard is full of people filling their plates with lamb and jacket potatoes with butter and sour cream and sauce. Always, so much sauce.

By ten o'clock, Hera and Donni have left, the guests have all settled around tables and, not feeling confident enough to plop myself down in their midst, I absent myself from the marquee, pull on an old t-shirt and get into bed. I am just dozing off when I hear a spoon clink against a glass: speeches. Panicking, I pull on jeans and a bra. I ought to be present, especially given what Pétur and Regína have done for me, how they have welcomed me back.

I make it inside the marquee just as Pétur is rising out of his chair.

'Jæja, þakka ykkur öllum kærlega fyrir komuna.' Thank you to everyone who has come. He turns and points to me. 'This girl has come all the way from Australia! Hannah, elsku dóttir okkar.'

Our dear daughter.

He gestures for me to stand by his side as he finishes his speech.

I don't know what I did to deserve this kind of love.

The party kicks off after the speeches. I contemplate going back to bed but get a beer instead. Everyone is a bit drunk – I can tell from the way their foreheads bump into mine and their effusive declarations about how good it is to see me back, how they are proud of me. It feels like a distinctly Icelandic trait to become ebullient when tipsy. I remember being puzzled at how, after a night out at the bar, all those who had professed their love for me were, in the morning, lukewarm at best. Still, I go with it. Someone gets out a guitar and the party is suddenly a huge singalong. I don't know any of the words but join in regardless. Someone gives me some snuff and I erupt in a bout of sneezing. Everyone crows with laughter. I take some more, and then soon I am in the groove of a distinctly Icelandic party. Beer, snus, song.

Back in Reykjavík, I return to the libraries, anxious to find *Enginn má undan líta*. One librarian assures me that they have it, then cannot find it on the shelf. She shrugs, apologetic. 'It should be there. Maybe someone shelved it somewhere it should not be?'

Another library tells me that their copy was destroyed in a fire.

I return to Eymundsson bookshop to see if I can just buy my own copy, but the book, published in 1974, is out of print. They tell me to try my luck in the north.

Exasperated, I return to the archives to see if I can find out more about the farm Agnes was held at in the last months of her life.

I find Kornsá in the soul registers of 1829. The farmer and his wife were in their late fifties, with a son and two daughters, all in their twenties. They had four servants. Down the bottom, listed as a sakapersóna, a criminal, is Agnes Jónsdóttir, thirty-four years old.

So, I think to myself. Jónsdóttir. She did know who her true father was.

I am struck by the information the priest has included about the behaviour of those at Kornsá. There is an exclamation of 'frábær!' (terrific!) next to the name of the youngest daughter, Sigurlaug. Her elder sister is simply 'well-read'. The mother is said to have good manners.

Agnes, the priest has written, is 'well-read', 'has good Christian knowledge' and, finally, is 'blendin' in behaviour.

I ask Jón what 'blendin' means in this context.

'It means mixed,' he says. 'She was both good and bad.'

I feel like clapping my hands together.

By the end of the week, I am forced to acknowledge what I will not find. After days of following Agnes through the archives and soul registers, there remain periods of her life where there are no records. I accept that it is unlikely I will discover what her life was like between the ages of six and twenty-one.

Some records don't begin until later years. Huge chunks are missing. There are acknowledgements of lost pages in the microfilm and clear examples of human error and oversight. The limitations of research make me so frustrated I could weep.

That night, I console myself by translating the local histories I have found in lieu of *Enginn má undan líta*. Hera and Donni help me translate unfamiliar and old-fashioned phrases.

> Agnes [...] was lively and enjoyable to talk to, quick-witted and particularly well-spoken. It's safe to say that she was well-liked, especially at first. But her temper was intense and her passions strong. It has also been said that she had been disappointed [in romantic relationships] more than once, and it is possible that because of this she had become insane.

One author posits that Agnes, in love with Natan and believing herself engaged to him, had been spurned once she came to his farm to work. 'Her burning love turned into burning hatred,' he writes. She was a woman of 'uncontrollable emotions'.

But I am more interested in the throwaway comment that she had been promised the position of housekeeper and, when she arrived, learned Natan had given it to the fifteen-year-old maid, Sigríður.

I think of Agnes's illegitimacy and her life of labour, and the fact that most children fostered due to pauperism were never able to become independent. I think of the many priests who refer to her intelligence over the years. What frustrated ambitions might Agnes have had?

Hera and Donni go to bed, but I am hooked. I can't stop. I read that Agnes requested a young assistant reverend to prepare her for death. She spoke calmly and plainly to him about her situation, and said she felt the district commissioner and her former priest had not presented the whole story during the trial. 'I cannot forgive them,' she said.

At one in the morning, I finish translating a paragraph about her execution and begin to cry.

The assistant priest had knelt beside Agnes as she lay on

the log. He had wrapped his arms around her and didn't let go until after she had been beheaded.

He consoled her until the last.

I decide to spend a day away from the archives and take two buses to get to Árbær Open Air Museum. My experience of such things is limited to the gold-panning and pantomime villainy of the old-timey schoolmaster at Sovereign Hill in Victoria's Ballarat, but this museum takes its task of recreating Iceland's past seriously. Several historic buildings and turf houses around Reykjavík have been relocated here. As I enter I see a young man in cap and black waistcoat and a girl in a white apron with a brown knitted shawl crossed over her chest. It momentarily feels as though the figures in those old Icelandic photos have been breathed back into life.

I follow the sound of a hammer upon an anvil to a turf house. A bearded young man is heating and shaping an iron rod outside.

'Góðan daginn,' he says.

I watch him work for a while, remembering that Natan, as well as a doctor, was reportedly a good smithy. Then I walk into the turf house, noticing the low ceilings, the dried dung set next to the hearth for fuel, the hard ropes made from horsehair. It is quiet in the turf house and I wonder about winter. About the loneliness of such deep and enduring silence.

Outside, the actors sit in the sunshine, knitting or occupied in other chores. Rhubarb grows in the shade. The grass is dotted with flowers. Yes, I think, you would grasp every bit of sun. You would escape the darkness of the turf buildings whenever you could.

Visiting the museum bathroom, I find the back of the stall door covered in an exhaustive history of the latrine in Iceland. People went outside, or in a wooden chamber pot. Urine was collected in barrels and fermented until it produced ammonia. Then it was used for washing hair or wool or for curing skins. I am so delighted to finally have my questions surrounding historic Icelandic toileting habits answered – and in such circumstances – that I cackle out loud.

On the day of Hera and Donni's daughter's christening, I spend the morning helping Hrafnhildur assemble her kornflexmarens, sandwiching the discs of meringue together with whipped cream, then looking after the baby while the families prepare for the afternoon's celebrations. At four o'clock we leave for the venue, which turns out to be Donni's place of work, the football and sports headquarters. I help Hrafnhildur set up the cakes and the caramel and chocolate sauces to go with them (!) and then walk with her to Friðrikskapella – Friðrik's chapel – opposite.

The christening begins with the singing of a psalm, and then the Lord's Prayer, somehow made more beautiful in Icelandic. The priest, full of sincerity and warmth, asks everyone to cross themselves and then the baby is dressed with holy water from a brass bowl. She doesn't cry, but Donni does. The priest invites him to tell everyone the name they have chosen for their child, but he is so choked up that no one can hear what he says. Hera leans over to wipe his cheeks and then we are all on the verge of weeping, in this gesture of love, in Donni's pride and happiness in his daughter.

'Hrafnhildur Kara,' he says again, voice clear.

The godparents are asked to come forward, the priest makes the sign of the cross, and it is concluded.

Afterwards everyone comes up to congratulate Donni and Hera. It is a happy occasion. How things have changed in Iceland since the nineteenth century, I think to myself. Hera and Donni are not married.

Friðrik and Agnes's grave at Tjörn

CHAPTER SIXTEEN

Illugastaðir

Mum and Dad arrive in Iceland, and Donni drives me to the airport to meet them. It is surreal to have them with me. Their presence in this country immediately solidifies my own experiences here; it is proof I have not been dreaming.

We hire a car, and I take them to the otherworldly waters of the Blue Lagoon, Geysir, Gullfoss and Þingvellir, that place of riven earth rich with a history of chieftains and law speakers, burning men and pools of drowning women. Then I take them north. During the drive we speak of my time living here.

'I remember when you came home from school in year twelve and announced to us that you were going on exchange,' says Dad. 'You were so excited and I didn't say anything at the time, but I remember looking at Mum and knowing we were thinking the same thing. "How the hell are we going to pay for this?"'

I frown. 'I thought Rotary mostly paid for it?'

'We still had to contribute some. We were skint back then.'

'We found the money, though,' says Mum. 'Somehow.'

I pull a face. 'I'm sorry. God, I didn't ever think of that. I was so selfish.'

Dad laughs. 'Hannah, you were seventeen.'

'And then I get there and complain about how homesick I am.'

Dad smiles at me in the rear-vision mirror. 'Things turned out pretty good though.'

Pétur and Regína embrace my parents as though they have known them all their lives. We sit at the kitchen table and share a dinner together amid the chaos and noise of all their children. My two homes, collided. I glow at this coming together of people I love, the people I owe so much.

Just before we leave to find our accommodation in the nearby town of Varmahlíð, Pétur mentions a letter I gave him when I left for Australia in 2004.

'Do you still have it?' Mum asks.

Pétur nods. 'I keep it in my bedside table.'

I have warned my parents that, since I'm in Iceland on the university's dollar, I will need to continue my research during their stay. I would love for them to come with me, but if they have better things to do than go look at a lot of Icelandic farms, I'll understand.

'Nonsense,' says Mum. 'We'd love to join you.'

Now that I have reached the limit of what the archives can offer, my plan is to leave the records behind. I want to see and smell and listen to the places where Agnes lived and worked. It is one thing to understand distances on a map, or chart people's movement from one dot to another and capture it in a neat timeline, another to bring it to life. I need to superimpose all I know upon the land. I need to note the mud lying in the wet places, imagine scraping off a journey from shoes of fish leather.

After only half an hour of driving, I am deeply glad of my parents' presence. Their total lack of familiarity with my research and with nineteenth-century Iceland forces me to haul up the knowledge I have accumulated and present it in tandem with the places we move through. I narrate our journey through the context of Agnes's story.

My parents are full of questions. I describe the work a vinnukona would have been expected to do, the living arrangements within a baðstofa and the injustice of the Danish monopoly on trading. As I do so, it is as though the words and maps I have spent so long gazing at are lifting off the page. I see the shape of Agnes's life among the mountains, its confluence and convergence with the stories of others.

We turn off the main road into Vatnsdalur, the narrow valley where Agnes spent much of her working life. I am immediately struck by its beauty and glad to see it in person: I could not have guessed that Flóðið, a lake at the mouth of the valley, is lit with swans, or known the fields of cut hay are thick with grazing ducks, how the sky is flecked with soft wisps of cloud.

'What beautiful country,' Mum remarks.

'Breathtaking,' agrees Dad.

The sunshine pulls the golds from the grass, makes the shadows purple. The air is sweet, and when we get out of the car to look around, rushing water from the many streams running down the mountainsides can be heard feeding into the river that winds through the centre of the valley. We take in Flaga, where Agnes entered the world, and Kornsá, where she lived the final months of her life. Now that I am here, I notice that Kornsá lies opposite Hvammur, where the district commissioner, Björn Blöndal, lived. I wonder if it was difficult for Agnes to look out and see the home of the man responsible for her death sentence.

Blöndal's home stands in front of a mountain braced steeply against the sky. It reminds me of a fortification, surrounded by tides of loose rock fallen from the heights. Kornsá is on a gentler slope. I imagine the family there fetching water from the stream I see emerging from a rocky cleft, the wet rock shining in the light.

We turn back into Vatnsdalshólar, the hundreds of hills at the mouth of the valley, and drive to the site of the executions at their periphery. We park the car on the side of the main road, untie the rope securing a gate in the wire fencing, and then walk through the grass towards the three hills. As we draw closer, my parents fall back and let me go ahead. We are all suddenly very quiet. I find a narrow track that rounds the bottom of the first hill and follow it as it circles upwards to the central mound.

At the top lies a rectangular stone carved with words hardly discernible through lichen.

Á þessum stað fór fram síðasta aftaka á Íslandi 12. janúar 1830.

The last execution in Iceland took place here on 12 January 1830.

I understand why this site was chosen for the beheadings. It would have allowed clear and uninterrupted witness. *Enginn má undan líta* is named for the order issued by Björn Blöndal to the one hundred and fifty men present.

No one may look away.

It is a sobering moment.

I realise that Agnes was brought towards her death in full view of her childhood.

Mum and Dad join me at the crest of the hill, and as we stand in silence a cold wind springs up from nowhere. Both my parents look at me and then each other as it sounds a low moan through the grass. Our skin breaks out in goosebumps.

It would have been very cold here on the execution day in January. There are no mountains to hold back the weather. I think of Agnes being kept beyond sight of Friðrik's execution and wonder if she was held behind the thicker clusters of hills. It is a longer way to walk than I imagined. Did she find it difficult to move through the snow and ice with her hands bound? I wonder if someone helped her, if the priest had his arm around her.

The wind blows harder. I am only wearing a t-shirt, and my teeth start to chatter.

'Come,' says Mum. She takes my hand and leads me back down the hill. 'Let's get you warm.'

We take the road west, then leave the highway to veer north on the road leading up the eastern flank of the Vatnsnes peninsula. I had known Illugastaðir was at a greater remove to any other farm Agnes had lived at before, but the distance seems even more significant now that I am travelling it. She believed something better was waiting for her, I think. Why else does anyone leave the place they know?

After only forty minutes, the landscape takes on a greater feeling of wildness. The road is gravel, hard and flinted, falling away on both sides to rock and bodies of water, eerie in their stillness.

We drive past Stóra-Borg, the farm where Agnes was held after she was first convicted. There is a modern house there now, tractors, bales of plastic-wrapped hay. It looks large, prosperous. I wonder why she was moved all the way to Kornsá. I have seen the records of Sigríður and Friðrik's imprisonment: both remained at their original farms of custody.

You could never run away from this place, I think. Where would you even go?

Just past Vatnsendi, we stop to let five Icelandic horses cross over the road. We are now on the stretch of peninsula abutting the ocean, the sandy coastal plain of Þingeyrar behind us. The horses, manes sun-bleached to white against rough coats of reddish brown, are in their summer roaming. Mum pulls the handbrake, but instead of moving on in front of the car, the horses circle back and crowd us. Mum rolls down her window and they immediately push their muzzles into her extended palm.

Mum laughs. 'Oh my goodness. They are so placid.'

Dad winds down his window too, and soon the car is filled with inquiring horse heads.

We continue rounding the top of the peninsula. The light is so clear we can make out Iceland's West Fjords across the ocean.

'I think this is some of the most stunning scenery I have ever seen,' murmurs Mum.

When we spot Tjörn in the far distance – a modest white church below the height of the mountains – I suggest we have a look.

'That's where Agnes's bones are,' I say.

The churchyard is walled, gravestones rising from lush grass starred with flowers. We open the gate and step inside. I hadn't known if it would be possible to find Agnes's grave, but we find it quickly. The burial site is surrounded by a low border, a black headstone bearing a cross over Friðrik and Agnes's names, their birth and death dates. The plots of others born in the eighteenth century are little more than white wooden crosses, and some have sunk into the ground completely. I wonder at this, at the modernity of Agnes's grave, until I remember that her bones were only buried here in the 1930s.

I stand at the foot of their final resting place. Someone has left some purple shells on the grave.

'There's that wind again,' says Dad.

When we entered the churchyard, the air had been utterly still. Now I feel the wind push against me in strange insistence. It ripples the long grass of the churchyard until it looks like the surface of the ocean, seed heads and small white flowers swimming in its current.

'It's sprung up out of nowhere again.'

I look back down at the grave and wonder why Agnes and Friðrik's remains were moved to consecrated ground. I have read the letters of Blöndal. I know the authorities had been adamant that they be buried facing south, without markers.

The wind follows us back to the car.

The road after the church becomes rockier and begs a careful approach. It is well over an hour since we left Þrístapar. The only way to reach Illugastaðir is to drive parallel to the shoreline, as though a journey with such isolated stretches needs the reassurance of the sea. The cant of the light is odd as we approach the farm. In the distance, the ocean appears almost white against a darkening horizon.

The radio signal dies before we arrive, and in the silence I feel a strange tugging of loneliness. I am not usually brought down by Iceland's inhospitable places. I think of Vatnsdalur, the throat of river at its centre, the farms tucked into the base of the mountains. The swans on the lakes. There was a greater sense of, if not cohabitation, then common dwelling there. This western flank of the peninsula feels unto itself. The animals here belong to the sea. Eider ducks and seals mark the seasons.

I am surprised, then, given the isolation, to see a large white bus parked outside the farm when we arrive. Tourists? I know that people sometimes come to these secluded places to watch the seals, who can be heard as soon as we get out of the car. But as we walk closer, I see the visitors are clustered beside the farmhouse, arranging themselves in some kind of order. A man steps onto the bottom of the concrete stairs leading to the house and lifts his arms in the air.

A choir, I realise.

They begin to sing.

Mum, Dad and I stand apart and listen. The words of the song are in Icelandic, but the rhythm is strange and unfamiliar to me. There is something very old about this music, something mournful. It sounds like a dirge, and my eyes prick with tears at the emotion it holds.

When the song is concluded, I approach the singers. 'Góðan daginn,' I say, and I ask why the choir is singing in the middle of nowhere.

A white-haired man tells me that every summer they take a bus to some of Iceland's most remote places just to sing.

A bearded man by the farmhouse steps is pointed out to me. 'That is our choir president, Steindór Andersen. Do you know him? He is a very famous singer, he collaborated with Sigur Rós. He sings rímur.'

I have heard of rímur. They are rhyming stanzas, often epic poems, their rhythm dictated by various meters. Some of the lost sagas survive only due to the rímur composed from them. It is an old form of Icelandic recitation, more akin to chanting than singing as we might recognise it. A spiritual music.

How strange to finally come here, the place of the murders and the fire and be greeted by song.

Illugastaðir sits on a rocky shore cluttered with driftwood. Bleached white by sun and salt, the logs resemble the bones of giants. Dad places a hand on the curve of a trunk.

'Where did this come from?' he says. 'No trees here.'

'Russia,' I say. 'Siberia.'

I think to myself that this is a place where things wash up.

The birds are loud here, the still air amplifying the cries of gulls and eider ducks. The seals, visible further down the shore as lolling, grey dumplings, sheen silver in the light. Their grunts are loud, a little frightening. Without any wind, the air feels heavy with the smell of rotting seaweed. There are masses of it on the shore, looped together not in tangled hanks but in reddish, combed twists. It turns in the water like the hair of the drowned.

Bones and hair, I think.

Suddenly the sun comes out and the sea becomes a mirror. High above us, birds fly in V formation.

We walk along the grassed edge of the shore where soil meets rock, looking for evidence of the earlier settlement. I do not think it will be possible to find the original farmhouse. But Jón Torfason at the archives did tell me that the ruins of Natan's workshop – the place where he prepared his herbal medicines – can still be found.

'It was on a little spit,' I tell Mum and Dad. 'Out to sea, at a remove.'

There are several such spurs of land protruding from the shore. One, I see, would become an island at high tide. Cut off. It seems to fit with the understanding I have of Natan as someone secretive and enigmatic. I know that he did not deny the rumours that he was a sorcerer.

'Let's look there,' I say.

We pick our way over the rocks and climb onto the grassy bulk of land, where I immediately see a sunken area walled with rocks and turf.

'I think this is it.'

I step down into the ruins. Long bones of driftwood lie against its highest point.

Something catches my eye, a smudge of dun amid the foliage growing out of the sway of the wind.

I prise the object from the dirt with my fingers, then hold it up to the light.

Shaped clay, circular and heavy in my palm. A stopper? The years have cracked and flaked the material, but there remains a black lacquering on its topmost surface.

I think of the stories I have read about Natan. The accounts of miraculous healing, of people drawn back from death's door – including Blöndal's own wife. Natan's extortionate demands for payment.

Mum steps down next to me and examines the clay object. A wind blows over us. The gust is suddenly, undeniably hot.

'Do you feel that?' I ask Mum.

She gives me a look. 'That's warm …'

'So warm.'

'As if from a fire,' she says quietly.

Then, in the next moment, it is gone. All is still once more.

'That was weird,' Mum says.

I place the object on an abandoned beam of driftwood. It doesn't feel right to take it with me.

We make our way back to where the current farmhouse stands. The choir are leaving for their next place of seclusion, to sing to the seals and the sky. I wander the farm, overlaying the landscape with what I know about the year Agnes spent here. Servants back then could only move during the fardagar, the 'flitting days', a time in spring when they had permission to leave their farms and settle in new places of employment. Agnes would have arrived in the fardagar of 1827. After that, she would not have been able to leave without Natan's permission.

I find the freshwater stream the original farm would have used, and here see a rubble of fallen stone, the diagonal pattern of a turf wall. Remnants of a vegetable patch are nearby, dark-leafed rhubarb enduring in the corner.

Illugastaðir is all sky and silver sea. It is all glass and light and calm suggestion of finality. The water holds the sky and the effect feels deceptive, as though the ocean is hiding its true face.

A burning farm would have reflected in a sea such as this, I think. Flames upon the water.

I cannot divorce what happened here from the landscape.

That night, back in our accommodation at Varmahlíð, Mum and I wonder why no petition was made for the commutation of Agnes's sentence. She was known to be intelligent. Was that it? Was Sigríður thought harmless because she was believed 'simple'? I tell Mum that historical accounts often seem intertwined with personal connection in Iceland, that what I have read is so often written by people who are bound to the story through genealogy or place. In such a small country, where interest in kith and kin is high, the past does not feel distant at all, and I cannot help but feel that every historian and commentator on the Illugastaðir murders has skin in the game. I am grateful that so many local histories speak of Agnes, but I am compelled to regard them as subjective. The proximity of the personal cannot be ignored.

Our conversation drifts to the accounts that describe Agnes as someone most people liked, at least initially. The speculation that she had been disappointed in love. At a time when the only way to gain independence was to marry someone who had their own farm, what else might have been lost in these failed prospects? Women servants were paid, at most, a quarter of what male servants were paid. Sometimes, they were paid *nothing.* I wonder about Agnes's ambitions, her desire to rise in the world. A home of her own, instead of the ceaseless movement from farm to farm, endless labour, and vulnerability to the whims of a household head.

We think Agnes might have had a sharp tongue. Might have been someone who found it hard to hide her anger. We think she would have encouraged Friðrik to confront Natan. Friðrik wished to marry Sigríður, but Natan refused to release her from his employment. I think it is likely Natan was sexually abusing Sigríður. Perhaps Agnes, too. People write of Natan's cruelty – it is hard not to read the euphemism in this. Certainly Agnes, promised the elevated position of housekeeper, would have been embarrassed to travel such a long way only for Natan to have given the position to Sigríður. But we are doubtful about Agnes being the one urging Friðrik to murder him. It seems a stupid crime, difficult to cover up. Clumsy.

'Perhaps, if Friðrik said he was going to kill Natan, she might have thought he was bragging or wouldn't go through with it,' Mum muses.

'She might have burned the place down in a panic then later realised she shouldn't have lied to the magistrate, realised how that made her look.' I put my face in my hands. 'I don't know. All I have is a gut sense that the whole thing was so much more complicated than the sources make out.'

'Remember, Hannah,' she replies. 'You're writing fiction at the end of the day. You don't have an obligation to the truth.'

I nod, but inwardly I reject this. All my life I have read fiction for its proximity to truths. Deep, complex, human truths. My obligation to bring understanding to the dead presses upon me.

The perfect place to write

CHAPTER SEVENTEEN

No One May Look Away

After four weeks of intensive research, and several days with my parents, Mum and Dad drop me at Ósar, a farm on the Vatnsnes peninsula. I want to be somewhere quiet and restful to consolidate all I have learned. We drove past Ósar on our way through to Tjörn and met the young farmer there as he was harvesting his barley. He had introduced himself as Knútur. When I told him I'd be staying at his farm in a few days' time, he'd asked what was bringing me out to Vatnsnes.

'I'm writing a book about Agnes Magnúsdóttir.'

Knútur had given me a studied look.

'Do you know about this story?' I had asked.

'Yes,' he'd replied. 'I think the murder and the executions are embedded in the psyche of this place.'

Now, as Knútur's mother Sesselja checks me in, she tells me that her son mentioned I was writing a book.

'We'd like you to have one of our cabins,' she says, gesturing to three summer cabins near the ridge of a lower cow field. 'The middle one is called Torfborg. You are very welcome to stay there.'

I tell Sesselja that I have booked a bed in a female dorm.

'Really,' she insists, 'it's no problem. There's no one else here. You will need a space of your own to write.'

My parents look through the cabin with me. It is distinctly Nordic in its outfit of knotted pine. Low-ceilinged, with a tiny kitchen, loft bedroom and a deck facing the sea, it is the perfect place to write. I am ecstatic at my good fortune.

'Someone is looking after you, Han,' Dad whispers into my ear as we hug goodbye. They are taking the car back down to Reykjavík before their flight home the next morning.

Shortly after my parents leave, Sesselja knocks on my door and asks if I can help her move a table into my cabin. She is concerned that I should have a proper desk.

Together we put the table in the corner of the kitchen, and then she leaves, reassuring me that she'll leave me 'í friði', in peace. The truth is that Ósar is possibly the most peaceful place I have visited in Iceland. The cows graze in grassy fields that slope down to the sea, clusters of angelica blossoms billowing white at their borders. In the distance, a river ribbons out over the black sand of Þingeyrar in streams until it reaches the wider maw of the fjord.

When I walk down to the shoreline I see puffins on the water. Later that evening I see the lights of Knútur's tractor harvesting late into the night under a sky emerald with aurora.

*

The next morning, I am woken at six o'clock by the cold. The quilt must have fallen off my bed in the night and I forgot to turn the heater on. Shivering, I put on a jumper and socks with the idea of returning to bed, but when I look out the kitchen window, I see a sunrise burning the fjord orange. It is a sky to be out in.

I dress quickly and walk down to the beach.

Low cloud and sea mist drift close to shore, allowing the light to pour through before muting it again. Turning north, I walk along the dark sand, spotting eider ducks as the tide flows out. The morning sunlight sharpens into fire and my skin turns golden. There is a small splash, and I turn to see a dark head looking at me from the shallows. The seal and I stare at each other. I can see the deep brown of its eyes. The slick shine of its fur. Its whiskers.

I raise my hand in greeting and the seal, as though satisfied, slips back into the flaming water.

By the time I return to the path, a long row of seals lie in single file where the black sand meets the shallows. I count over one hundred of them, before I give up and instead marvel at their profusion, the gleam of their fat bodies in the light.

The days at Ósar pass in a gentle rhythm. The only people I see are Knútur and Sesselja as they wave to me from tractors, cars or harvesters. I work in the mornings, translating new sources, reviewing my notebooks and collating the story of Agnes's life.

Some of the information I found before coming to Iceland has been contradicted by the primary sources here. Sometimes the priests get it wrong in their records, too. I have always accepted that historical records might contain mistakes, but now I see they can be positively error-riddled. Records suddenly seem fallible, filled with prejudice, insistent on singular truths. History, I decide, is prismatic, multifaceted. It needs to be regarded from many angles.

It also becomes clear to me that I will need to begin my manuscript again from scratch. There is so much I now know. At first, dumping the 40,000 words I wrote before this research trip feels like a terrible loss. I have never written so much before. But I realise that everything I have written, even if it no longer belongs in the manuscript, has led me here. No draft is a waste. Writing a novel perhaps comprises writing off the page as much as on.

I feel close to the story here at Ósar. Agnes's voice is loud in my ear. Some scenes appear fully formed in my mind's eye. I write down what comes to me.

Most days I walk down to the shore and watch the seals, who regard me with thoughtful expressions before sighing and throwing themselves back down on the sand. Sometimes I walk north along the fields, the ocean before me in a long low hand of metallic grey. The clarity of the air brings every stalk of grass into view like a revelation. Looking back, I see the languorous curve of the fjord, the suggestion of the mountains. Ahead is the oddity of Hvítserkur, a three-legged basalt outcrop. Knútur has told me it is the most famous attraction on the peninsula. It is a steep drop to the rocky beach below, but I always spot sheep halfway down the cliff face, nibbling grass growing in clefts of stone, wandering heights as though to fall is an impossibility.

One morning I wake to a deep grey fog that fills the basin of the fjord. It grows thicker as I work. I decide it would be unwise to go walking in it, so instead I make myself a coffee and go sit beside the fields. Knútur and a young girl are driving the cows below my cabin, and when Knútur sees me he raises his hand and waves. As the cows trudge closer, he sings out a greeting.

'How is the writing going?'

'Good, thanks!' I reply.

He leans against the fence. 'Are you still doing your research or are you writing the book now?'

'A bit of both.'

Knútur opens his mouth to ask another question but, glancing back at the cows, realises they are going in the wrong direction. 'Sorry,' he says and runs after the girl.

'Do you need any help?' I call.

'Sure!'

I set my coffee down, pull on my boots and run after them. Together we take the two dozen cows up into the milking shed.

'You know, I am so interested in this old case,' Knútur tells me. 'I was thinking about it just the week before you came.' He attaches milking cups to a soulful-looking cow.

The cat that lives in the milking shed winds its way between my legs as I follow Knútur along to the next stall.

'There is an evil that lingers in it,' he continues. 'A bad feeling. Not so much in the murders, but in the executions.'

'I feel the same way,' I say, stroking the damp flank of a cow.

As we move between the stalls, Knútur tells me an interesting story about Natan Ketilsson.

'He was summoned by a farmer who had got his servant pregnant. The farmer asked Natan for something to kill the baby and Natan gave him a small bottle of liquid. The farmer paid him a lot of money for it, and so was very angry when, a few months later, the maid's belly started to show. He went and found Natan and told him he had paid for something that didn't work.'

Knútur pours a little milk for the cat into a dish on the floor.

'Natan pointed to the label on the bottle and told them that it said, in Danish, "Rent Vand". Pure Water. The farmer was furious and threatened to tell everyone Natan had swindled him. Natan responded by threatening to tell everyone that the farmer was the father of the child and had asked Natan to kill it.'

As we drive the cows back down to the paddock, Knútur tells me about farming in the nineteenth century.

'Times were colder then. Every possible bit of land was used. The farmers did not have machinery for smoothing the land or draining it. No fertiliser like we have. People fought over tiny mounds of grass. And society was strict.'

I nod. 'I have been learning a lot about this.'

'It was very bad to have, you know, unlawful children, even though it happened often enough.'

'Ingveldur, Agnes's mother, had four illegitimate children.'

'Yes, she might have been whipped for that. And you know, it was quite common for children to be named after others if their fathers weren't supposed to be their fathers.' Knútur raises an eyebrow. 'This happened in my own family.'

'I found the soul register from Agnes's last year of life,' I say. 'She gave her last name as Jónsdóttir, not Magnúsdóttir.'

'You see?' Knútur says. 'You know, I read a story about Agnes from when she was young. She was a foster child, working on a farm where she had been given the job of looking after the home field, making sure the horses didn't eat the grass. She fell asleep, and when she woke up she saw that a traveller had set up camp nearby and his horse was grazing in the field. She became very angry and marched over to his tent, lifted the flap and recited a poem at him. Something along the lines of, "Move your stupid horse and go away," to which the man replied, "An axe will fall on your head one day."'

I am thrilled.

'Come,' Knútur says. 'I have something to show you.'

I follow him to the farmhouse, where he makes us coffee and places a spread of cakes, waffles, biscuits, juice and milk onto the table before me. The hospitality of the Icelanders, I think to myself.

'Gjörðu svo vel,' he says. 'Help yourself. I'll be back in a minute.'

I take a cup of coffee and Knútur soon returns, holding a book in his hands.

I nearly drop my cup. The book is *Enginn má undan líta.*

'I read this just one week before you arrived,' Knútur explains. 'That is why I was so surprised when I met you and you told me you were here to write a book about Agnes Magnúsdóttir. The coincidence seems very strange. I had just been thinking about these bad old things.'

I set my coffee on the table and tell Knútur of my failed attempts to find this very book.

Knútur nods slowly. 'And here it is. In this farmhouse.'

He watches as I open it. There, as promised, is the chapter on Agnes.

'I can help you translate it,' he offers.

'Thank you,' I say. 'But I know how busy you are.'

Knútur picks up a biscuit, shaking his head. 'No, I would enjoy it. Now that the barley harvest is in, I only must milk the cows. We can do some now, if you like?'

I run back to the cabin to grab my laptop, and when I return to the farmhouse Knútur tells me that he has rung a farmer who lives nearby.

'I think you should come and speak with this man,' he tells me. 'Let's go.'

Knútur grabs his keys and I follow him to the car. We drive three minutes south to Hrísakot, and there Knútur introduces me to Agnar, a thin man wearing a traditional Icelandic sweater. Hlíf, his wife, welcomes me inside like she has already known me for years, exclaiming how exciting it is that I speak some Icelandic.

They sit me down at a table. I notice, then, that the entire farmhouse is filled with books.

'I think there are maybe four thousand?' muses Agnar, before launching into a conversation about the 1828 murder and the poetic skill of so many of those involved. I am soon completely in awe of Agnar's own formidable intellect. He tells me about ring rhymes, about their patterns of stressed syllables, and tells me Agnes would have composed many verses like this – alliterative rhymes of strict metrical form. She was reputed to be an excellent poet, he tells me.

I ask Agnar for his opinion of Agnes and Friðrik. Knútur and I have both wondered if Friðrik was a bit of a lout.

'Nei,' he says, shaking his head. 'Friðrik's younger brother and his nephew were fine poets, too. I don't think he was stupid.'

We spend the night talking, until everyone starts yawning and Agnar sends us back to Ósar with four more books he says I am welcome to borrow. By the time I am back in my cabin, it is two o'clock in the morning.

Knútur comes to my door the following afternoon with coffee and snúðar from the farmhouse, and a novel about Björn Blöndal, *Yfirvaldið*, by Þorgeir Þorgeirsson. We sit at my table and begin by translating the foreword of *Enginn má undan líta*. The author speaks of a 'web of destiny' everyone became stuck in, woven by one individual.

'Is he talking about Agnes?' I ask Knútur.

He nods. 'Like she's a spider.'

Despite this inauspicious start, it turns out that the book is unusually considerate of Agnes's early childhood. It draws from documents of the trials, Blöndal's letters and other local manuscripts, and confesses to some speculation. Certainly, most of the information listed about Agnes's early years is correct. She was illegitimate, in foster care, 'introverted, very intelligent and trustworthy'.

> Soon people found out that she was ambitious, that she didn't want to be subservient to anyone and that she didn't care if other people

> suffered as a result of her actions. She was fast to learn to read and write, and to learn Christian theology. She loved books and she loved the old sagas the most. She soon started composing poetry.

Knútur, it turns out, also has the soul of a poet. He helps me translate the poems Agnar was talking about last night, the stanzas composed by those involved in the events. My own attempts at translating these have produced unintelligible assemblages of words and phrases. Even Donni and Hera, who had tried to help me back in Reykjavík, were not sure what the authors were getting at.

'It's just a bunch of words,' Donni had said.

Knútur, it turns out, has an excellent understanding of these poems' unique composition and their literary allusions. Together we translate the poem composed about Agnes when she was working at Litla-Búrfell as a young woman:

> Handar-vagnar-Freyjum fljóð
> flytur sagnir ljóða
> kennd við Magnús, blessað blóð
> Búrfells-Agnes góða.

'Freyja's handcart floods?' I say to Knútur.

He takes a sip of coffee. 'It is like she is holding up the wagon for the women of the world. You know, holding up their reputation.'

'There is no way I would have guessed that.'

'The rest of it goes something like, "presenting poems, named for Magnús, his blessed blood, Búrfells-Agnes the good".'

'The good?'

Knútur nods.

Before I know it, the hour approaches midnight.

As he rises to leave, Knútur repeats his unease with the case, his dislike of the executions, his sense that people are still not at peace with what happened.

'You know about the mysterious incidents of 1934?' he asks.

'I know that this was when the bones were moved,' I say.

'Do you know why they were moved?'

I shake my head.

'Agnes wrote through a medium called Sesselja. She requested their bones be moved.'

'Sesselja?'

'No, Agnes requested it.'

My mouth falls open.

Knútur's expression is thoughtful as he picks up the coffee cups. 'Guðlaugur Guðmundsson has written about this in the book,' he says. 'Let's see what we can translate tomorrow.'

The next day Knútur returns with photocopied pages from the books Agnar lent me.

'I have been thinking of Björn Blöndal this morning,' he says. 'I think he used the murders as an opportunity. You know, to stop all the stealing that was happening in the district.'

I tell him I think the same. I know from Henderson's journal that it was standard practice for Iceland to send those convicted of serious crimes to Denmark for execution, but Björn Blöndal decided to hold the beheadings in the very district in which the murders had occurred. Some sources say that this was to save money, but among the letters in the archives there is one from Blöndal apologising for overdrawing funds by commissioning a purpose-built axe, and I found another which details the expenses accrued in keeping Friðrik imprisoned. It mentions the cost of iron and coal required by a blacksmith to build him leg irons with chains, and new clothes. Friðrik, still a teenager, continued growing while in custody.

Knútur and I agree that Blöndal was conscious of the rise of petty theft within his district – of which many sources speak – and was determined to set an example for the local population. He ordered all local farmers to attend the execution, or to send a grown male in their place. He also requested that Natan's brother, Guðmundur Ketilsson, perform the executions. Some sources claim that Guðmundur asked to swing the axe, but his family vehemently deny this, and it is true that he gave away the money he was paid by Blöndal for the executions. Why choose Guðmundur? It has the feel of something out of the Sagas.

We turn to translating Guðmundsson's account of the execution. It is hard to know what is drawn from eyewitness accounts passed through families, or what has been imagined or falsely remembered. But the scene has the feel of truth, and I find, translating it, that many details line up with what I have already read.

Agnes, Guðmundsson says, was farewelled at Kornsá, and many members of the family 'had tears in their eyes'. She was very emotional on the journey to Þrístapar and a local farmer gave her some hard liquor to calm her. While she couldn't see Friðrik's execution, she apparently heard the singing of the hymn. When Agnes's time came, Reverend Þorvaður was prevented from removing her shawl by Blöndal, who asked if he was going to make himself a servant to her. Other men dragged Agnes to the block and held her hair away from her neck, but Guðmundsson says she reached for the priest's hand, and he gave it to her – a slightly different account of their last moment together from what I have previously read.

After her head was cut from her body, Reverend Þorvaður 'stood slowly up and walked out of the crowd, stumbling on his feet, as though he was going to fall over'.

I pause my typing at this and tell Knútur I remember reading that the priest was haunted by Agnes's death for many years.

'I think he truly felt for her,' says Knútur.

The heads were placed on wooden poles but were found missing the next day. Over time, rumour spread that a local housewife had ordered a young servant to remove the heads in the night and bury them in the Þingeyrar churchyard.

I ask Knútur if we can return to what he spoke of the previous evening, namely the story of the medium and the reason why Agnes's bones were moved.

'Is it true?' I ask him.

Knútur smiles at me. 'I believe so.' He flips to several accounts relating to the reburial of the bones. They include several journal entries made by Guðmundur Sigurjónsson, the man who facilitated the requests made through the medium, the sworn affidavit of the two men who found the bones, an interview with a woman who witnessed the reburial service at Tjörn and, finally, the last known message the medium received from Agnes, produced verbatim.

It takes us a few days to finish translating the documents. Together they form, without a doubt, one of the eeriest stories I have ever heard.

In 1932, a woman living in Reykjavík, Sesselja Guðmundsdóttir, found herself producing involuntary writing. Sesselja had psychic abilities that she largely kept secret, but the urgency of the psychography, and the consistent requests within the letters she was writing, troubled her. The voice speaking through her was that of Agnes Magnúsdóttir. She wanted, among other things, for her and Friðrik's bones to be exhumed and buried in consecrated ground in the churchyard at Tjörn.

Sesselja was reluctant to do anything about these communicated requests. For two years she told no one about them, but when the writing intensified, she asked Guðmundur Sigurjónsson for help in fulfilling Agnes's wishes.

Guðmundur was a man sympathetic to the idea of placing the bones in consecrated ground, although he was not entirely sure whether to believe the medium. Tjörn was a long way from Vatnsdalshólar, and the heads were believed by everyone to already be buried in the Þingeyrar churchyard, which was much closer to Þrístapar.

On 13 June 1934, Guðmundur wrote in his diary:

> I thought it preferable that the bones be buried – if they are found – in Þingeyrar. I asked the medium today, when I was entrusted with the journey north, to seek Agnes and Friðrik's permission for that change. The medium agreed to pass on my request and invited me to attend her writing that night. Unfortunately, I had to work, but I came to speak with her afterwards. I was told Agnes and Friðrik had held to their wish that they be buried in Tjörn, and that the priest Sigurður

> Jóhannsson from Hindisvík should administer the rites. They said that their heads had not been moved to Þingeyrar churchyard, even though 'the woman of good quality' – the 'Þingeyrar priestess' – had indeed instructed her worker to do exactly that the night after their execution. The worker failed to do so and had never told anybody, taking his secret to the grave. Instead of taking the heads to Þingeyrar and burying them secretly as he had promised, he had buried them in a place that 'corresponds to a foot north of the cairn, in a bore of gravel'.

Guðmundur was unsure if it was possible to find the bones at all. The only account of the burial following the executions came from a local farmer, who said that the bodies 'were placed in coffins and buried not far from there, but the heads were put on poles because that is what was decided in court'. No one actually knew where the coffins were buried in that wide stretch of land. The medium said that Agnes had provided directions which included the words 'í hásumars-sólsetursátt, sjéð frá aftökupallinum og skammt frá honum'. At the place of high-summer sunset, seen from the execution platform and not far from it.

The night before he went north to begin the search, Guðmundur acknowledged in his diary the futility of trying to find the bones by any other means. 'I must therefore obey Agnes's guidance when it comes to the search,' he wrote.

> Another thing. Agnes mentioned tonight, in connection with the story about the heads, that the worker had not taken her head off the pole, but had broken it off, leaving a piece of wood in her head. She said it was still there. Then she had given me this advice, among other things. 'Guðmundur should get the help of old Magnús in

> Sveinsstaðir, because he will prove to be a good searcher.' Who this Magnús is, or if he exists, I do not know.

Guðmundur was troubled by the conflicting information about the heads.

> The stories about the heads being in Þingeyrar churchyard are so unanimous I fear what I thought might be nonsense will actually prove the medium's connection [to the dead]. On the other hand, the reference to 'Old Magnús' in Sveinsstaðir is so vague that I doubt he exists, let alone is as resourceful as Agnes wants him to be.

Two days later, however, when Guðmundur arrived at the farm of Sveinsstaðir, he learned that 'Old Magnús' *did* exist. 'An intelligent and careful man, it seems to me. He is not, judging by appearances, anything more than forty years of age, although Agnes calls him old.'

Guðmundur introduced himself to Magnús and explained his mission, including Agnes's request that he help search for her bones. Magnús was happy to help, but doubtful about Agnes's supposed guidance in the matter. When Guðmundur told him Agnes's claims about the heads being buried near the bodies and the broken wood in her skull, Magnús found it hard to hide his amusement.

'I have never heard anything other than that the heads are in Þingeyrar churchyard and that they were moved there by people the night after the execution,' he responded.

The next day, at half past nine in the morning, Guðmundur was joined at Þrístapar by Magnús and his grown son, Ólafur. With no outward sign of disturbed earth, Guðmundur, Magnús and Ólafur began exploring the soil north of the execution site with iron rods. After fifteen minutes, Magnús drove his rod down onto something. The men began digging in a large area to avoid doing any damage, and at a depth of sixty-five centimetres found the skulls lying next to one another.

One of them held a long fragment of wood.

The skulls were only a little decayed and were undamaged, although one was missing three teeth. The soil in which they were buried was gravelly, which corresponded with Agnes's description, but further down the pit was pure earth. The men dug there and found the coffins, lying north-west to south-west. The lids were broken and had fallen in, but the coffins were otherwise intact. One was 1.65 metres, the other 1.45 metres. Inside, only the hardest and the largest bones remained. Two dress clasps were found in Agnes's coffin, which suggested she had worn her best clothes to die.

When the bones were removed, Guðmundur looked up and noticed that the summer sun 'kissed' the place they lay. Their location was exactly where Agnes had said it would be.

Magnús and Ólafur certified Guðmundur's account regarding the exhumation of Agnes and Friðrik's bones.

> We also certify that we and our local people were aware, from his account, before we set off with him from our home this morning to Vatnsdalshólar, that Agnes and Friðrik had claimed through involuntary writing – referring to their heads – the gravel-laden soil and the broken wood in Agnes's head.

'Do you believe it?' I ask Knútur.

It is close to midnight. I have extended my stay at Ósar, and Knútur and I now have an easy way between us. We are in accordance with all that we discuss. Both of us are deeply moved by what we have been translating.

Knútur nods. 'I do,' he says. 'How else could they have known where the bones were?'

I flip to the slender collection of photos included in *Enginn má undan líta*. Among them are the four pages comprising Agnes's last message to the medium, who asked to remain anonymous until her death. The handwriting is neat but there is an urgency in the message's composition. The sentences run on and the language is unlike any I have come across. In a stream of consciousness that refers to Illugastaðir as 'the place of misery' (hörmungastöðum), and to her own reputation during her lifetime, Agnes notes:

> my sign has been seen cold and bitter before you parted from me now you have crowned my cause with a great victory wreath which is far more perfect now than if I had lived the particular life I was supposed to fulfil here which I never completed but drifted and drifted as a wicked woman could have but Holy God heard my prayer when I wanted to understand how badly I had acted but I didn't think that I deserved all of this it is a terrifying sight to look back but now I am free from those high torments that I endured yes as I said for almost half if not the entire time since I went through the ordeal of always enduring the same misery and everything that tore my life away from this earth

I am struck particularly by a line which refers to a man who 'attacked my soul and turned me into a wolf which ended my life'.

'She refers to signs a lot,' I say to Knútur. 'I wonder if she uses wreaths to signify the way in which she has been remembered. Agnes refers to her own wreath as one of "crowberries".'

'Like a black stain,' he suggests.

> you may say dear daughter that your victory is owed to me by greeting me with friendship for the call has come and quickly as you wished to do for me one thing I wish to ask of you dear woman is that you fulfill as far as is within your power to resolve the great sign that comes with good and noble deeds the reed that speaks is a play that could be described in broad strokes if there were time

That night, once Knútur has returned to the farmhouse, I go outside to stand in the dark. The long hours of talk and work have left my face flushed, my head hot.

The wind picks up. I feel the force of it against my body. I think about Agnes's voice, her desire for people to remember her kindly, the clasps found with her remains. I realise that they were not included in the list of possessions she had with her when taken into custody.

Someone gave them to her, I think. And I wonder at that, the grace of a gesture. Light in the dark, I think. Light in the dark.

When I leave the next morning, Knútur refuses to let me pay for my accommodation.

The letters and lists of those who judged Agnes

CHAPTER EIGHTEEN

Dreams

2010–2011

Back in Australia, I begin writing the first draft of *Burial Rites* in a converted wardrobe on the second floor of a Fitzroy share house in Melbourne's inner north. The space is just big enough for my scuffed pine desk, which a housemate had rescued from hard rubbish. I jam it in against the wall under a window. The outlook is limited to the red brick of the neighbour's house, but sometimes, when I throw open the sash to admit the morning air, a wren comes and sits on the sill.

I write first thing in the morning. A new day fills me with optimism and, unencumbered by any domestic responsibilities, it is possible to move quickly from bed to desk. I like to hold on to my dream space for as long as possible; my mind softened and receptive, a little out of time.

I listen to music as I write. The open window admits a chorus of tram bells and pigeons and the homeward stagger of drunk and vocal backpackers, so I choose music which conveys the same atmosphere I am hoping to capture in my manuscript. The songs offer rapid entrance to emotional landscapes. I turn again and again to Sigur Rós, to Laura Marling's second album, *I Speak Because I Can*. The deep feeling within the music strikes me to the bone. It holds the marrow of what I have intuited from my time in Iceland.

After reading Agnes's words written through the psychic, devastating in their imagery and so breathlessly intimate in their flow, it feels natural to write in her voice.

She speaks in images, I write in my journal. *I have chosen to give her a tongue of landscape. She speaks in stones and in dirt. In ashes and in snow. And water. Especially water. I am once again walking to the river's edge and the ocean's shore to find her waiting, the wind whipping her hair, the storm gathering above. I find her at the water's edge, trailing her fingers through the language that belongs to her.*

I think a great deal of poetry's centrality within the culture of nineteenth-century Iceland as I draft, of Agnes's poems that survive her. Even those who wished to denigrate Agnes's character did not deny her love of literature. I want to honour this and I also want to remark on the difference between Agnes's voice as it is in the psychic's letters, its full-bloodedness, and the thin bureaucratic language within the letters of the authorities who judged her.

Each day I acknowledge that my work is empathic, but to create an angel of Agnes would be as much of a disservice as to make a devil of her. We are, all of us, 'blendin' – complex and contradictory, and capable of good and bad in action and in thought. I decide to move between Agnes's own perspective and a third-person narration. This, I hope, will allow me to show such contradiction. The difference between what we say and what we think. The stories we tell and those we withhold.

I am aware, always, that who I write is the Agnes of my imagination. I am aware of literary theorist Mikhail Bakhtin's warning of 'that simple-minded self-appreciation which uses its own sincerity as a standard of truth'. It feels annoyingly relevant. I decide, however, that I am not trying to replace the many accounts of the murders of Illugastaðir with my own. I want to invite a dialogic approach to the events, and to an understanding of Agnes's perspective. And yet, I feel a truth in my approximation. One of many truths, perhaps. I make my peace with this. If what I write is false, it is no more a lie than the many others which abide within the sources I have read. In my notebook I sticky-tape a quote from German Romantic thinker Novalis's collection of writings, *Fragmente und Studien*: 'Novels arise out of the shortcomings of history.'

Halfway through writing *Burial Rites* I am woken in the night by the sound of my own name. I sit bolt upright in the dark, heart pounding. There is the shadow feel of another's mouth near my ear.

'Hannah.' Whispered and not a dream at all.

'Hannah.' A voice, clear and urgent.

It takes me hours to fall asleep again.

A few weeks later I dream I am standing in a snowy landscape; I can feel the soft brush of snowflakes against my cheeks. My hands are tied, and I am surrounded by men.

One of them steps forward and slits my throat. It does not hurt, but I am shocked at the violence inflicted on my body and the ease with which it was done. For a moment I feel that I am only injured, but then a warmth expands across my chest, and I realise that it comes from my own blood. I know I will die soon; there must be so much blood for me to feel so warm. As I die, I wake, and when I wake, I lie for some time, breathless, hands around my throat, trembling. When the shock of the nightmare passes, I cry. And then I get up and I draw the dream rather than write it down, because the horror is something I do not want to put into language.

Dreams were historically seen as symbolic or prophetic in Iceland, and during my time in the country I have noticed a heightened respect for and interest in dreams. In the Icelandic Sagas there are many who receive dreams of warning or foretelling, including Njáll, who foresees the violent deaths of his sons in Njáls Saga, and Guðrún Ósvífrsdóttir, who has four dreams foretelling each of her four future marriages and the fate of each husband in Laxdæla Saga.

It is also hard to ignore my dreams when the people I am writing about were so vocal about their own.

Natan Ketilsson was supposedly a 'draumamaður mikill', a big man for dreams. It was said to run in his family. He related many of his dreams to other people, but two in particular seem specifically linked with his death.

In the winter preceding his murder, Natan told several of his friends that he would have a 'short life to live' and would die by human hands. When they asked him why he believed this, he told them he had dreamed he was standing by an open grave. At one end he saw his soul and at the other end his body, and his body was singing the hymn, 'Wake, My Soul'. It made him deeply ill at ease. He also told others that he had dreamed he was standing by a fire when two or three vipers leaped out of it and bit him.

The night before the executions, Natan's sister Ketilríður dreamed he came to her. She asked him how he was feeling and he said, 'I feel well, my plover! And today Friðrik and I will become the best of friends.'

'And Agnes?' she asked him.

'How might it go?' he replied. 'Who has no desire to sympathise with men, who mistrusts God?'

At this point Ketilríður woke up and recounted her dream to others in the baðstofa.

Guðmundur Ketilsson, Natan's brother who performed the executions, was also a man who put great store in his dreams, but when he dreamed he would die on the same day as Björn Blöndal, the magistrate who bade him behead Agnes and Friðrik, he doubted whether his dreams were significant, as the likelihood of that was so slim. Yet, he did indeed die on the same day as Blöndal, on 24 June 1859.

Even years and years after Natan's death, there are accounts of his relatives dreaming of him in times of illness. Often, he would tell them how they might be cured, and then introduce himself as Natan. Sometimes he would offer to show them the stab wounds on his body as proof. Although frightened by these dreams, those who did as Natan instructed recovered.

There is also the famous story of the dream Agnes had as a teenager.

When Agnes was being held in custody at Kornsá, she puzzled people by asking for a young, relatively unknown assistant priest to attend her. Þorvaður Jónsson was surprised when told she had requested him, but he travelled to Kornsá. There, Agnes asked him if he remembered meeting her.

'I don't,' he is said to have replied.

She then told him that, when she was sixteen, she had a deeply unsettling dream. She was walking alone and barefoot on a wasteland of snow and ice. She didn't know where she was going but continued in desperation and bewilderment. Then a man came to her. He was young and beautiful and wore a priest's collar and robe, although he was bareheaded. He offered to lead her for a while, and she accepted. He gave her strength. They continued in the same direction as before. Suddenly, she fell down a crevasse in the ice. Her hand slipped out of that of the unknown man, and ice closed over her. Yet even in the darkness, she knew that he remained there, above the crevasse.

She woke up then, but the dream worried her for a long time.

At Kornsá, Agnes told Þorvaður that, four years later, when she was twenty, she had been walking barefoot in Gönguskörð. The river there was swollen, and as she hesitated at the ford, she saw a man tying his horse near a stretch of new-grown grass. She greeted the man and then stared at him – it was the man from her dream.

'Why are you staring at me like that?' he asked her. 'Do you want help across the river?'

Agnes agreed and he helped her cross. They parted ways then, and afterwards, realising she had not asked his name, she found it out from others. When she learned he was studying to become a priest, she knew her dream would come to pass.

Agnes told Þorvaður that this was why she had requested that he attend her in the months before her death.

The priest then recognised Agnes as the same girl he had helped across Gönguskarðsá the spring he had ridden north into Skagafjörður. He stayed with her until the day of her execution, and accompanied her there.

In April 2011, with very little of the manuscript left to complete, I have a terrifying dream while staying at my parents' house. I am condemned to be executed and every fibre of my body, every thought that fires through my head, is fighting to stay alive. I cannot comprehend that my consciousness can be extinguished by others. It seems an impossibly cruel barbarity, so irreparable as to strike me into paralysis. My legs will not work properly, my fingers are clumsy, and I am crying out. But even then, I have some hope for my continuation, for ongoing life. I think, This cannot really be happening. Perhaps if I beg them, they will see that they must not do this to me. Perhaps someone will talk to them for me, explain that I am not to be killed. I cannot, even as my time grows closer, accept the certainty of everything I am being extinguished. Extinguished! There is no other word that conveys the absolute dissolution I fear. It is a horror. Then I see that there is a priest with me and his kind eyes are a comfort, a small light in the dark. He sits down next to me, and I can feel the weight of his hand on my back. I want him to tell me that he will fix this, that he will talk to them, but all he says is, 'I am here for you. I am here.' My soul enters my mouth and cries out, and my horror grows and grows until my body wakes itself up.

It is a dream like no other I have ever had.

I sit in the half-darkness of my old childhood bedroom. My face is wet.

When I walk out into the kitchen, Mum is standing there. She takes one look at me and asks what is wrong. I tell her about my dream.

'Go write it down,' she says softly. 'Go on. Go write.'

So I do. I return to my old bedroom and open my computer and write the final scenes of my manuscript.

After that there is nothing more to write. I print out a copy and place the pile of paper under my desk. I have always thought I would feel euphoric when I finally finished a first draft, but I do not. All I feel is grief.

I rest my forehead on my desk, and I weep.

We married under the trees of my childhood

Endurkoma
Return

2022

Stella Soffía is as good as her word. In 2022 I receive a formal invitation to the Reykjavík International Literary Festival to be held in April the following year.

I am thrilled. When I tell Heidi and the kids that I'll be going, Anouk tells me she misses Iceland.

'But, baby,' I say, 'you've never been.'

'I miss the snow,' she says.

When I relay our exchange to Pétur, he is delighted. 'Anouk is raised the right way – with Iceland in her heart.' He tells me he'll drive me everywhere when I come. 'There is so much to talk about. So many things have happened on both sides.'

The last time I saw Pétur and Regína was at our wedding. Heidi and I were married in 2019 under the trees of my childhood home, surrounded by our friends and family and a koala who watched the ceremony from a nearby candlebark.

I had not believed Pétur and Regína would come when I invited them. Regína has a great fear of flying, and the prospect of so many separate flights all the way from northern Iceland to South Australia was too much to expect of her. But Pétur had been hopeful.

'I'm going to talk to her,' he said. 'She might make an exception.'

When he got back to me to say that, yes, they would come, I was elated. I told him I would pay for their flights. It was the least I could do after all they had given me in the years of our knowing one another. I could never repay their generosity in full.

'I can't wait for you to meet Heidi,' I told Pétur. 'She's nervous! She knows how much you both mean to me.'

'Segðu Heidi að hafa ekki áhyggjur. Við elskum hana fyrir að vera móðir dóttur ykkar og tilvonandi tengadóttir okkar.' Tell Heidi not to worry. We love her for being the mother of your daughter and our future daughter-in-law.

Time seemed a great fallacy during that visit. Having Pétur and Regína at our wedding made me feel as though my life no longer extended out into the distance but spiralled around me. I felt the years press upon the present, every happiness of my life concentrated. My joy in marrying a woman I loved beyond measure was amplified by the past's proximity. Everything felt a confluence of fate.

As a wedding present, Pétur and Regína gave us a pillow embroidered with a shelf of Icelandic novels. 'Kanóna: úrvalsrit íslenskrar alþýðu.' Canon: the best writing of the Icelandic people. The embroidered titles on the spines of the books included the works of Halldór Laxness, Böðvar Guðmundsson, and Jón Kalman Stefánsson. I had laughed when I unwrapped it. How wonderful to be known. What a gift to be seen.

The organisers of the festival ask me if, alongside my planned events, I might take part in a panel being organised by a women's literary collective in Eyrarbakki, a small village on Iceland's south coast. I agree. Then I am asked if I would consider making the festival's opening remarks.

'The Icelandic Minister for Culture will be officially opening the festival, but would you be willing to make a short speech afterwards? Perhaps something about the relevance of Icelandic stories globally?'

I say yes. The prospect of doing such a thing in the country that first propelled me towards writing feels like an act of both synchronicity and kismet. Of things coming full circle.

Drafting my speech, I write of the centrality of storytelling to Icelandic culture, that it was witnessing this deep respect and love and hunger for language and its power as an exchange student that eventually gave me what I had hoped to find through the experience: conviction and direction. I write of the many Icelanders who encouraged me personally, and others whose stories have reached readers across the world. How does such a remote island offer so many narratives that represent the local and yet speak to the universal?

Many Icelandic authors are known and celebrated internationally, all deservedly, all for singular voices. Two weeks ago, I reviewed a novel set in Reykjavík written by Rijn Collins, an Australian, and in it the narrator – a visitor – remarks, 'For such a small, solitary land, Iceland had a strong magic.' It is true. It does. But what is this magic, and why does it lend itself to writers? Why is it so readily summoned?

I wonder if it has something to do with the exquisite natural beauty of Iceland, its cruelties and its benevolence. A country where you can often see for great distances, where the sky is astonishing in the quality of its light or the lack of it, and where nature is not cordoned off, separate, or controlled. Is it simply because winters are dark and long, or is it because it is easy to feel vulnerable in Iceland, aware of life as precious and precarious, human existence as both insignificant and full of meaning? Might it have something to do with Iceland's history as an island of immigrants – Scandinavian farmers, Irish slaves – or the fact that, despite its relative isolation, it has always been connected with the wider world? Has always produced people who have travelled across the seas, sometimes willingly, sometimes not, some returning, some not, but nonetheless opening channels of exchange?

I am not Icelandic, I write, *but I feel that, for a long time now, I have swum in its currents of story. I often feel raw with the need to press life to paper when surrounded by Iceland's unbearable beauty, its many enduring ghosts. In a world where it is increasingly difficult to find the rare and the wild, Iceland offers both rarity and wilderness. In a world where so many are dissuaded from using their voice, how fortunate to come together in such a place, to celebrate stories and those who tell them, words and those who wield them.*

A few days after I send the draft of my speech so that it might be translated, I receive an email from the festival's manager.

A quick question in the small world of Icelandic literature, she writes. *Your teacher with the poetry book … Was it Geirlaugur Magnússon by any chance? His daughter is the cousin of the festival director and will actually be hosting one of the off-venue events at her bookshop, Kanínuholan.*

I smile at the name of the bookshop. The Rabbit Hole.

Yes, that is him, I reply. *Small world indeed.*

PART III

Heima / Heimurinn
Home / The World

2011–2023

Nadarstund is launched at Café Rosenberg

CHAPTER NINETEEN

Reckoning

2011–2021

The first draft of *Burial Rites* sits under my desk for five months before I bring myself to pick it up again. I tell myself that I am busy, that I am distracted by all the $20 review commissions and part-time contracts I've been taking on to build my writing resume, but the truth is that I have needed time to mourn Agnes, and to also recover from writing her story. I was unaware of how much the creative process would ask of me. It has taken me almost half a year to consolidate my writing self again.

The reason I, one day in October 2011, pick up the printed draft and wipe the dust bunnies from its bulldog clip, is because a friend of mine has asked me if I plan to enter the new Writing Australia Unpublished Manuscript Award. Initially I said no, I was too busy writing book reviews.

'Sure, those are great,' she said. 'But maybe it's time for you to take advantage of the bigger opportunities out there. Hey, you might win $10,000! And you get a mentorship, too.'

I pointed out that I had not yet redrafted my novel and the deadline for the award was only one week away. 'Also,' I added, 'I have a review due the same day.'

'Email the editor and tell them it will be submitted late. Honestly, Hannah, don't prioritise a 250-word column over your own book.'

I begin redrafting *Burial Rites* that night and continue for seven days, working with the kind of intensity only an impending deadline can bring. I cut 20,000 words from the original manuscript. Fifteen minutes before the competition closes, I enter the novel and its synopsis.

A few weeks later I receive a phone call telling me I have won the award.

Burial Rites is acquired simultaneously in Australia/New Zealand, the United Kingdom and the United States of America after a series of bidding wars orchestrated by my new literary agent. Pippa emailed me shortly after the award was announced and, despite my accidentally emailing her twenty-three copies of *Burial Rites*, took me on as a client. The whole affair – the news of early offers, the auction – is thrilling. It is also completely beyond the wildest dreams I have ever harboured for my manuscript. The novel is, after all, indisputably dark. It is set in a country few people are familiar with. Even Geraldine Brooks, in her gentle mentorship, urged me to 'let in a little more light'.

That people have embraced Agnes's story, despite its bleakness, feels akin to exoneration.

*

Burial Rites is published in 2013. It is both an exhilarating and an overwhelming experience, and my learning curve as a newly published author is steep. I am pushed into an unfamiliar world of public speaking, praise and criticism, and I soon realise that I am both grateful for and deeply anxious about reader responses to my work. It does not take long before I begin to hear from Icelanders. I had braced myself for this as soon as I heard that my novel would be available in Iceland in English. What I had not anticipated was that so many of my readers would hold such close personal connection to the story. When Knútur, who read an early version of the manuscript, had reminded me of Icelanders' particular genealogical awareness, I had taken his reminder only within the context of it being necessary to avoid making false allegations about any of the people represented as characters in the book. I did not expect relatives to get in touch with me. When they do, I am relieved at their graceful and generous responses.

> Thank you for your kind portrait in your novel of my forefather, Reverend Jónsson, who is my mother's great-great-grandfather. [...] I have heard so many stories of him and his contact with Agnes.
>
> I had no idea how Icelanders would take to you writing this book and taking the story up first in English, but I knew from the time I heard about it that it was going to be great. I'm happy they have embraced you.

> Tóti [Reverend Jónsson] is my great-great-great-grandfather. My gran thought you might appreciate the biography of Tóti that our

family has passed down the generations through storytelling, and this portrait of him, drawn in Copenhagen.

Later in the year, while on tour, I come across an unexpected crowd of Icelanders at an event in Minnesota, that epicentre of Nordic migration. They thank me for my interest in their country, then one of the women lowers her voice and says in Icelandic, 'Of course, you know it isn't coincidence. We who know, know it isn't coincidence. We know about the parallel worlds.'

In 2014, the Icelandic translation of *Burial Rites* by Jón St. Kristjánsson is published by Forlagið. It is called *Náðarstund* (*A Moment of Grace*). Having already agreed to promotional travel in Germany, Spain and Italy, I am able to ensure I am in Iceland for its release. It is important to me that I be there. To be translated into Icelandic feels like a great honour. I am also glad to return to the country having fulfilled Geirlaugur's prophecy.

Some publicity is arranged to support the publication of *Náðarstund*. In the course of one afternoon I am taken out into a spectacular lava field by Spessi, an iconic Icelandic photographer, interviewed for *Morgunblaðið*, and driven to the National Museum so that I might be interviewed for the RÚV evening news standing before the axe and block.

'Was she an evil killer?' the journalist asks me, camera in my face.

'Sometimes in history people are reduced to stereotypes,' I respond. 'And I think that this has perhaps happened to Agnes. People thought of her as wicked, whereas I think that she was guilty, but I also believe people's behaviour is shaped by the times they live in – they influence how people behave and what they feel they can do.'

The following day I am brought to a television studio to be interviewed on the country's book program, *Kiljan*, one of the great influencing forces for the Christmas book flood. As I sit in hair and make-up, it occurs to me that it is extraordinary for such a small country to have a weekly program entirely devoted to literature and author interviews. It shows just how seriously Icelanders take their stories. I immediately feel nervous. How seriously might they take my own?

Before we begin, *Kiljan*'s host, Egill Helgason, asks if it would be okay for us to converse in Icelandic initially. 'To show everyone that you do speak a little,' he says, thus confirming my suspicion that Icelandic is a passport, a possible way of validating what I have done.

Egill is a generous interviewer and our conversation goes well. I appreciate the opportunity to acknowledge to the Icelandic public that I understand the story of Natan's murder to be well-known, and that I am aware some people might not agree with the way I have told it.

'But,' I say, 'I have always hoped it would be a recognisably Icelandic novel. Even though I'm Australian, I have such a great love and respect for this country. I wanted to represent it in a true way. Even though this book is fiction, even though this story is one of many that could be told about this case, I wanted it to be Iceland within the pages.'

When *Náðarstund* is launched at Café Rosenberg in Reykjavík later that night, the room is crowded. Pétur and Regína come down from Sauðárkrókur, bringing Birgitta, Fannar and their sixth child, Sigurbjörn Darri, born in 2012. I am relieved to have them in the room with me during an event of such personal significance. During the signing after the reading, many of those who approach me are relatives of people depicted in my book. They are polite, but curious as to why I, an Australian, have been drawn to the story.

As the crowd filters out into the night, I look up to see a woman I recognise but cannot place.

She sits down across from me at the signing table, smiling.

'Hæ, Hannah,' she says. 'Ég heiti María Ellingsen.'

It is then that I recognise her. María had played the role of Agnes in the 1995 film.

We speak of our attempts to communicate Agnes's story. It feels surreal to have María opposite me. An enduring image of her from the film, as Agnes lying upon the block, plays through my mind as she tells me that, while inhabiting the role, she had felt Agnes's presence very strongly.

Just before she gets up to leave, María leans forward and lowers her voice. 'I can see Agnes has visited you, too,' she says.

Three years after the publication of *Náðarstund*, at the beginning of September in 2017, I receive an email from Icelandic journalist Egill Bjarnason, asking whether he might interview me. He is covering a staged trial of Agnes Magnúsdóttir scheduled for the following week, and wants to incorporate my comments into his piece.

I write back quickly, agreeing to answer his questions in exchange for some more information about the event. I have not heard anything about a new trial.

Bjarnason replies that the Icelandic Lawyers Association is holding a mock retrial of the historic case. The idea is to use the old court documents, but to try Agnes, Friðrik and Sigríður under modern Icelandic law. The judges will include Davíð Þór Björgvinsson, a former judge of the European Court of Human Rights. Tickets have already sold out.

When he interviews me a few days later, the journalist emphasises a question I have by now heard many times from Icelanders: what is it about this case that continues to haunt people? We speak about the changing nature of justice, whether I find Icelanders' perception of the story different from my own, if there are aspects of the case not raised in the original trial that should be considered.

After the mock trial, he introduces me to Eyrún Ingadóttir, the manager for the Icelandic Lawyers Association, who came up with the idea. She is a novelist as well, and, having read *Burial Rites* in both English and Icelandic, kindly sends me a transcript of what happened on the day. Over two hundred people attended.

Reading verbatim reports of what was said during the original nineteenth-century interrogations and court trials is thrilling. I had not been able to access these when researching *Burial Rites*, and my curiosity in the case has not abated over time. I have accepted that I will always be fascinated by Agnes, that I will always grieve for her. I carry her in a way that is different to the other characters I have since written. She remains close to me and will always inhabit a corner of my mind. To finally know what she was reported to have said in court is riveting.

There is one point when, reading the transcript, I feel my heart stop. It says that, when Agnes stood over Natan's body, she reportedly said something like, 'Now Natan won't be able to "laspúvera" me or any other women anymore.' According to the transcript, the lawyers spent some time discussing what this word, 'laspúvera', meant. It does not appear in dictionaries, although the world 'lasputera' does, meaning to scold, as does the term 'laspa til', meaning to attack with hard words or abuse, including physical violence. Eggert Þór Bernharðsson, an author who had transcribed the original court documents, thought Agnes was referring to the harsh verbal abuse she and Sigríður suffered from Natan, while literary scholar Helga Kress believed Agnes was referring to sexual exploitation.

It was noted that, in those days, farm workers were not permitted to leave the farm where they had been hired. And yet, the defence pointed out, Agnes had fled Illugastaðir on two occasions before Natan's murder.

> And where did she flee to? First to Tjörn, where the priest lived – seeking refuge with the local authority. But she did not seem to receive much understanding there, so she went to Ásbjarnarstaðir, where she stayed for a week, too afraid to return home. Nothing in the case's records indicates that Agnes was asked about these escapes; she was never asked why she felt compelled to flee to the local authority.

When she returned to Illugastaðir after her efforts to flee had failed, Agnes was forced to apologise to Natan.

Natan, the defence argued, had not only subjected Agnes and Sigríður to repeated physical and verbal abuse, he had also sexually abused both women. Sigríður had testified that she 'was often made to sleep with him at his command'. Natan's actions would be punishable by up to sixteen years' imprisonment under contemporary Icelandic law.

Despite the women's frequent allusion to the repeated 'scoldings' they received from Natan, there was never any inquiry into his treatment of Agnes and Sigríður, despite 'ample opportunity'. Blöndal's questioning repeatedly focused on the valuables reportedly taken after the murders and what they might have been worth – demonstrating the different priorities between the early nineteenth century and today, the defence explained. It may not have been considered unusual for a household head to mistreat his servants in this way.

The defence also noted that Agnes's testimony was never recorded in the first person, but instead written entirely in the third. None of her words were transcribed verbatim, as was done with Friðrik and Sigríður.

'We don't know today why this was the case, but it is noteworthy,' the defence argued, 'especially considering that the same scribes recorded all the testimonies in the case.'

The accounts of the three were generally consistent regarding the sequence of events. The main difference was that, according to the women, Friðrik had made most of the decisions, while he emphasised that they had been full participants. Friðrik and Sigríður both mentioned a desire for Natan's money, whereas Agnes's involvement was said to be motivated by 'her resentment towards Natan for how he had treated her'.

I am struck, reading the transcript, by how similar some details are to parts of *Burial Rites*. I had thought I had invented the scenes in which Agnes flees from Illugastaðir in the middle of winter and Natan forbids Sigríður from readmitting her, but it happened. And Friðrik, in his testimony, said that Agnes had 'lost her nerve and dropped the lamp' during the murders, that Natan had muttered in a delirium and called out for mercy, and that, after he had dragged the bodies out of the beds, 'Agnes helped me lift them both onto Natan's bed. We smeared the bodies with oil, set the bed on fire, and left.' I thought I had imagined these details, too.

The court documents support the impression I received early in my research, namely that 'since Agnes was intelligent, she was seen as the primary instigator who strengthened Friðrik's resolve'. During the retrial the judges did not necessarily agree with this, but acknowledged her intelligence as something that should have given her 'the wisdom to dissuade her much younger co-accused from their plans'.

In forming their verdict, the judges said that they would overlook the fact that the same person, Blöndal, investigated the case, prosecuted it and adjudicated it in the first instance – something that the European Court of Human Rights has ruled does not comply with the Human Rights Convention.

At the conclusion of the mock retrial, Friðrik was sentenced to seven years in prison and Sigríður to five, as both were underage at the time of the murders, which limits sentences to eight years. Agnes was sentenced to fourteen years in prison, a reduced sentence from a possible sixteen, in recognition of the likelihood of Natan's cruelty towards her. Had she served the entirety of that sentence in her lifetime, Agnes would have been free at forty-eight, not dead at thirty-four.

Afterwards, Davíð Þór stated that, in the original trial:

> No one cared about the motivation behind the murders – that wouldn't happen in a modern court. Today we would try to understand [...] how the two women, who had no other place to live, were treated by their master.

I sit in a reverie for a long time after reading the transcript. I am both spooked by the coincidences between the revelations of the mock trial and my own intuition, and also haunted by the thought that I might have not made enough of Natan's ill treatment of Agnes.

Would I have written Agnes's story differently had I known these details? I ask myself. Would I write it differently now?

It is surely no coincidence that this mock trial has occurred during this time of the #MeToo movement on social media, and numerous sexual-abuse allegations against those in positions of power and influence. Our understanding of the past changes in accordance with our understanding of the present. Yet, a book written in time, remains fixed in time. Even a historical novel that represents a period over one hundred years ago is equally – if not more so – a representation of the era in which it is created.

It is the first time I have truly understood that I cannot bring my writing into the present with me.

The tradition of silence

CHAPTER TWENTY

Independent People

2023

In the months before I leave for the festival, I become terrified that my Icelandic has evaporated through neglect. I test myself throughout the day. What is the word for table? For strawberry? How would I say that I am anxious, that I am hungry, that yes, thank you, I would like a receipt? Too often, my mind comes up blank or, rummaging around, feebly offers something else entirely: Swedish or French.

I find an app that allows me to listen to Icelandic radio and play the national broadcast station every morning as I shower. The voices speak quickly, flattened by impenetrable Reykjavík accents, which lack the singsong cadence of the north. The lag in my comprehension is excruciating. This is language learning at its most uncomfortable, when the words must be translated back into English to be understood, not recognised on their own accord. It smacks of the futility of running after a departing bus.

My anxiety mounts. I enrol in a free online course offered by the University of Iceland and, after wading through the first few classes of greetings and polite introduction, the insidious grammatical complexity gums over my mind. I feel stupid at my ignorance of syntactic terms. I mourn my old fluency. I know I have never spoken Icelandic like a native speaker – my conversation has always been pockmarked with grammatical error and the foreigner's manner of jamming in known vocabulary at the expense of clarity and precision – but I have always been told that my Icelandic is good for an utlendingar, an outlander.

The night before I leave for Reykjavík, it occurs to me that my anxiety about Icelandic may be connected to my desire to be accepted. It is, after all, my hard-earned currency of belonging. The longer I sit with my dread, the more I understand I am concerned I will be forced to defend *Burial Rites* during the course of the festival. Two years ago, Þórunn Jarla Valdimarsdóttir, an Icelandic historian and novelist, wrote a book called *Bærinn brennur*, or *The Farm Burns*. Icelandic friends wrote to tell me about its publication, advising that it was a very different take on the murders and executions. Þórunn has recently been named as the other speaker on the panel in Eyrarbakki. If I no longer have any Icelandic under my belt, how will I prove that I did the work? How will I prove I spent the required time here to earn the right to author *Burial Rites* and write it in the way that I did?

*

I arrive in Iceland at midnight. As I walk towards customs among a throng of tourists in outdoor clothing and puffer jackets, my phone buzzes.

Pétur has texted: *Welcome home.*

The word sends a thrill through my body. Home.

Despite the late hour, everyone from my plane seems excited. I overhear snatches of conversation in American and British accents, Spanish, German. The airport is unrecognisable as the one I had landed at twenty years before. It is now designed for visitors: English dominates, and the corridor from our arrival gate is filled with spectacular photographs of Icelandic nature alongside bright advertisements and portraits of Icelanders wearing traditional lopapeysur. It makes sense. Last year more than 1.7 million international visitors passed through this airport. A combination of the 2008 Kreppa Hrunið financial crisis and the 2010 eruption of Eyjafjallajökull pushed Iceland into the global spotlight. The devalued krona made it an affordable holiday destination. Since then, tourism to Iceland has quadrupled and for every Icelander in the country, there are approximately four and a half tourists. It not only accounts for a solid third of Iceland's GDP, but it has also shared Icelandic culture with the world. It feels surreal to me that, while in 2002 most Australians knew nothing about Iceland, last year my daughter's kindergarten held a 'jólabókaflóðið' event at Christmas time. The world is smaller now. I am no longer alone in my love of Iceland.

It is one o'clock in the morning when I reach my hotel, a building by the harbour I have no memory of ever seeing before. My room is small, cosy. Lamplit. I leave my suitcase by the door, take off my shoes and climb onto the bed to better peer out the window. I can make out the dull shine of streetlight on the massive hull of a ship at harbour not thirty metres away, the slick of light on puddles. It is raining. I push open the window so that I might properly empty my lungs of the grimy sum of travel. The night smells scrubbed with salt. I let it breathe into the room as I undress and step into the shower. The water is scalding, sulphuric. I remind myself that this water has been piped from a magma-restless ground and bears its mineral signature. All those years ago, when I returned to Iceland for the first time, Pétur showed me where in Sauðárkókur they cooled – not heated – the water before piping it into homes.

It is very late by the time I crawl into bed. I leave the window open, better to transfuse the north back into my blood.

The first thing I notice on waking is that the walls of my hotel room are papered with illustrations of knots. They lead my mind to a sleepy consideration of my father, who is a wizard with a piece of rope, and then to Iceland's fishermen.

I think of the 2012 film *The Deep* (*Djúpið*), based on the true story of Guðlaugur Friðþórsson. His story was already familiar to me, related during a trip to Vestmannaeyjar with the other Rotary exchange students in the summer. Jón Ásgeir told us that Guðlaugur had been a fisherman based on Heimaey, the largest island of Vestmannaeyjar. In 1984 he had been working on a boat that capsized after its trawl net caught on the sea floor. The four other crew members died in the accident – two never resurfacing after the boat went down, and the other two drowning after ten minutes of swimming in cold water – but Guðlaugur had somehow managed to swim the six kilometres back to shore, and then walk another three, barefoot across volcanic rock, before he found help and finally collapsed. His survival – particularly the total absence of any symptoms of hypothermia after six hours in the sea and then an additional three, soaked to the skin, in air temperatures of minus two degrees (not including wind chill) and a body temperature of below thirty-four degrees Celsius – had so puzzled doctors that he had been studied.

Guðlaugur's story, as it was first told to me, had been endowed with a mystical edge. Researchers found his body fat more closely resembling that of seals than of humans. During his swim he had called to a bird for help, and the bird – an arctic fulmar – had stayed with him the whole way, leading him to shore.

As I lie in bed, hearing the sounds of the harbour beneath my window, it makes sense that the tragedy has been cast into something supernatural. Certainly, Guðlaugur's courage was epic in scope. His – and his community's – pain, too, for the loss of the other four fishermen. All of them had been young.

Most of the stories I have heard while travelling throughout Iceland have been like this: bound in tragedy, often mysterious and bordering, if not outright entering, the domain of the uncanny. Most of the time these stories were told in the moment without forethought or plan. The teller had been reminded of them by their connection to the places we were passing through. They have frequently been offered to me as actualities, mystery and all. Certainly, hearing them while staring out at the vast weight of a sullen, shifting ocean, or in a valley filling rapidly with descending fog, they seemed very real and not mythical at all.

It occurs to me that these are the stories which have shaped my own interests as a writer. My novels veer towards the liminal and the transitional, are firmly rooted within the natural world as purveyor of the uncanny. I have always credited Iceland with turning me towards writing, but this is the first time I understand that my own storytelling has been endlessly cast within the mould of Iceland's own myths, its ever-shifting back and forth between known and unknown, what is said, what is kept silent.

How far down, this tap root, I think. This influence, this island.

After an interview with a journalist from *Morgunblaðið*, I return to the hotel bar to meet Alda Sigmundsdóttir, the author of the very popular *Little Books on Iceland* series, and one of several Icelandic writers I have corresponded with but never met in person. I am hoping to meet as many of them as possible during this trip.

It is lovely to finally meet Alda. Over coffee and tea, we talk about her latest book, *Daughter*, a memoir about her abusive and narcissistic mother. The subject matter has resonated with Icelanders.

'I have been surprised by this,' she tells me. 'But I think that it might have something to do with a need for modern Icelanders to have negative family experiences represented.' Icelandic culture, she reminds me, has historically not been one in which you speak of such things.

I nod and tell her that Hallgrímur Helgason, author of *101 Reykjavík* and *The Woman at 1000 Degrees*, gave a lecture in 2019 called 'The Icelandic Tradition of Silence'. In it he explained

Iceland's culture, 'where literature is a religion, writers are holy figures and the Sagas are the Bible,' and spoke of Icelanders' peculiar way of preserving language through silence.

'We are a silent bunch,' he said.

> The age-old tradition of silence spilled over to every aspect of our society. If there was a problem within the family, people shut up about it, no matter if it was sexual abuse, adultery, bankruptcy, homosexuality, or an alcoholic problem. No one spoke about it. People went to their graves without asking who it was who really conceived them. Many wives silently endured an abusive husband, children grew up carrying heavy secrets inside them. In the political field all possible scandals were silenced, and as a poet you gained the most respect if you did not publish a book for at least twenty years and never gave interviews. [...] We were not just very good with words. Except on paper. Because our big national tradition, beside the cult of silence, was literature.

For centuries, he argued, Icelanders were a text-based people. Fluent on paper, silent in tongue. But then, in his lifetime, he noticed it changing. Hallgrímur attributed it to greater contact with the world, which made Icelanders 'realise how strange our behaviour was', and finding true independence once George W. Bush closed the Keflavík US army base – originally established in World War II – in 2006.

Alda thinks that Covid, too, has done something to open Icelanders, both psychically and emotionally. 'It stripped some of the pretence from us, and now we want to get rid of the bullshit, be more real. Be honest. Speak honestly.'

Alda tells me that she believes the tradition of silence comes from deep trauma carried by Icelanders. We talk of the way families were dissolved in the past when the breadwinner died, children sent to foster families who received a stipend for caring for them.

'It was a way to prevent further children, although children will, of course, be born regardless,' Alda tells me. 'The shame of unwed motherhood was similarly devastating. So different from modern Iceland.'

She shows me a photo of her great-grandmother with her four children a few weeks before the family was split up. Her husband had drowned.

'She knew what was coming,' Alda says. 'You can see it.'

Her great-grandmother does not look at the photographer but into the distance, face charged with a harrowing unhappiness.

I think of Agnes's mother, Ingveldur. The four illegitimate children she could not keep with her. I think of Agnes separated from her mother, her siblings. In all the official records I read, there was never any indication of the emotional toll of such dissolution, and yet here it is, writ large in this woman's eyes.

'They let her keep one child of the four,' Alda says quietly. 'She chose the eldest.'

Our talk turns, then, to the ways in which trauma might have shaped Icelandic cultural beliefs.

'I think the huldufólk, the hidden people, might have been a means for communities to console themselves over the loss of children who, due to a lack of supervision while their parents worked or a dangerous environment, have gone missing: washed into rivers, fallen off cliffs, into crevices. Better to imagine them taken and cared for by the huldufólk.'

Following the publication of *Daughter*, Alda received a furious 3500-word email from an Icelandic family member she had never met, never knew existed. She says she feels her book has untapped something in some people in her family, that it has to do with this trauma. She does not take it personally.

'I am a false target,' she explains.

Later that evening I walk through downtown Reykjavík to Iðnó, a cultural venue by the city pond, for the opening night of the festival.

I am greeted by Stella, the festival director, and her colleague Fanney. They greet me in English, but when I respond in Icelandic they switch too.

'I have forgotten ogeðslegt mikið,' I say to Fanney. I have forgotten a disgusting amount.

She laughs and says that 'ógeðslegt mikið' is such an Icelandic way of expressing things.

As I am introduced to locals, I realise that attitudes to language have changed since I was here as an exchange student. Then, no matter how much Icelandic I spoke, most people insisted on speaking English with me. During coffee with Alda, she had remarked about the increasing prevalence of English in hotels and restaurants. I wonder if this has changed things. Now, no matter how grammatically incorrect or confused or slow my speech, people seem happy to speak to me in Icelandic.

A few minutes before the speeches are due to begin, I am taken backstage by Stella and introduced to Lilja Alfreðsdóttir, the Icelandic Minister for Culture and Business Affairs.

'Hello, it's nice to meet you,' she says in English.

As we head to the wings, Lilja speaks in Icelandic to Stella, then turns and explains in English that she has just come from the opening of a centre for the Icelandic language.

'Í dag?' I ask. Today?

Lilja does a small double take. 'Talarðu íslensku?'

'Ekki mikið,' I respond. Not a lot.

Her entire manner changes then to become informal and friendly, and we chat until she goes onstage to formally open the festival.

And then it is my turn.

After the speeches, a tall man grabs my hand and introduces himself as Einar Már Guðmundsson, the author of the novel *Englar alheimsins* (*Angels of the Universe*). I love his book and am thrilled to meet him. He tells me that he has written a novel called *Hundadagar* (*Dog Days*), about Jørgen Jørgensen, and that there is a connection with Tasmania in his story. It has not been translated, but he says he will email me a piece he wrote about the book for the University of Tasmania.

I tell him I have heard of Jørgen Jørgensen. 'Isn't he the man who proclaimed himself King of Iceland in the 1800s?'

'That's him,' Einar Már says.

I came across an account of this man in my research. Originally born in Copenhagen, Jørgensen ended up being transported to lutruwita (Tasmania) as a convict. Marcus Clarke, author of *For the Term of His Natural Life*, supposedly found his autobiography.

Einar Már asks me about *Náðarstund*, which he has read, and we discuss our common interest in this period of Icelandic history, in how there is so much which has gone unsaid about this time.

We are, by now, in the close press of people surrounding the bar in the entrance hall of Iðnó, and the conversation around us is a cacophony of Icelandic and English. People keep interrupting us to introduce themselves, and I give Einar my email address so we can continue our conversation that way. The crowd is filled with Icelandic writers I recognise and admire, but when the volume reaches a level where I cannot understand either English or Icelandic, I feel overwhelmed and head to the quiet second floor of Iðnó on the pretence of fetching my bag.

I am, however, not the only person who has climbed the stairs to escape the crowd. A pale, dark-haired girl is sitting with a tall man beautifully adorned with gold jewellery. I smile at them as I pass, but the girl stops me.

'I read your book,' she tells me, in what is clearly a British accent. 'I loved it. You probably hear that all the time.'

'Not really,' I say, and introduce myself properly. Her name is Katie, and the man is Jakub Stachowiak, a Polish-born Icelandic poet.

An anthology has just been launched as part of the festival; *Writers Adrift* in English, *Skáldreki* in Icelandic, it is a collection of essays written by foreign-born writers in Iceland. Jakub is one of the contributing authors.

I ask Katie if she is a writer, and she says that she is a poet. I ask for her last name, then, so that I will know her poems when I read them. I have never forgotten when someone asked me for my own name.

'Katie Metcalfe,' she says, and then gives me a zine of her poems. Titled *The Darkest Days*, the first poem is in the voice of the ogress Grýla, mother of the yule lads.

We talk together about the pull of Iceland, of our attraction to its stories.

'I don't know why, but I always find myself coming back,' Katie says.

I know exactly what she means.

Icelanders aren't shy of late nights. I have another event at nine thirty in the evening with the writer Haukur Már Helgason and the poet Kristín Svava Tómasdóttir, moderated by Halla Oddný Magnúsdóttir. All of us have written stories of Icelandic history, and together we talk about private and public spaces, justice and freedom, and the relationship between research and writing. Halla asks us about the imagination required to illuminate perspectives not necessarily recorded in historical documents. I have had experiences of sitting on literary panels with a translator, but this is my first experience of a truly bilingual festival. Translations are projected behind us, but I am glad that I can understand Haukur and Kristín as they speak their own language. At one point, I have the strange feeling that all my Icelandic is coursing back, synaptic connections suddenly flaring back to life. It feels as though someone has switched out a memory card in my brain.

By the time I walk back to my hotel that night, it is late. I kick my shoes off and eat a dinner of flatbread and cheese, then gaze out at the harbour, eating blueberries, wondering if it is easier to be myself in Iceland than anywhere else in the world.

I pick up my copy of *Skáldreki* in the morning while still lying in bed. I am struck by how these writers – born in Russia, India, Poland, Palestine, USA, Switzerland, Venezuela, Canada and

Brazil – all of whom have come to Iceland for their own reasons, nonetheless circle around the same anxieties I struggled with when publishing *Burial Rites*. How might I convince this country I have something to contribute? How do I tell the stories of Iceland if I am not Icelandic-born?

Several essays make mention of Iceland's Artist's Salary Fund, something I know nothing about. I put the book down and google it.

To promote artistic creation in Iceland, the Ministry of Education and Culture offers over 1600 monthly salaries, or 133.3 annual salaries, to artists across six disciplines. Writers receive the most allocations out of any other discipline. Last year, a total of 555 months' salary was allocated to writers, with each artist receiving the same salary of ISK507,500 a month, the equivalent to A$5305. Twelve writers, I read, received a full year's salary equivalent to A$63,660.

This, in a country of 375,000 people.

The equivalent for Australia's population, I figure out, punching numbers into my phone's calculator, would be 858 writers being supported to write full-time for a year. It would cost over $54 million.

Eight hundred and fifty-eight fellowships awarded to Australian writers would be culture changing. It would require a massive, earth-shattering shift in attitude towards literature on a societal and political level in Australia.

I understand that simply adapting Iceland's numbers to Australia's much bigger population and publishing industry, its different budgetary demands, is a little simplistic. The size of the Icelandic book market is much smaller and Icelandic publishing friends tell me that book sales have also dwindled over the last decade. Support is necessary. But what I find myself bristling most at is the news that the Icelandic government awards the *most* allocations to writers. Literature is the least-funded artistic discipline in Australia. Even before the Covid pandemic devastated artistic communities and livelihoods, the Australia Council for the Arts (now known as Creative Australia) awarded only $5 million total to support all successful literary applications. Theatre, on the other hand, received nearly three times that amount.

When I return to *Skáldreki*, I read Joachim B. Schmidt's essay 'Application Rejected'. He notes that grants are primarily awarded to established Icelandic authors with recognised names, regardless of financial need.

At a meeting of the Icelandic Writers' Union, Schmidt asks whether an application for a work not written in Icelandic would stand a chance of being accepted. He is met with laughter.

The Icelandic government *is* hyper-protective when it comes to Icelandic. There are several institutions responsible for promoting its development and celebrating its history, such as The Icelandic Language Committee (Íslensk málnefnd) and the Árni Magnússon Institute for Icelandic Studies. Icelandic neologisms have traditionally been preferred over the adoption of loan words from other countries, such as 'tölva' for computer, drawn from tala (number or figure) and völva (female seer or prophetess), and 'útvarp' for radio, a compound word from út (out) and varp (throw or cast). One of my favourites, 'mörgæs', literally meaning 'fat goose' for penguin, was created by the poet Jónas Hallgrímsson.

Iceland's insistence on linguistic purism has made international news from time to time, especially when it comes to the naming of babies. Iceland's Personal Names Committee requires that names not already on its approved lists be submitted for approval. If they cannot adapt to Icelandic's structural and spelling conventions (such as a genitive ending), they are rejected by law. A quick look at the committee's rulings shows me that Harriet, Duncan, Theo, Zelda, Damien, Candice and Natasha have never passed muster.

This deliberate prudence when it comes to the Icelandic language can, at first, seem a bit much. But I do think it is understandable, especially when considered in the light of Iceland's five hundred years of colonisation by Denmark. Throw in Iceland's very small population and the country's pride in their literary history, and it makes sense that the country comes across as anxious in this age of increased globalisation.

But I think Schmidt has a point when he asks, 'Is an Icelandic novel still an Icelandic novel if it isn't written in Icelandic?'

It is a question I have asked myself.

The great wonder of books

CHAPTER TWENTY-ONE

Storytelling

It is the twentieth of April and the First Day of Summer: Sumardagurinn fyrsti. The old calendar year of the Icelanders only had two seasons – winter and summer – and the First Day of Summer was a time to celebrate. Today is a public holiday, and as a special treat, the festival is taking guest writers to a garden party at Gljúfrasteinn, the home and workplace of Halldór Laxness. Although it is a museum now, and open to visitors, the Nobel Prize winner's home is unchanged from when he and his family lived there.

I love the place immediately, particularly the vast collection of Icelandic artworks, but I am keen to see where Laxness wrote, and go upstairs as soon as I am able. His library is lined with bookshelves and the ceiling is painted green, sunlight slanting in the windows. His study is smaller. A typewriter sits on a desk of blond wood and the walls are filled with photographs and portraits and abstract impressionist paintings.

It seems extraordinary to me that I am standing in the room where some of my favourite novels were written. This, I think, is the great wonder of books. That stories might be conceived in one place, in one time, by one mind, only to then be flung into the world, into the years to come, taken up by the imaginations of many. I think of when I lay on my bed in the attic at Syðri-Hofdalir as an exchange student, reading Laxness. That moment had its source here, I think.

As I make my way back downstairs, I hear singing. Stepping into the living room I see an Icelander has sat down at the piano and is playing. No performance was scheduled; it is just that Icelandic proclivity towards a spontaneous singalong. The song must be well known, for every other Icelander in the room – sprawled on couches, leaning against doorways – joins in. The foreign guests, myself included, are gaping. This feels special. Here we are, a group of writers from around the world, gathered in Halldór Laxness's home, listening to his countrymen lift their voices.

The next morning I make my way outside and get on a bus with the rest of the festival's writers. Each of us, on arriving in Iceland, were given an envelope of thick paper that we were told not to lose. It turned out to be an invitation.

> The President of Iceland Guðni Th. Jóhannesson and Ms Eliza Reid kindly invite Hannah Kent to a reception at Bessastaðir, the President's residence.

While it was very exciting to see the Icelandic coat of arms on the letter, with its bull, eagle, dragon and giant – the four 'guardian spirits' of Iceland from the Heimskringla – I know that most Icelanders wouldn't bat an eyelash at the prospect of meeting the President. There is very little hype about fame. I remember once bumping into Björk at the airport (physically bumping into her because I wasn't looking where I was going), and when I mentioned it to an Icelandic friend, they just nodded, as if waiting for me to begin my story. There is a strong sense in Iceland of everyone being just like everyone else and deserving to be treated as such. Also, Iceland is so small that lots of people have met the President at some time or other.

Bessastaðir is the most understated official residence I have ever seen. As the bus drives towards it I notice a small gate has been opened to admit us, but there is no adjoining fence and no security detail. The country surrounding Bessastaðir is strikingly flat and the home stands out. It is lovely and completely accessible.

As I get out of the bus it occurs to me that this building was where Björn Blöndal was educated. During the first half of the nineteenth century, Bessastaðir was the only formal school in the country.

Once inside, we are greeted by the President and the First Lady. The home is white-walled, hung with gilt-framed paintings and chandeliers, but otherwise restrained.

We gather for the presentation of the Orðstír Prize, an award given to translators in recognition of their support of Icelandic literature abroad. After the ceremony I take a flute of champagne and slip away to explore the house. Many of the other writers have congregated in the library, a long, narrow room filled with wooden shelves and beautiful leather-bound books, including collections of the Sagas of the Icelanders. The rest of the house is filled with photos of world leaders displayed on mantels and side cabinets. The paintings by Icelandic artists are breathtaking. One of a woman and a swan holds my attention so deeply, I do not notice that the First Lady of Iceland has come into the room.

We are introduced then, and I tell Eliza I recently read her book *Secrets of the Sprakkar: Iceland's Extraordinary Women and How They Are Changing the World.*

She tells me that she is also a co-founding director of the Iceland Writers Retreat, an organisation that offers people around the world the opportunity to come to Iceland and learn from local and international writers through intimate workshops.

As I tell Eliza about *Kill Your Darlings*, the literary magazine I co-founded twelve years ago, I brush up against something soft in the stairwell. Turning, I see a massive polar bear skin hanging from the banister of the floor above.

'Oh my god,' I say. The pelt of the head is still attached. I am sure that touching things is frowned on at the presidential residence, but I can't resist pushing my fingers into the fur. The paws are massive.

'A gift from Greenland,' Eliza says. She points out some other curiosities as we continue upstairs. 'That owl is from Ronald Reagan. That clock from Gorbachev.'

Our talk turns to *Skáldreki*. Eliza contributed the introduction to the collection, and I tell her that I enjoyed her argument that immigrants to Iceland 'can deepen and widen the reach of this ancient and beautiful language'.

'I'm a writer,' she says. 'And I'm foreign-born. It's an interesting space to occupy.'

The Icelandic crime writer Yrsa Sigurðardóttir once jokingly dubbed me 'Icestralian'. We'd been (at least, I had been) very drunk, smoking cigarettes on a hotel balcony during a Canadian writers' festival. I have no idea if she meant it as a compliment or as a nod to my unlikely interest in her home country, but the term stayed with me.

It feels rude to ask but, as we politely sip our drinks, I wonder whether Eliza Reid feels herself to be 'Icenadian'.

'I liked your consideration of what it might mean to define an "Icelandic writer", too,' I say instead. 'Is it someone who writes in the Icelandic language? A writer who holds Icelandic citizenship? A writer who creates stories set in Iceland or about Icelandic topics?'

We are interrupted then – the First Lady of Iceland is in high demand. But as I walk back to the stairwell, it occurs to me that I might, arguably, be an Icelandic writer. The idea thrills me in the moment for the way it troubles the notion of nationality and art. For eight years, before *Devotion* was published in 2021, I was frequently asked when I would set a book in Australia. Never 'if'; always 'when'. The question was well intentioned, but it made me feel uncomfortable, as though I must be more cognisant of the country stamped on my passport. The idea that one might, through creative dedication, enable one's own belonging is much more interesting to me. I know there are things I will never write about – boundaries exist and must be respected; I am not, nor should I be able to speak to all spheres of experience – but I quite like troubling any binary categorisation.

Let the waters be muddied, I think, brushing my fingers against the polar bear skin. Let me be many things.

My remaining festival sessions pass smoothly. In one, Alexander McCall Smith challenges crime writer Eva Björg Ægisdóttir and me to a competition. Whoever can fit the words 'lightning' and 'sharks' into our conversation seamlessly will be declared the winner. He triumphs five minutes in.

My event in Eyrarbakki is scheduled to take place after the festival has officially ended in Reykjavík. As part of my press commitments, I am interviewed by Egill Helgason, who remembers me from 2014. After the filming is finished, he asks me how I feel about being on a panel with Þórunn Valdimarsdóttir, the historian who wrote *Bærinn brennur.*

'I'm sure we'll have lots to discuss,' I say.

'You know, she thinks you're wrong about some things,' he says cheerfully. 'Þórunn wrote the book after the death of her husband, Eggert Þór Bernharðsson. It's based on his research.'

Eggert, I recall, was the author who'd transcribed the documents from the original trial of Agnes and the others.

Egill must see the blood drain from my face, because he smiles reassuringly. 'I'm sure it will be a great session.'

Walking back to the hotel, I can't help but feel as though this upcoming Eyrarbakki panel is being touted as some kind of boxing match. A novelist in one corner, a historian in the other. I have never been placed on a panel with a historian before. Einar Már Guðmundsson, after our meeting at the opening night, emailed me some information about his writing and I was struck by his comment, 'Fiction is a search for an inner meaning in the outer world and an outer meaning in the inner world.' Yes! I thought. This is exactly it. The interior world, largely unknown and rarely documented, is the prerogative of the novelist. The silences. What has not been said.

I wonder if Þórunn might be disdainful of the licence I took in creating Agnes's inner world. I wonder if she disagrees with a creative philosophy that, the more stories and perspectives we share, the closer we might come to an approximation of truth. I wonder what else we might disagree on.

Towards the end of the festival there is a Book Ball. We have been told that this event is usually considered the highlight of the festival, and after the DJ starts up, I realise why. The Book Ball is essentially a big party. There are no speeches, no formalities, just music and dancing and alcohol. The Icelanders are ready for a good time, and the visiting writers follow suit. It doesn't take long before everyone is dancing with the kind of abandon and glee you normally see at weddings rather than literary festivals. Dancing is a great equaliser, I realise, throwing myself into the fray. It's hard to feel intimidated by literary giants when they're grinding to Robyn. I am sweaty and drunk and having the time of my life when, around midnight, I am tapped on the shoulder. It is Maríanna, the chair of the session with Eva Björg and Alexander McCall Smith.

'Hey, Hannah, there is someone out by the bar who wants to talk with you!' she shouts over the din of the music.

'Who is it?' I shout back, picking up my beer.

'You'll see!'

She leads me off the packed dancefloor and into the smaller front room. There, in the crowd of people standing around and drinking, is an older man. He smiles at me.

'Sæl og blessuð,' he says, stepping forward and shaking my hand. He introduces himself to me as Magnús Ólafsson from Sveinsstaðir.

Then I see, behind him, a familiar face. It is María Ellingsen, the actor who played Agnes. 'Good to see you again, Hannah,' she says.

My mouth drops open.

Magnús, María and I escape the thudding music from the dancefloor and the roar of conversation and go upstairs to the second floor of Iðnó, where we settle ourselves around a table by the window. It is then that Magnús Ólafsson tells me he is the son of Ólafur, grandson of 'Old Magnús'. His farm, Sveinsstaðir, was where Agnes's bones were stored before being taken to Tjörn.

I am a little shaken to find myself sitting across from the man whose grandfather found Agnes and Friðrik's heads, unearthed their remains. I ask him if what I read about his grandfather in *Enginn má undan líta* was true.

Magnús nods. 'Já. My grandfather did not believe the story about the medium at first. But it all happened as it is written.

I believe that the farmer's wife at Þingeyrar wanted the heads buried in consecrated ground. The bodies had already been interred at the site of execution, of course. But I think the farm worker who came was afraid to hold them, that's why he just buried them there. Who would know the difference?'

'Did Agnes's skull really have a piece of wood in it?'

He nods. 'Já.' He holds up his hands to indicate its size. 'It was ten centimetres long.'

Magnús and María mention tomorrow's panel with Þórunn. I tell them that I'm a bit nervous about it.

'We think your book comes very close to the truth,' María tells me. 'Þórunn's book uses Eggert's research, and he made many good discoveries, but it is largely based on the court documents. These are true, of course, we don't dispute that, but these documents also ignore a lot of other things.'

Magnús tells me that both he and María believe greater context needs to be given to Agnes's actions.

'I believe she was trying to get help,' Magnús says. 'Natan had put both women in a búr and was abusing them both.'

'What is a búr?' I ask, thrown by the unfamiliar word.

'A cage,' explains María. 'Figuratively speaking, but also literally. They were stuck at Illugastaðir. It also doesn't make sense to me why they would kill anyone for money. They can't leave the land. They can't go to a shop. Besides, they were known to be destitute people. Everyone would know where they got their money from.'

I agree with this, and I tell them both that I have always been confused about the theories that put great weight on Natan's supposed wealth, on Friðrik, Agnes and Sigríður's desire for it. Wouldn't everyone be suspicious if their wealthy master died and then they suddenly had money and goods? Agnes was supposed to be particularly intelligent. Surely she would have realised that everyone would work out what had happened?

Þórunn's book, they tell me, places the same emphasis on the desire for wealth and the role of theft in the murder as the authorities of the time, highlighting who stole what from whom. It reminds me of the mock retrial, when the modern judges noted that the endless questions about what might have been taken and how much it was worth was representative of the pecuniary interests of the original authorities.

'No one ever asked Agnes why she had run away. No one wrote down what she said to the priest. They didn't think it was relevant!' Magnús says.

He tells me that he now spends a lot of time taking visitors around the sites on horseback, telling this old story as they pass through. María tells me that she is now writing a play about Agnes. 'I thought she was finished with me after the film, but no!' She adds: 'It is filled with her rage. It comes out in the writing like a flood.'

I ask María what she meant when she told me nine years ago that she could see Agnes had visited me. Did she mean it metaphorically?

'I meant it as I said it,' she says, giving me a careful look. 'Literally.'

She tells me of her experiences during the filming of *Agnes*, the times she had felt Agnes's presence. Even after production had finished, she had difficulty letting go of Agnes. 'It was as though she wanted my body to talk for her. I couldn't sleep. I thought I would go mad from not sleeping.'

'How did you get over that?'

María raises her eyebrows. 'I had help from a medium.'

After my conversation with Magnús and María I find my anxieties about the panel have dissipated. It is enough to know that they, too, have harboured the same doubts as me and asked the same questions.

I turn around to head back into the Ball, checking my phone for the time. A notification has popped up on my screen. Clicking on it, I realise *Burial Rites* was published exactly ten years ago to the day.

The next morning I am picked up by Valdi, the husband of one of the organisers, Anna. He has volunteered to drive me the forty-five minutes to Eyrarbakki. We speak in Icelandic the entire way down the coast, which seems remarkable to me given that, one week earlier, I couldn't remember the word for strawberry. Yesterday, at the party, an Icelander told me that if I stayed in the country for three months I'd be fluent.

One day, I think. The prospect of coming back here with my family for an extended period is not something I have contemplated, but what an adventure that would be, it occurs to me now.

Valdi drops me off and I meet Anna. Then we go to meet Þórunn at Rauða Húsið, the Red House, the restaurant where our session will be held.

Þórunn is not what I expected. She is friendly and embraces me when we are introduced. Over lunch we talk of our lives, and she speaks a little of her late husband. Eggert, I learn, was a descendant of Guðmundur Ketilsson, and when he was a boy he was shown a book which claimed that his great-great-grandfather had offered to execute Agnes and Friðrik. This was not true, but the rumour that Guðmundur had wanted to be the executioner was widespread. Eggert, filled with shame, wanted to rectify this. That was the motivation for his research, Þórunn explains.

She grips my hand. 'We shall have a good talk,' she says.

Before we step into the room, the moderator asks if Þórunn is willing to speak in English for my benefit. He can translate if necessary. Þórunn agrees, but ten minutes into the discussion she returns to Icelandic. My mind flares white-hot as it tries to keep up with her while, at the same time, formulating responses to her criticisms and commentary.

At one point a woman stands up and, in Icelandic, speaks vehemently in support of Þórunn's representation of Björn Blöndal. She glares at me as she does so.

When invited to speak, I reiterate that my novel is a work of fiction. Although based heavily on research, it necessarily privileges the point of view of Agnes.

'Björn is seen as Agnes sees him, which is not in a complimentary light. He is, after all, the man who has sentenced her to death. It's not my job as a novelist to ensure he is portrayed in a neutral way. It's my job to honour the way my protagonist would have felt about him.'

During question time, when a man asks me in Icelandic how I knew what happened in the murder scene, I remind him that I do not know. No one truly does. We were not there. Besides this, only so much was indicated by the records I had available to me, and many details were inconsistent. That is why, in the description of the murder in my novel, I use both first- and third-person narration. 'Agnes is an unreliable narrator,' I remind everyone. 'That's not to say she is untrustworthy, but the context of her narration is such that she is desirous of understanding and compassion. It affects what she says and how she says it. When Agnes describes the murders, her narration is also coloured by everything that has happened since they occurred.'

By the time the session closes, my head is pounding. I excuse myself to the bathroom, where I see the lady who expressed her displeasure at my representation of Blöndal. After she leaves, another woman who is washing her hands tells me that the lady was a direct descendant of the judge.

Ah, I think. The past is always personal, especially in Iceland.

When I return upstairs, I am taken aback to see Sjón, one of my favourite Icelandic writers, in the crowd. He comes up to me and introduces himself, and we talk a little about the writer's prerogative and imagination.

I feel myself relax a little when he tells me I spoke well.

'You're a novelist, after all,' he says. 'You must honour the interior world. You must honour what is not known.'

I can feel the layers of time
upon this place

CHAPTER TWENTY-TWO

Words in the Landscape

The next day Pétur picks me up from Eyrarbakki. He gets out and hugs me and I am so happy I can't stop smiling. It's been four years since I last saw him, but within a few minutes it feels like no time has passed at all. He's got an electric car now, and when we pull over to charge it in Reykjavík, ready for the four-hour drive back home to Sauðárkrókur, we catch up on family news and I try the new energy drinks Pétur says are now really popular in the country. They seem distinctly Icelandic – some potent combination of caffeine and fish collagen.

Pétur and Regína have three grandchildren now. Gunnar Stefán's girl is four, Óli Björn has a toddler with another on the way, and Birgitta had a little boy in January. Jón Arnar is also expecting a child with his wife.

'How do you like being a grandfather?' I ask Pétur.

He smiles. 'It's great. But you left out Anouk and Rory. They're also my grandkids, right?'

'Right.'

Other things have been changing, too. Pétur and Regína sold the house where they lived for more than twenty years and have moved a few blocks away. I'm excited to see their new place, although it feels strange knowing that I won't be returning to the home of my memory.

'I think you're going to like it, Hannah,' Pétur says. He and the boys have been working hard on renovating it.

When we pull into Sauðárkrókur, something in my soul, as always, is comforted by the sight of the mountains. Pétur tests me on their names.

'That one is Molduxi, remember?' he says. 'And that one is …'

'Mosfell. And I would never forget Tindastóll.'

The mountain tops are streaked with snow, tinged pink in the late spring sunset. The valley is brown, waiting for the eruption of green. I know the seasons here. I understand how they arrive.

Pétur pulls up to the new house, which is set on the higher slopes of the town. I kick off my boots in the entryway and follow him up the stairs. Regína is in the lounge room, and when I appear she envelops me in a hug. Birgitta waves to me from where she and her baby boy are cuddled up on the couch. It is astonishing to see the baby with her own baby. I feel like a time traveller.

That night, over pizza, I meet more of the grandkids and see how much Fannar and Sigurbjörn have grown, too. I am aware that, to at least half of these kids, I am something of a stranger, a relic from before their own memories began, but they seem to accept my presence. Pétur has told me before that they have been raised with stories of me, that they know who I am. I go to sleep that night thinking about my host family, how easy it always is with Pétur and Regína, and how even someone like Birgitta, who was a baby when I lived with them, holds space for me in the family lore. I am never made to feel unwelcome.

Pétur has taken a few days off work to spend with me during this brief visit. We decide to take a few day trips to visit places in the north country, such as Mývatn, an extraordinarily beautiful nature reserve comprising wetlands and volcanic landforms about two and a half hours away.

I'm grateful to play the tourist, but the best part of our travels is the opportunity to chat in the car. In between stops at Goðafoss, the waterfall of the gods, and the Forest Lagoon, new hot pools surrounded by birch and pine trees with spectacular views of Eyjafjörður, I catch Pétur up on news of Heidi, of our children, of work and what I have planned. He tells me that he knows Heidi and I have a great love between us, that our wedding was something special.

'She is special,' he says. 'She has a beautiful mind.'

He asks how the festival went, and I tell him about speaking with Magnús Ólafsson and María Ellingsen at Iðnó the other night.

'You know, when news of your book first came out, Magnús was cross about it. I think he even went on television to say that he didn't think an Australian would be able to write this story.'

My heart sinks. 'Really? I didn't know that.'

Pétur nods. 'But then he read it. And he made a point of making sure everyone knew he stood corrected.'

We talk of Pétur's kids, too, of how much they have accomplished, of their beautiful, clever children. In Akureyri we drop in to Gunnar Stefán's house and I sit on the floor with his little daughter, chatting away in Icelandic.

'You know, she can already speak some English,' Gunnar Stefán tells me proudly.

I grin at him, remembering my conversations with him twenty years ago when he was a shy eleven-year-old. Gunnar Stefán is a body builder and strength trainer now, as is his partner, Rannveig. I have never seen a couple with more impeccable musculature. Gunnar tells me about his time training celebrities who come to shoot films in Iceland, although, like a true Icelander, he doesn't bother telling me who the celebrities are.

During the evenings, back in Sauðárkrókur, I sit at the table in the living room, letting myself be with the family as they come and go. It is a wonderful thing to see Birgitta be a mother, to have her plop her own baby down on my lap in the same way her mother did with her, to listen to her tease her brothers. Fannar speaks in English with me, shows me what he's doing on the computer and asks me some questions about Australia.

'You should come visit, one day,' I tell him. 'I would show you around.'

'Yeah,' he says, nodding. 'Cool.'

I watch Tindastóll – the name for the town's sporting teams – play basketball on the local broadcast with Regína, and chat with her as she makes waffles. They taste exactly as I remember. She asks me about my children, and I remember how, during her visit for my wedding, she sat with Anouk for hours amid the chaos of preparations. My daughter, not one for strangers, had been drawn to her instantly.

'I've really missed you,' I say. 'I wish we could have had more time together in Australia.'

'We miss you too,' she says. 'You have to bring Heidi and the kids here.'

People drop in, too, much in the same way as they used to twenty years ago. Hera and Sylvía come around, and we cry and hug. I am overjoyed to see them. We sit around the table, catching up on news, until Hera springs up and tells me she wants to surprise Mæja.

'You know, she's back here now, working at the hospital with me. Hold on a second, I'm going to see if she's finished her shift.'

A few minutes later, Hera bundles me into her car and we drive the two minutes to Mæja's family home. 'I haven't told her you're here,' Hera says. 'She's going to be so surprised.'

Mæja opens the door as we're walking up the path to her house. She looks at Hera, then at me, eyes widening.

'Whaaaat?'

I haven't seen Mæja for twenty years. She is one of the few Icelanders who is not especially active on social media, and we have not caught up during any of my previous visits.

'I can't believe you're here,' Mæja says, hugging me.

We go inside. Hera can't wipe the smile off her face.

'I can't believe that you look exactly the same,' I reply.

'I know, right?' says Hera. 'Not like us hags. Pick the ones who had kids!'

Later that night, Hera asks me when I am going to move to Iceland. She laughs, tugging at the sleeve of my jumper, but says, 'Hannah, I'm serious! When are you going to move? You need to bring your family here first, to show Heidi. She will love it, of course. But then I really think you should all live here for a little bit.'

'I've thought about it,' I admit, 'but I don't know how I would get a visa.'

Hera pulls a face. 'We would work it out. You know Pétur would find a way. Hannah, please think about it.'

My visit is short. I must return to my own family, my own children. On my last day in Sauðárkrókur I stop at the supermarket and pick up as many Icelandic treats as I can fit in my suitcase. I have promised Anouk and Rory chocolate and mittens.

Then, after a kleina at the bakery, Pétur and I get in the car for the trip back to Reykjavík. We'll stay at an apartment he owns there tonight, and then he'll take me to the airport first thing in the morning.

'If you did want to move here with your family,' Pétur says as we head out of Sauðárkrókur, 'we would help you. It could be really great. You could rent out your house in Australia, and we'd find you something here. You could write about Iceland again, and I could help Heidi to find work. But, Hannah, you have to give me notice, okay?' He winks at me. 'You can't just let me know a few weeks out.'

I wince. I did not give Pétur much of a heads up about this particular trip.

'I'm sorry. I'm not very good at replying to emails or texts. Sometimes I can't even bring myself to read them. Every new year I resolve to be better at it, to be more social.'

Pétur smiles. 'I don't think it is possible for people to change who they are. Sure, maybe you could try to check in a bit more. But you're never going to be a social butterfly. You are what we would call "someone who is connected to the earth". You are happier watching. Taking it all in.'

'I'm quiet,' I agree. 'I think that's why I found it hard when I first came here. I probably wasn't extroverted enough.'

Pétur gives me a gentle look. 'You know, we weren't actually supposed to be one of your host families.'

I stare at him.

'No. You were only supposed to stay at Guðný and Þórir's and then with Gísli and Steinnun. Two host families. But I could see you were unhappy. I knew you were finding it hard, so I told everyone that I was going to take you in for a bit. You were going to be our foster kid.'

I don't say anything then. I can't. But I reach over and squeeze his hand.

As we approach Þrístapar, Pétur tells me he wants to stop.

'I haven't seen it yet,' he tells me. 'They've been developing the site as a memorial. It's changed a lot since you last saw it.'

I am astonished to see that the site of Agnes's execution is now clearly visible from the road. There is now a car park and a bitumen path leading to the three hills.

We climb out of the car and start walking along the new path. The sun is shining, but it is bitterly cold, and my eyes stream in the wind that is pouring over the hills from the north. Because of this, I don't see the plaques until Pétur stops me.

'Look,' he says.

There, in the middle of the pathway, is a rust-red metal placard bearing a quote from *Burial Rites*.

Pétur and I look at each other.

I notice then that plaques have been set at intervals along the journey to the execution site. Several bear passages from my novel, and at the end, as the path curves up to the original stone memorial, one lists *Burial Rites* among the books written about the murders of Natan Ketilsson and Pétur Jónsson. The plaque lies next to an artwork of two large metal poles, rising into the sky. Beneath them is a statue of a woman lying on her side.

On the hill where the execution took place I see that one final quote from *Burial Rites* has been embedded in the ground. It was written after my terrible dream, and is in Agnes's voice.

> I don't think I'm ready. I don't think that they can do it. Can you make them wait? They have to wait.

The wind has grown stronger. My face is wet. I sit down on the grassed earth beside Þrístapar in my enormous jacket and feel the wind buffet my body. My hair writhes in the air. The wind dries my tears, then blows harder and makes them water anew.

'I didn't realise it would be like this,' I say to Pétur when he sits down beside me.

'It's something special.'

We rest there for a moment, letting the wind knife us. It is as though I can feel the layers of time upon this place. Against this moment of Pétur and myself sitting upon the dun grass, backs against the rise of Þrístapar, there exists, too, every other time I have been here. I am looking out of the window of a car to the lowering light. I am climbing the summer green to the lichen-scarred stone while my parents hang back, watching. I am trying to climb the summit in the snow, boots slipping on the ice beneath so that I fall and crawl to the top, losing feeling in my hands. Against these ghost selves, pressed closely upon one another, like a pile of photo negatives, I feel the things I have never seen with my eyes but have imagined. Axe fall. The cry of ravens. A priest stumbling into the snow. Three men digging.

I lean against Pétur's side and look back at the three hills, now so changed and yet not changed at all, and I see my past selves there in a tableau that is also populated with everyone else who has stood at this place in a deep crisis of feeling. And I get up, and as I leave I know that I am also remaining. I have imprinted again upon this place, like so many others have. The air is dense with remembrance. And as I walk back to the car with Pétur I farewell the hills and all who exist there in the layers of time that cover it like a company of ghosts.

ACKNOWLEDGEMENTS

When I was first contemplating whether I should write this book, two Little Ravens moved into my backyard. Our place had long been home to a pair of Grey Currawongs, but one day I heard a caw above my head and looked up to see a raven peering at me, black feathers sleek in the sun.

'Hæ Krummi,' I said, using the Icelandic nickname for a raven.

It stared at me, white-eyed, then offered a hoarse call.

When the raven returned, it brought a partner, and the two of them set upon cawing at me each time I left the house. I named them Huginn and Muninn after Odin's ravens, the pair that flew all over Midgard and returned to that one-eyed Norse god with tidings. Thought and Memory. I began to find their black feathers waiting for me on my doorstep. They felt like omens.

Okay, fine, I thought one day, picking up yet another feather. *I'll do it.* I started writing this book that same day, the feather on my desk as a reminder to centre memory and thought, and to better carve a path back to Iceland which has always, for me, been a land of ravens.

So, first of all, thank you to Huginn and Muninn for your work in both harassing me and summoning the first words of this memoir onto the page.

Thank you to the brilliant editors who generously honed, queried and bettered this book. Thank you to the incredibly kind and enthusiastic team at Picador: Ingrid Ohlsson, Danielle Walker, Grace Carter, Ali Lavau, Susin Chow, Lily Cameron. I'm very grateful to you all. Thank you to my wonderful UK publisher, Sophie Jonathan, for every astute suggestion – you are inevitably always right. Thank you to Sunna Dís Másdóttir for a forensic read, for ensuring my (now rusty) Icelandic was at least intelligible, and for your insights into the contemporary Icelandic literary scene. Thank you to Tracey Cheetham for everything you do.

Thank you to Knútur Óskarsson, María Ellingsen, Magnús Ólafsson, Hallgrímur Helgason, Stella Soffía Johannesdóttir, Alda Sigmundsdóttir, Eyrún Ingadóttir, Einar Már Guðmundsson and the authors of *Writers Adrift* for so generously allowing me to reproduce your words here. Thank you to the organisers and guests of Bókmenntahátið 2023 for having me. Thank you to all those who helped me as an exchange student, or as a research student, not least Jón Ásgeir Jónsson and Jón Torfason. Thank you to Jón St. Kristjánsson for your exquisite translation of *Náðarstund*. Thank you to the late Ruth Starke for her guidance and for being one of the great forces behind *Burial Rites*. You are missed.

Thank you to my brilliant and ever-wise literary agent, Pippa Masson, and the team at Curtis Brown Australia. I am forever grateful for the faith you have in me. Thank you to the wonderful

Gordon Wise and team at Curtis Brown UK, and to Dan Lazar at Writers House. Thank you to Leslie Conliffe at Intellectual Property Group.

Thank you to those who offered their homes to me so that I might better write about my own. Thank you to dearest Bev and Michael Eaton for the shack at Middleton, and to Kinchem Hegedus, Peter Barge and the Stella Prize for the time at Springfield.

Thank you to those I worked with at Matilda Bookshop. Your support of my writing has meant so much to me. Thank you to my literary witches, Margot McGovern and Lisa Bennett, for the gift of your friendship. Thank you to Bec Starford for being an early reader and for your encouragement.

To my Icelandic friends and family, this is as much a love letter to you as it is to your country. Thank you for your generosity and friendship and for always welcoming me back. You all know who you are (your names are in this book) – knús frá mér. Pétur and Regína, you changed my life. I am honoured to be your Australian daughter. Hjartans þakkir til ykkar beggja.

To my parents, sister and brother-in-law – Pam, Alan, Briony, Owen – thank you for your love, steadfastness and for always believing in me. I love you all.

Thank you to Anouk and Rory, for the wondrous gift of yourselves.

Thank you, Heidi, my love. Without you and all you do, this book would not be here. Home is where you are.

FURTHER READING

Agnes (motion picture), dir. Egill Eðvarðsson, Pegasus Pictures, 1995.

Árni Magnússon Institute for Icelandic Studies, 2025, www.arnastofnun.is

Artists Salary Fund, 2025, en.rannis.is

Auden, W.H. and Louis MacNeice, *Letters from Iceland*, London: Faber & Faber, 1937.

Boucher, Alan (trans.), *Icelandic Folktales*, Reykjavík: Almenna bókafélagið / Edda Publishing, 2007.

Brynjúlfur Jónsson, *Natans Ketilssonar og Skáld-Rósu*, Reykjavík: Sigurður Kristjánsson, 1912.

Einar Ólafur Sveinsson, *The Folk-Stories of Iceland*, Exeter: Viking Society for Northern Research (Short Run Press), 2003.

Gísli Konráðsson, *Sagan af Natan Ketilssyni / Húnvetninga saga*, 1892.

Grétar Fells, 'Agnes og Fríðrik', *Morgunn*, vol. 16, no. 5, 1935.

Guðbrandur Jónsson, *Dauði Natans Ketilssonar*, Reykjavík: Söguféag, 1936–1939.

Guðlaugur Guðmundsson, *Enginn má undan líta*, Reykjavík: Örn og Örlygur, 1974.

Halldór Laxness, *Independent People*, trans. J.A. Thompson, London: The Harvill Press, 2001.

Helga K. Einarsdottir (ed.), *Cold was that Beauty: Icelandic nature poetry*, Reykjavík: Salka, 2002.

Iceland Writers Retreat, 2025, icelandwritersretreat.com

Icelandic Literature Centre, 2025, www.islit.is

Icelandic Naming Committee, 2025, island.is

Icelandic Tourist Board / Ferðamálastofa, 'Tourism in Iceland in Figures', 2025, www.ferdamalastofa.is

Kent, Hannah, *Burial Rites*, Sydney: Picador, 2013.

Larrington, Carolyne (trans.), *Poetic Edda, The*, Oxford: Oxford University Press, 2014.

Magnús Ólafsson, *Öxin, Agnes og Friðrik: verkið er byggt á heimildum um morð og aftöku*, Reykjavík: Veröld, 2024.

Marcinek, Ewa and Natasha S. (eds.), *Writers Adrift: Essays by foreign born writers in Iceland*, Reykjavík: Una útgáfahús, 2023.

Reid, Eliza, *Secrets of the Sprakkar: Iceland's Extraordinary Women and How They Are Changing the World*, Naperville: Sourcebooks, 2022.

Sagas of the Icelanders, The, Iceland: Leifur Eríksson Publishing Ltd., 1997.

Sigrún Huld Þorgrímsdóttir, 'Agnes og Friðrik fyrir og eftir dauðann', *Morgunblaðið*, 21 May 2005. www.mbl.is

Snorri Sturlason, *Heimskringla*, 2025, www.gutenberg.org

Tómas Guðmundsson, *Friðþæging (frásögn af Natani Ketilssyni)*, 1967.

Þorgeir Þorgeirsson, *Yfirvaldið*, Reykjavík: Iðunn, 1980.

Þorúnn Jarla Valdimarsdóttir, *Bærinn brennur*, Reykjavík: JPV, Forlag 2021.

SELECTED BIBLIOGRAPHY

Please note that this bibliography honours the Icelandic convention of listing Icelandic authors in alphabetical order of first name.

Aðalheiður Amundadóttir, 'Baráttukonan Agnes', *Fréttablaðið*, 9 September 2017.

Agnes og Friðrik (song), Bubbi Mortens, 1980.

Alcott, Louisa M., *Little Women*, Middlesex: Hamlyn Publishing, 1986.

Alda Sigmundsdóttir, *Daughter: A Memoir*, Reykjavík: Little Books Publishing, 2022.

Anderson, Robert. 'Defining the Supernatural in Iceland', *Anthropological Forum*, vol. 13, no. 2, 2003.

Aron Daði Þórisson, 'Skrifaði bókina fyrir eiginmanninn heitinn', *Heimildin*, 22 December 2021, heimildin.is

Atwood, Margaret, *Alias Grace*, London: Virago, 1997.

——, 'In Search of *Alias Grace*: On Writing Canadian Historical Fiction', *Curious Pursuits: Occasional Writing*, London: Vintage Press, 2005.

Baum, F.L. and John Harryson, *Galdrakarlinn Í Oz*, trans. Hulda Valtýsdóttir, 1966.

Benedikz, B.S., 'Basic Themes in Icelandic Folklore', *Folklore*, vol. 84, no. 1, Spring, 1973.

Bjarki Bjarnason and Sigríður Harðadóttir, *Island i aldanna rás 1800–1899*, Reykjavík: Mál og menning, 2006.

Björk, *Homogenic* (album), One Little Indian Records, 1997.

——, *Post* (album), One Little Indian Records, 1995.

Björn Bjarnason, *Brandsstaða Annáll*, Reykjavík: Sógufélag Húnavetningur og Húnavetningafélagið í Reykjavík, 1941.

Björn Valur Gíslason, 'Rósa Guðmundsdóttir: Vatnsenda-Rósa', 2009, www.bvg.is

Bödvar Gudmundsson, *Where the Winds Dwell*, trans. Keneva Kunz, Winnipeg, Manitoba: Turnstone Press, 1997.

Brynjólfur Pétursson, et. al. *Fjölnir. Árs-Rit Handa Íslendíngum*, Copenhagen: J.D. Kvisti, 1835.

Caveng, Barbara, *Final Meals* (exhibition) in *Aftökur og utrýmingar*, Akureyri: Listasafnið á Akureyri, 2003.

Collins, Rijn, *Fed to Red Birds*, Sydney: Simon & Schuster, 2023.

Cunningham, Michael, *The Hours*, London: Fourth Estate, 1999.

Dagskrá: Ákæruvaldið gegn Friðriki Sigurðssyni, Sigriði Guðmundsdóttur og Agnesi Magnúsdóttur, 9 September 2017.

Dancer in the Dark (motion picture), dir. Lars von Trier, Fine Line Features, 2000.

Dasent, George Webbe, *The Story of Burnt Njal or Life in Iceland at the End of the Tenth Century*, Edinburgh: Edmonston and Douglas, 1861.

Djúpið (motion picture), dir. Baltasar Kormákur, 2012.

Edvinsson, Soren, Ólöf Garðarsdóttir and Gunnar Thorvaldsen, 'Infant Mortality in the Nordic Countries, 1780–1930', *Continuity and Change*, vol. 3, 2008.

Egill Bjarnsason, 'Iceland riveted as notorious 1828 murder case is retried', *Associated Press*, 8 September 2017, www.mprnews.org

Einar Már Guðmundsson, *Englar alheimsins*, Reykjavík: Mál og menning, 2016.

——, *Hundadagur*, Reykjavík: Mál og menning, 2015.

Elsa Jónasdóttir and Þuríður Helga Gunnarsdóttir, 'Þrístapar', *Húnavatnshreppur*, 2006.

Englar Alheimsins (motion picture), dir. Friðrik Þór Friðriksson, Icelandic Film Corp., 2000.

Eyrún Ingadóttir, email with Hannah Kent, 13 September 2017.

Friðrika Benónýsdóttir, 'Myrkt ástarljóð til Íslands', *Fréttablaðið*, 20 September 2014.

Gísli Ágúst Gunnlaugsson, '"Everyone's been good to me, especially the dogs": foster-children and young paupers in nineteenth-century Southern Iceland', *Journal of Social History*, vol. 27, no. 2, Winter, 1993.

——, *Family and Household in Iceland 1801–1930: Studies in the Relationship Between Demographic and Socio-Economic Development, Social Legislation and Family and Household Structures*, Uppsala: Acta Universitas Upsaliensis, 1988.

Gísli Ágúst Gunnlaugsson and Loftur Guttormsson, 'Cementing Alliances? Witnesses to Marriage and Baptism in Early Nineteenth-Century Iceland', *The History of the Family*, vol. 5, no. 3, 2000.

——, 'Transitions into Old Age: Poverty and Retirement Possibilities in Late Eighteenth- and Early Nineteenth-Century Iceland' in John Henderson and Richard Wall, eds. *Poor Women and Children in the European Past*, London: Routledge, 1994.

Guðrún Bjartmarsdóttir, ed. *Bergmál: Sýnisbók* Íslenskra Þjóðfræða, Reyjkavík: Mál og Menning, 1996.

Gunnar Karlsson. 'Hvenær var síðasta aftakan á Íslandi?', *Vísindavefurinn*, 8 December 2004, visindavefur.is

Gunnar S. Þorleifsson, 'Dauði Natans Ketilssonar', *bindi 2 Syndi feðranna*, 1987.

Gylfi Guðmundsson. 'Vatnsenda-Rósa', 2009, www.ismennt.is

Halldór Laxness, *Iceland's Bell*, trans. Philip Roughton, New York: Vintage Books, 2003.

——, *The Atom Station*, trans. Magnus Magnusson, London: Vintage Books, 2004.

——, *The Fish Can Sing*, trans. Magnus Magnusson, London: The Harvill Press, 2001.

——, *Under the Glacier*, trans. Magnus Magnusson, New York: Vintage Books, 2004.

Hallgrímur Helgason, *101 Reykjavík*, Reykjavík: Mál og menning, 1996.

——, 'The Icelandic Tradition of Silence', *Hallgrímur Helgason*, 2019, www.hallgrimurhelgason.com

——, *The Woman at 1,000 Degrees*, trans Brian FitzGibbon, London: Oneworld, 2018.

Hardy, Thomas, *Jude the Obscure*, London: Penguin Classics, 1998.

Hávar Sigurjónsson, *Ertu Hálf-Dán?*, 2003.

Helgi Gunnlaugsson, 'Hvar Er Dauðarefsing Leyfð? Hvers Vegna Er Henni Beitt? Fækkur Hún Glæpum?' *Visindavefurinn*, 2001, www.visindavefur.hi.is

Helgi Gunnlaugsson and John F. Galliher, *Wayward Icelanders: Punishment, Boundary Maintenance and the Creation of Crime*, Wisconsin: The University of Wisconsin Press, 2000.

Henderson, Ebenezer, *Iceland; or the Journal of a Residence in that Island, During the Years 1814 and 1815, Containing Observations on the Natural Phenomena, History, Literature, and Antiquities of the Island; and the Religion, Character, Manners, and Customs of its Inhabitants*, Edinburgh: Waugh and Innes, 1819.

Hermann Pálsson and Paul Edwards (trans.), *Egil's Saga*, Middlesex: Penguin, 1976.

Hoffmann, Eline, *Dauði Natans Ketilssonar: Sögulegt Leikrit Í Sjö Sýningum*, Akureyri: Útgefandi Þorsteinn M. Jónsson, 1928.

Holland, Sir Henry, *The Iceland Journal of Henry Holland, 1810*, London: Haklyut Society, 1987.

Ingimar Friðfinnsson, 'Að Þrístöpum' in *Heimasloð: árbók hreppanna í Möðruvallaklaustursprestakalli*, Akureyri: BOB 1983–, vol. 8, 2006.

Jón Torfason, 'Svipast um á Illugastöðum', *Hunavetningur*, 1991.

Kent, Hannah, *Devotion*, Sydney: Picador, 2021.

——, *Náðarstund*, Trans. Jón St Kristjánsson, Reykjavík: JPV, 2014.

Kolbeinn Óttarson Proppé, 'Kaldi Blása Norðanvindur', *Múrinn*, 2001.

Kyzer, Larissa, 'Annual Artist Salaries Allocated for 2023', *Iceland Review*, 17 December 2022, www.icelandreview.com

Lárus Jóhannesson, *Blöndalsættin*, Hafnarfirði: Skuggsjá Bókabúð Olivers Steins, 1981.

Loftur Guttormsson and Ólöf Garðarsdóttir, 'The Development of Infant Mortality in Iceland, 1800–1920', *Hygiea Internationalis*, vol. 3, no. 1, 2002.

Magnús Magnússon and Hermann Pálsson (trans.), *Laxdaela Saga*, London: Penguin Books, 1969.

Manntal á Íslandi, 1801, Reykjavík: Prentsmiðjan Hólar, 1980.

Manntal á Íslandi, 1816, Reykjavík: Prentsmiðjan Hólar, 1980.

Matthías Johannessen, 'Maður má ekki ljúga í lóði', *Morgunblaðið*, 14 April 1964.

Olafur Gudmundsson and Anna Gudrun Thorhallsdottir, 'Extensive Sheep Grazing in the North', *Grazing and Pasture Management in the Nordic Countries*, vol. 126, 1999.

Ólöf Garðarsdóttir, 'Naming Practices and the Importance of Kinship Networks in Early Nineteenth-Century Iceland', *The History of the Family*, vol. 4, no. 3, 1999.

——, 'The implications of illegitimacy in late-nineteenth-century Iceland: the relationship between infant mortality and the household position of mothers giving birth to illegitimate children', *Continuity and Change*, vol. 15, no. 3, 2000.

Porter, Dorothy, *El Dorado*, Sydney: Picador, 2008.

Rúnar Kristjánsson, 'Á Þristöpum', *Húnavaka*, p.163–164.

——, 'Agnes', *Húnavaka*. p.43.

Sigurður Gylfi Magnússon, 'From Children's Point of View: Childhood in Nineteenth Century Iceland', *Journal of Social History*, vol. 29, no.2, Winter, 1995.

Simmonds, Jane (ed.), *Insight Guide Iceland*, London: Discovery Channel, APA Publications, 2000.

Stefan Jonasson, 'Icelandic Spiritualism: Mediumship and Modernity in Iceland', *The Icelandic Canadian*, 2009.

Stella Soffía Jóhannesdóttir, 'Hvaða heimildir eru til um Vatnsenda-Rósu og hvað er vitað um hana?', *Visindavefurinn*, 2008, www.visindavefur.hi.is

Svein Nielsson, 'Björn Auðunsson Blöndal', *Merkir Íslendingar*, 1957.

Theodór Arnbjörnsson, *Sagnþættir úr Húnaþingi*, Reykjavík: Ísafoldarprentsmiðja, 1941.

Thorvaldsen, Gunnar, 'An International Perspective on Scandinavia's Historical Censuses', *Scandinavian Journal of History*, vol. 32, no.3, 2007.

Tomasson, Richard F., 'A Millenium of Misery: The Demography of the Icelanders', *Population Studies*, vol. 31, no. 3, 1977.

——, 'Premarital Sexual Permissiveness and Illegitimacy in the Nordic Countries', *Comparative Studies in Society and History*, vol. 18, no.2, 1976.

Turville-Petre, G, 'Dreams in Icelandic Tradition', *Folklore*, vol. 69, no. 2, 1958.

Woolf, Virginia, *To the Lighthouse*, St Albans: Triad, 1997.

Æsa Sigurjónsdóttir, *Ísland í sjónmáli*, Reykjavík: JPV Forlag, 2000.